T0205887

The Global Politics of Artificial Intelligence

Chapman & Hall/CRC Artificial Intelligence and Robotics Series

Series Editor
Roman Yampolskiy

For more information about this series please visit:
https://www.routledge.com/Chapman--HallCRC-Artificial-Intelligence-and-Robotics-Series/book-series/ARTILRO

The Global Politics of
Artificial Intelligence

Edited by
Maurizio Tinnirello

CRC Press
Taylor & Francis Group
Boca Raton London New York

CRC Press is an imprint of the
Taylor & Francis Group, an **informa** business

A CHAPMAN & HALL BOOK

First edition published 2022
by CRC Press
6000 Broken Sound Parkway NW, Suite 300, Boca Raton, FL 33487-2742

and by CRC Press
4 Park Square, Milton Park, Abingdon, Oxon, OX14 4RN
CRC Press is an imprint of Taylor & Francis Group, LLC

Library of Congress Cataloging-in-Publication Data

Names: Tinnirello, Maurizio, editor.
Title: The global politics of artificial intelligence / edited by Maurizio Tinnirello.
Description: First edition. | Boca Raton, FL : CRC Press, 2022. | Series: Chapman & Hall/CRC artificial intelligence and robotics series | Includes bibliographical references and index.
Identifiers: LCCN 2021054756 | ISBN 9780429446672 (hardback) | ISBN 9781138314573 (paperback) | ISBN 9780429446726 (ebook)
Subjects: LCSH: Artificial intelligence.
Classification: LCC Q335 .G556 2022 | DDC 006.3--dc23/eng/20211213
LC record available at https://lccn.loc.gov/2021054756

ISBN: 978-0-429-44667-2 (hbk)
ISBN: 978-1-138-31457-3 (pbk)
ISBN: 978-0-429-44672-6 (ebk)

DOI: 10.1201/9780429446726

Typeset in Minion
by Deanta Global Publishing Services, Chennai, India

Contents

Preface

TECHNOLOGIES SUCH AS ARTIFICIAL intelligence have led to significant advances in science and medicine, but have also facilitated new forms of repression, policing, and surveillance. AI policy has become, without doubt a significant issue of global politics. The development and use of AI pose a myriad of challenges to the body politic, social constructs such as democracy, and economic activity, affecting seemingly every aspect of our lives, even how we relate to reality and to each other—in short, how we construct the future. This is already visible as powerful actors such as Apple, Alphabet, Microsoft, Facebook, and Amazon appropriate our data, and affect how we exert our agency. This impacts societies, as we are in constant interaction with different types of AI: in our phones, in our social media accounts, and every other trace of ourselves that we leave in the Internet of Things. How to deal with these interactions from a personal perspective as well as a wider perspective is a matter that touches the political. It is from the field of politics that humanity should decide where to go with AI. As pointed out by historian Yuval Noah Harari, the COVID-19 pandemic has highlighted the limitations of scientific power, as it is in the political sphere where decisions take place.[1] This is also very true about AI.

As states and corporations are racing to create better AI, questions arise regarding its use and purpose. Whom does it benefit and how? What can societies do to deal with AI, so it serves them and not corporations and states? How do we deal with the various stakeholders developing and using AI? These questions are not exhaustive but pinpoint some of the political challenges surrounding AI. Even whether there is already an AI race is a matter of debate; some object to and/or reject the term "race" in favour of AI cooperation.[2] Yet, a militarised AI race already exists, and powers such as the United States (US) and China have programmes to achieve hegemony in this field. Discussions about whether the race to achieve militarised AI can be stopped fall within the complexities of the political sphere.

This is not to say that economic imperatives do not play a major part in militarised and commercial AI use, but this also dwells within the political; the separation of economics and politics is at best non-existent in the interconnectedness of a globalised world. While drives have been made to make much of AI research open access, there is no question that corporations expect capital returns on their investments, and thus financial considerations drive how AI tech firms see the use of their AI. The economy of AI is expected to be around $15.7 trillion by 2030. Who owns the AIs that create so much capital is a key question linked to power, and so to the study of global politics.

It is from thinking about these issues that the idea of this volume came about. The nagging question of how we are going to secure that AI fits our societies for the benefit of all humankind, and not just be a tool for *politics* as usual. The literature on how to make AI good for society is growing, and much has been done from the technical, law, and philosophical fields, amongst others. A first example comes to mind, by the hand of those working towards banning lethal autonomous weapons (LAWs). The Future of Life Institute lists 247 organisations and 3,253 individuals calling for the ban of LAWs. They pledge:

> we will neither participate in nor support the development, manufacture, trade, or use of lethal autonomous weapons. We ask that technology companies and organisations, as well as leaders, policymakers, and other individuals, join us in this pledge.[3]

From computer scientists to AI tech firms worth hundreds of millions of dollars, all vowed to distance themselves from LAWs. This by all means is a powerful political statement; however, it reflects a myriad of interests and visions of the world, and perhaps an omission of understanding of the workings of the international system, i.e. states will use any methods to keep and obtain hegemony.[4] Even our international institutions fail to secure a lasting resolution to world problems. The challenge of climate change can illustrate this, as it has been decades since the first global calls for tackling climate change and environmental degradation were uttered—around the time of the Vietnam War. And yet, we still do not have a stable and strong institution to deal with climate change, even in the face of global climate related catastrophes. The way power has been exerted has allowed for this! How can we respond to the great challenge of AI and its impact on humankind? Will we need to wait decades for concrete political actions to secure its good and beneficial use? This is possible, but as political beings we must not leave this to chance, and tirelessly we must work, so AI is not misused for private interests alone, away from a global common good.

This volume tackles some of the issues linked to AI development and use, contributing to a better understanding of the global politics of AI. This is an area where enormous work still needs to be done, and the contributors to this volume provide significant input into this field of study, to policymakers, academics, and society at large. Each of the chapters in this volume work as a freestanding contribution and provide an accessible account of a particular issue linked to AI from a *political* perspective. Contributors to the volume come from many different areas of expertise, and of the world, and range from emergent to established authors. I am sure they will continue to enrich the study of the global politics of AI with original approaches.

I am very grateful to all authors represented here, for their contributions and also for their patience, especially as the pandemic brought disarray to many activities, including the production of this volume. This volume will certainly not be the last to tackle AI challenges from within the study of global politics, and it does not claim to have solved all ongoing debates, but it does hope to make an important addition to the debate on the global politics of AI for years to come.

In Chapter 1, Mona Sloane presents an exhaustive and compelling review of AI national strategies, and the nuances of how ethics are linked to and inform them. In particular how ethics inform national AI strategies. She engages in regulation debates and how the lack of strategy is not necessarily the absence of other interventions such as those provided by policy. She identifies five issues linked to AI ethics and proposes ten cues to contribute to developing approaches to mitigate the potential harms of AI for society as a whole.

In Chapter 2, Inga Ulnicane, William Knight, Tonii Leach, Bernd Carsten Stahl, and Winter-Gladys Wanjiku provide a substantial analysis of AI governance, what is driving it, and the main frames of emerging AI policies. The authors do well in telling us that most policy debates have been carried out from an ethical and philosophical view and less from the actual view of policy and governance, and point out that AI greatly impacts politics, labour, and the welfare state. They argue that a transformative view of AI affects how policy is conceived, and this leads to a policy frame that focuses on emerging global competition and collaboration, and on the role policy has in weighing the benefits, risks, and responsibilities in AI development as a revolutionary technology. Finally, the authors call for international collaboration to address the challenges brought by AI. There is a huge gap in the AI and public policy literature, and this chapter goes a long way towards filling this gap and bringing AI public policy research up to speed.

In Chapter 3, Eugenio Vargas Garcia discusses the possibilities for multilateralism to provide effective governance to AI. Despite numerous initiatives on AI principles by civil society, the industry, and some governments, the international governance of AI lacks coordination and has been plagued by competition. He argues that the UN is the right organisation to provide effective governance. However, he tells us that this is not a straightforward path, showing us the many difficulties that already exist in terms of governance to deal with the complexities of world problems, in particular in relation to AI regulation. He shows us the different initiatives that have been put forward to pursue AI governance, and their limitations, and other types of coordination drives that have proven more successful, such as those implemented by the European Commission. On AI governance, he points out that in times where multilateralism is under great pressure worldwide, it is the UN and its institutions that could provide such framework, and that there are already initiatives in place to address the challenges of AI governance. Furthermore, he points out that governance is not just about regulation but about fomenting prevention and foresight. Finally, he makes the point that the AI governance debate should include a broader collation, not just influential actors but "the Rest," as he calls the many not present in the debate.

In Chapter 4, Alfredo Toro Carnevali addresses issues concerning the global governance of autonomous weapons systems and the various challenges that they bring to our ability to create and apply norms to their use, and gives us an extensive overview of the positions of several international and national committees on their use. He uses principles codified in International Humanitarian Law, such as the principles of distinction, proportionality, and precaution in attack situations to analyse their use, providing a clear taxonomy, clarity, feasibility, and applicability of the challenges we are facing in regard to these systems. He addresses three questions on autonomous weapons systems' operational capability to comply with the principle of distinction, on whether they should be allowed to make life and death decisions without human control, and on what is the best avenue available to regulate the development and use of such autonomous weapons. He concludes that none of the existing instruments form a governance mechanism that can comply with IHL, and proposes a combination that perhaps could. Meanwhile, a moratorium on their use in civilian-populated areas is the way to go. Finally, this work provides a comprehensive recommendation on the way to regulate autonomous weapons systems, and issues a rich set of pointers to whoever wants to get deep into this topic.

In Chapter 5, Seth Baum, Robert de Neufville, Anthony M. Barrett, and Gary Ackerman examine the possibility of transfer learning from previous experiences of global risks that can be applied to avoid risks arising from AI development and use. They emphasise the importance of historical successes, and point out that humanity is not doomed to repeat the same mistakes if lessons from the past are carefully considered. They draw our attention to the way four global risks have been addressed: biotechnology, nuclear weapons, global warming, and asteroid collision. They point out that the severity of the risks does not translate into successful actions, and that perception of global risks is dependent on people's cultural and intellectual positions. An interesting case is made for an analogy between the nuclear weapons race being held in secrecy, and the possibility of something similar happening with AI technologies. They argue that the way to tackle global risks depends on how to secure the participation of those set to lose out from risk reductions actions, and that risk reduction efforts can be moulded by broader and complex socio-political conditions. They argue that from this understanding, the study of AI as a potential risk for society and policy can be fast-tracked. These lessons will help mitigate risk from AI by providing useful insights and a range of options that can be considered for future research on, and practice of, AI governance and policy.

In Chapter 6, Mark Coeckelbergh addresses questions regarding being-at-risk in the COVID-19 pandemic, and issues of power in relation to the use of technologies such as AI. He raises the subject of how AI and data science can shape and transform the experience, and create new vulnerabilities, of being-at-risk. He argues that AI technologies, amongst other powerful technologies, can encourage and shape a distant understanding and acceptance of the presence of death and vulnerability. Science and technology turn the risk into something that has been interpreted and experienced. He identifies how science and technology, including AI, not only shape our understanding of being-at-risk but steer human behaviour, and the effects this has on power—more precisely, on actions taken by states to deal with the challenges posed by the pandemic, including using technologies such as AI and machine learning. He advances important questions here on what AI technologies do to discipline and control individuals, and what effects this has on freedom. Moreover, he raises the possibility that AI will augment the vulnerability of those who are already in precarious circumstances, leading to a continuation of various forms of injustice and inequality. He concludes by providing recommendations on how to tackle the challenges presented, including calls for global actions to bring technology into politics, and politics into technology.

In Chapter 7, Vassilis Galanos applies the metaphor of royal (or state) and nomadic (or curiosity-driven) science to explore the relationship between researchers and the state in the development of artificial intelligence. He uses interviews, documents, and history to argue that there should be more room for curiosity-driven research. The chapter draws on a range of literature on long-term and more recent AI history, as well as interviews with people who work in AI-related areas. He also explores AI winters, the role of DARPA and recent predominantly-UK AI funding, documents and media statements that suggest that AI is largely developed as a nomadic science, yet at the same time is in a complex relationship with royal science.

In Chapter 8, Mahendra Prassad vouches for approval voting as opposed to plurality voting as a solution for a fairer political system, and also a better design of AI systems. The chapter describes at length, from different philosophical and ethical perspectives, the advantages of approval voting, with a specific focus on primaries in the US. Towards the end, the focus shifts onto artificial intelligence, and he argues that approval voting should be adopted as a general framework to conceive and design AI systems, because it ensures a better alignment between human values and the values encoded in the AI systems, and also allows for safer AI systems.

In Chapter 9, Thanasis Apostolakoudis examines the future of artificial intelligence in relation to the future of work. He sets off to investigate whether the replacement of human labour is imminent, and whether the use of AI is a source of celebration or worry for labour. He presents a balanced argument, addressing the hopes and fears around fully automated, labour-replacing AI technology. He then argues that any predictions are best-situated within the historical and material parameters of value and profit, and how these set the pace and shape the limits of the use of AI and labour replacement.

In Chapter 10, Maurizio Tinnirello addresses whether it is possible to achieve beneficial or *good* artificial general intelligence within capitalism, and in particular addresses how this system has shaped democracy in a manner that cannot be said to favour the global common good. He argues that if AGI is developed within the existing framework, then it is unlikely to act in a beneficial way. The paper concludes that to secure AGI's beneficial use, humankind needs to ensure that its development does not reflect capitalism, or otherwise humankind must accept that an AGI future within a form of capitalist democracy will be marked by great crises, and the continuation of a plutonomic order.

NOTES

1. Yuval Noah Harari, "Lessons from a Year of Covid," *Financial Times*, 26 February 2021, https://www.ft.com/content/f1b30f2c-84aa-4595-84f2 -7816796d6841.
2. Stephen Cave and Seán ÓhÉigeartaigh, "An AI Race for Strategic Advantage: Rhetoric and Risks," Paper presented at *AAAI/ACM Conference on Artificial Intelligence, Ethics and Society 2018*, New Orleans, 2018. doi:10.1145/3278721.3278780.
3. "Lethal Autonomous Weapons Pledge," accessed 12 January 2021, https:// futureoflife.org/lethal-autonomous-weapons-pledge/.
4. Maurizio Tinnirello, "Offensive Realism and the Insecure Structure of the International System: Artificial Intelligence and Global Hegemony," in *Artificial Intelligence Safety and Security*, ed. Roman Yampolskiy (Boca Raton: CRC Press/Taylor & Francis Group, 2018).

Acknowledgements

Foremost, I would like to express my sincere thanks to all the contributors in this volume, whose names appear in the table of contents. I also want to express my gratitude to all those who helped to review, edit and take this volume from an idea to reality, including Randi Cohen, Talitha Duncan-Todd, Danielle Costa, Seth Baum, Roman Yampolskiy, Mahendra Prassad, Vasileios Galanos, Robert de Neufville, Inga Ulnicane, Mario Verdicchio, Alex Grigor, Luke Kemp, Katharina Höne, Michael Klare, Thanasis Apostolakoudis, Alfredo Toro Carnevali, Eugenio Vargas Garcia, Mona Sloane, Dongwoo Kim, Alexey Turchin, and Christopher Markou. I apologise to those I forgot to mention.

Editor

D R. TINNIRELLO is an independent researcher and visiting lecturer in International Relations, Conflict and Security at Northumbria University in Amsterdam, and Member of the Ghent Institute for International and European Studies (GIES), Department of Political Science—Ghent University. Belgium. He has held academic positions in both the Global South and North, and he has also worked as an international researcher and policy consultant on global security and military corruption issues. He has been the Vice-Chair and Programme Chair of the Science, Technology and Art in International Relations section at The International Studies Association since 2019.

Dr. Tinnirello holds a PhD from the School of Politics and International Relations, and an MA in International Conflict Analysis from the University of Kent, UK. He was a recipient of a Marie Skłodowska-Curie Action Initial Training Award, and a visiting PhD fellow at Coimbra University. His research has primarily focused on how global capitalism and its ideology have affected global politics and security, as well as intellectual thought and what societies can do to free themselves from capitalism's grip. Dr. Tinnirello applies his understanding of our historical, intellectual, and political era to address international political challenges arising from an epoch-transforming technology like artificial intelligence.

List of Contributors

Gary Ackerman
College of Emergency
    Preparedness, Homeland
    Security and Cybersecurity
University at Albany
State University of New York
Albany, New York

Thanasis Apostolakoudis
Independent Researcher, Lawyer
Social Sciences and Humanities
University of Amsterdam, MSc/
    Leiden University, MA
Edinburgh, UK

Anthony M. Barrett
Global Catastrophic Risk Institute
Washington, DC

Seth D. Baum
Global Catastrophic Risk Institute
Washington, DC

Alfredo Toro Carnevali
Department of Political Science
    and Law
Montclair State University
Montclair, New Jersey

Mark Coeckelbergh
Department of Philosophy
University of Vienna
Vienna, Austria

Vassilis Galanos
Science, Technology and
    Innovation Studies
School of Social and Political
    Science
University of Edinburgh
Edinburgh, UK

Eugenio V. Garcia
Tech Diplomat
Consulate General of Brazil
San Francisco, California

William Knight
Centre for Computing and Social
    Responsibility
De Montfort University
Leicester, UK

Tonii Leach
Centre for Computing and Social
    Responsibility
De Montfort University
Leicester, UK

Robert de Neufville
Global Catastrophic Risk Institute
Washington, DC

Mahendra Prasad
Department of Political Science
University of California, Berkeley
Berkeley, California

Mona Sloane
Department of Technology,
 Culture and Society
Tandon School of Engineering
New York University
New York, New York
and
Tübingen AI Center
University of Tübingen
Tübingen, Germany

Bernd Carsten Stahl
Centre for Computing and Social
 Responsibility
De Montfort University
Leicester, UK

Inga Ulnicane
Centre for Computing and Social
 Responsibility
De Montfort University
Leicester, UK

Winter-Gladys Wanjiku
Centre for Computing and Social
 Responsibility
De Montfort University
Leicester, UK

CHAPTER 1

Threading Innovation, Regulation, and the Mitigation of AI Harm

Examining Ethics in National AI Strategies

Mona Sloane

CONTENTS

DOI: 10.1201/9780429446726-1

1

1.1 INTRODUCTION

The development of artificial intelligence (AI) will shape the
future of power. The nation with the most resilient and productive
economic base will be best positioned to seize the mantle of world
leadership. That base increasingly depends on the strength of the
innovation economy, which in turn will depend on AI.

(US NATIONAL SECURITY COMMISSION ON ARTIFICIAL
INTELLIGENCE, 19 MAY 2020).

Over the past three to five years, AI technologies and AI research have
become a major focus of private and public funding initiatives.[1] This heightened attention is paralleled by a growing proliferation of AI technologies
across social life. Today, these technologies are embedded into many devices
and services that people use on a daily basis, ranging from e-mail spam filters
to navigation devices or shopping websites. This development is advancing at
a rapid pace, which has led to the competition for (national) leadership in the
AI field becoming so fierce that it has been referred to as a "global AI race."[2]
In this "race," AI has become the strategic focus of many global technology
companies who commit substantial resources to push AI innovation,[3] and
the amount of capital invested in AI companies in the US came to a staggering $9.3 billion in 2018.[4] In Europe, the investment into tech companies (not
only AI companies) reached $23 billion in 2018,[5] while Chinese tech giants
Baidu, Alibaba, and Tencent equally investing heavily into AI technologies
and start-ups, backed by a government plan to build a domestic AI industry
worth around $150 billion by 2030 (Mozur, 2017).

Other nations and regions are not lagging behind. Although much
attention has been on the heated AI competition between the United
States of America and China (Metz, 2018), there is investment and policy activity in other regions and countries as well. For example, the EU
Commission pledged investment into AI of €1.5 billion for the period
2018–2020 under the Horizon 2020 research programme, expected to
trigger an additional €2.5 billion of funding from existing public–private
partnerships and eventually lead to an overall investment of at least €20
billion by 2020 (European Commission, 2018a). National European examples include France announcing a €1.5 billion pure government funding
for AI by 2022 (Cerulus, 2018), Germany outlining €3 billion aimed at
spending on AI research and development by 2025 (Delcker, 2018), and
the United Kingdom forging the AI Sector Deal (part of the Industrial

Strategy) worth £1 billion (British Government, 2018). In Asia, China's government is leading with US$7 billion minimum AI investment by 2030 (Ravi and Nagaraj, 2018), well ahead of South Korea, intending to invest US$2 billion in AI by 2022 (Synched, 2018). Canada has pledged C$125 million (CIFAR, 2017), while Australia announced an AUD$29.9 million investment into AI over four years in its 2018–2019 budget (Pearce, 2018).[6] While governments have to foster innovation, they are also tasked with mitigating the potentially adverse effects of AI through regulation and governance.

1.2 ARTIFICIAL INTELLIGENCE: THE ETERNAL DREAM

Despite the recent "AI hype" (Spencer, 2019), the idea of an "artificial intelligence" is not new: it could be claimed that it dates back to Homer's Iliad (Cave and Dihal, 2018; Royal Society, 2018). Between the 1950s and the mid-1970s, as computers became faster and cheaper, AI flourished, which was followed by an "AI winter" in the 1990s and 2000s and a dip in interest and funding in AI, despite the many AI advancements made during that time (Anyoha, 2017). The new AI hype is based on three developments that coincided and that are deeply connected: the availability of large datasets, the rapid advancement of computational machinery and processing power, and the invention of self-learning algorithms[7] based on artificial neural networks ("deep learning").[8]

The success of new AI technologies has reignited the imaginary of conscious machines or robots that have agency (Royal Society, 2018) and the fear that they may overthrow humanity (Bostrom, 2016). But we are far from that type of "general artificial intelligence" (Knight and Hao, 2019). All of the AI systems in place or under development today are what can be called "narrow artificial intelligence"; basically, statistical models that can (teach themselves to) detect correlation, but not causality.[9] This means that AI technology can be very good at very specific tasks, such as identifying the pixels in a photograph to help doctors diagnose a malignant mole.[10] But it also means that AI does not possess the capacity to deal with the sheer complexity of social life.[11]

1.2.1 Harmful AI

AI systems can be riddled with high error rates (especially facial recognition or object detection systems), which can disproportionately affect certain groups, such as people with darker skin tones.[12] AI systems can also be very vulnerable to outside influence, for example, to adversarial attacks,[13] which can have devastating consequences in high-stake contexts, such as diagnostics, autonomous driving, or combat. These attacks do not need to be digital, "physical world attacks" can also affect deep learning visual classification, such as stickers on stop signs.[14]

Over the past years, new research has demystified the account that algorithms and AI are de facto neutral and shown that existing power imbalances, inequalities, and cultures of discrimination are mirrored and exacerbated by automated systems. Important works include, but are not limited to: Virginia Eubanks'[15] research on how data mining, algorithms, and predictive risk models exacerbate poverty and inequality in the US; Safiya Umoja Noble's[16] work on how search engines discriminate against women of colour; Cathy O'Neil's[17] work on how the large-scale deployment of data science tools can increase inequality; Marie Hicks[18] demonstration of how gendered inequalities in computation are not accidental, but derive from a particular cultural landscape and a series of policy decisions; the work of Joy Buolamwini and Timnit Gebru[19] on discrimination in image databases and automated ender classification systems; research by Wilson, Hoffman, and Morgenstern[20] on higher error rates for pedestrians with darker skin tones in object detection systems; and Bolukbasi et al.'s[21] research on gender stereotypes in word embeddings.

The concern for ethics in AI, algorithms, and automated systems is also amplified by scandals that have shaken the tech industry, such as the Cambridge Analytica scandal involving Facebook user data, civilian deaths through driverless cars or the automated replication of the live-streaming of the Christchurch mosque attacks on social media. Meanwhile, the rollout of Europe's General Data Protection Regulation (GDPR) has brought data protection issues to a broad audience.

1.3 NATIONAL AI STRATEGIES

Many efforts to address issues around AI and society are now streamlined in and through national AI strategies. Therefore, this chapter provides a qualitative analysis of existing national AI strategies with a specific focus on ethics, and ethics-related concerns. It sets out to examine what work "ethics" do in national AI strategies and identify broad patterns of AI ethics interpretation and representation within these strategy documents.

The empirical material for this study is comprised of national AI strategy documents that were sourced through an online search[22] (between

February and March 2019[23]). In order to be included in the sample, a nation had to have a formal strategy in place, and the AI strategy documents had to be available in English. After the completion of the data collection, the AI strategy documents were analysed to identify aspects of "ethics" or related concerns and approaches and define core themes that cut across the sample. To account for the AI innovation landscape beyond formalised national AI strategies, additional data was gathered from policy documents, reports and news articles. This chapter should not be read as a comprehensive analysis of all AI strategies that have been proposed globally. It focuses explicitly on how concerns around AI and society, and ethics specifically, are articulated in the national AI strategies that were available at the time this study was conducted. It is therefore limited in its scope.

1.3.1 Defining National AI Strategies

At the most basic level, national AI strategies are frameworks that facilitate the distribution of public funds and incentivise research and innovation, as well as private funding, in certain areas and into certain directions. Bradley, Wingfield, and Metzger[24] broadly define a national AI strategy as

> a strategy, ordinarily developed by a government [...] which sets out its broad approach to AI, specific areas of focus, and activities that it will undertake which relate to AI [...] [and which represents an] attempt to coordinate government policies in order to maximize the potential benefits for the economy and society, while minimizing the potential costs.

There are, of course, cultural aspects that shape national AI strategies. For example, Finland and Sweden treat the potential of AI for the public sector as equally important as the potential for business, while Germany is focused on reaping the benefits of AI for its large sector of medium-sized businesses ("Mittelstand"), China is oriented towards integrating AI strategically into large-scale planning of economy, culture, and society and the USA is concentrating on funding (directly or indirectly) military-related AI innovation.

Broadly, there are two major elements that drive AI investment patterns and intentions in national AI strategies: *economic concerns* around competitiveness and developing or retaining global technological leadership. Across the board, these tend to be focused on developing and retaining research capacity, talent attraction, and retention,[25] innovation (especially via start-ups) as well as hardware development (especially chip production and supercomputer innovation); and *national security concerns* that include cybersecurity and the advancement of military technology.

1.3.2 No Strategy, No AI?

The presence or absence of a national AI strategy is by no means the only indicator of activity in the AI space. For example, until recently, the US was without a national AI strategy and yet was dominating the AI research space by being home to technology giants such as Alphabet Inc., Amazon, and Facebook. Similarly, Israel to date lacks a national AI strategy and yet was boasting a growing AI ecosystem of 1,150 companies by the end of 2018,[26] following $1.8 billion of AI investments in 2017, which was only topped by the US and Europe, and presumably China.[27]

Where (federal or state) government funding or strategic direction in terms of AI is less pronounced, other players move into the AI (ethics) space. These players often are *multinational corporations*. For example, in February 2019, IBM announced it would open an AI research centre in Brazil;[28] in Nigeria, the non-profit organisation Data Science Nigeria (DSN) runs AI-focused capacity building programmes;[29] in Rwanda, the African Institute for Mathematical Sciences (AIMS), a Pan-African network of centres of excellence for post-graduate training, research, and public engagement in mathematical sciences, offers an "African Master's in Machine Intelligence (AMMI)," a fully funded one-year graduate programme, offered in partnership with Facebook and Google.[30]

Another dominant picture that emerges is that the have-a-national-AI-strategy countries are also, predominantly, among the most powerful countries. We could argue that we are seeing some of the well-trodden paths of colonial power resurface in the AI arena. This, for example, materialises in the form of cobalt mining in Congo[31] or AI data training in Kenya,[32] but also in strategic ties that are (re-)forged between colonial powers and their former colonies through AI, such as the "International Panel on Artificial Intelligence (IPAI)" that is to be set up between Canada and France.

1.4 TO REGULATE, OR NOT TO REGULATE?

An absence of a national AI strategy does not indicate an absence of regulation or other (policy) interventions that may relate to the AI space. Prominent examples are the EU's General Data Protection Regulation, or

South Korea's strict data protection laws, or the US's Communications Decency Act of 1996 (CDA) that exempts tech firms from being liable for the content created on their service by third parties. Furthermore, some countries chose not to treat AI as a separate digital technology, but focus on broader digitisation strategies and funding initiatives that may include AI, particularly in Europe, but also in some African countries, such as South Africa. Others are en route to developing a national AI strategy, such as Bahrain or Malaysia.

Falling outside of national AI strategies, and very much related to concerns of mitigating potential AI harm, is the question of how to *regulate large tech firms* (who also tend to be those controlling the AI research and deployment space). Much of this is focused on addressing the issue of monopolisation (particularly in the EU context) and the related large-scale collection of data from users. For example, the European Commission has repeatedly fined Google for antitrust violations in the online advertising market[33] and Facebook may face a substantial fine for a large-scale data breach.[34] Existing regulatory frameworks around data collection and privacy, such as the GDPR, affect the design and deployment of AI systems, because they mitigate potentially predatory data collection practices that underpin the "big data" that is needed to train AI models. Therefore, they often form the basis for these strategies. Regulators may also focus on particular AI products and their underlying business models, such as social media or facial recognition technology. For example, regulators in the UK[35] and in Australia[36] have recently put a strong focus on regulating social media platforms in terms of controlling the spread of extremist content, misinformation, hate crimes, and dangerous material, especially when aimed at children. Germany already has strong anti-hate speech laws in place which extend into the virtual space, including social media, and has recently moved to fine social media companies if they do not remove hate speech swiftly enough.[37] The US is currently seeing a strong movement of academics, activists, and politicians against the use of facial recognition technology, with some commentators framing this AI technology as dangerous as nuclear technology, requiring similarly strong regulation.[38] Similarly, US Senators Cory Booker and Ron Wyden, along with Congresswoman Yvette D. Clarke, recently introduced the "Algorithmic Accountability Act of 2019," which sets out to "direct the Federal Trade Commission to require entities that use, store, or share personal information to conduct automated decision system impact assessments and data protection impact assessments."[39]

1.4.1 AI Tensions: Between Innovation and Regulation

Against that backdrop, it is evident that national governments find themselves in what seems like a field of tension: they must foster innovation and stay in the "national AI race" while having to mitigate the adverse effects of AI through regulation and governance.[40] In the context of national AI strategies, threading the fine line between innovation and regulation is complicated political work. Here, the notion of "ethics" has become essential: many national AI investment strategies and policies tend to entail a concern for "AI ethics" as an umbrella strategy for both boosting the AI industry and protecting citizens from AI harm. That is to say that "ethics" does important work in and through national AI strategies. This work can broadly be classified into three main areas: risk mitigation, design and deployment concerns, and governance approaches.

1.4.2 Risk Mitigation

One dominant pattern is that ethics within national AI strategies are represented as a tool for mitigating risks[41] and potential harms, particularly in the context of individuals that are or could be negatively affected by AI technology or in the context of society at large.[42] In other words, the need for ethics is rationalised by a potential risk or harm to an individual or to society. What exactly constitutes a risk or harm in the context of AI ethics, and what does not, however, remains abstract or vague in most strategy documents. But despite this vagueness, we can broadly extract three core risk/harm themes that are articulated in relation to AI ethics: (robot) safety, data privacy, and bias. They are not featured in all strategies, but permeate across the majority of the documents that were assessed.

(Robot) Safety most often relates to the physical harm that can potentially be inflicted upon humans in and through interaction with robotic systems that are equipped with automated decision-making systems or AI. Prominent and much-quoted examples are potential harms that could occur in the context of automated driving and autonomous weapons.[43]

Data (privacy) is a major theme in the context of AI technology, ethics, and society. In national AI strategies, privacy concerns usually relate to AI technologies that depend on the collection of vast amounts of data for the development of algorithmic models and for their deployment and future functioning—especially when this data is personal and thus sensitive, such as health records.[44]

Bias is often depicted as a potential harm that may affect individuals or groups of individuals. It commonly refers to social, cultural, and economic biases that show in databases which, in turn, are a building block for AI technology development (e.g. an over-representation of certain groups and traits that lead to AI systems "learning" that these groups are the "norm" and others are "outliers"). Some AI strategies acknowledge that these biases may exacerbate socioeconomic polarisation and existing inequalities, but there also is a commercial concern that biased AI may lead to bad product quality.

The theme *"security"* is also featured prominently across the documents; it is not related explicitly to ethics, but to the broader treatment of AI technology within a specific national context (often relating to issues like cybersecurity or cyber warfare). For example, the US AI strategy document (produced by the Department of Defense) is firmly located in the military context and aims to develop "military ethics and AI safety" as part of the mission to "address the technical, ethical, and societal challenges posed by AI and leverage its opportunities in order to preserve the peace and provide security for future generations."

1.4.3 Design and Deployment Concerns

Within the data that was collected for this study, a wide array of ethics themes emerged[45]. We can attribute these themes broadly to two main areas of action: either ethics concerns that focus on AI design and deployment, or AI ethics concerns that relate to AI governance.

Design and deployment concerns relate to the way in which the AI system is rationalised, created, and used. There are a number of building blocks that make up this ethics element. First, there is transparency relating to clearly defined processes and responsibilities within the AI design process. This is closely related to new questions that are arising in the context of (human) accountability or responsibility (e.g. in the context of data privacy, see above) and, by extension, liability. Transparency can also relate to the need for explainability in the context of the "black box problem,"[46] whereby it is unclear how an algorithm working based on an artificial neural network arrived at its prediction or behaviour. There are calls for AI systems that are transparent via explainability by design, meaning that the inner workings of AI are explainable to a non-expert, for example, for the sake of an audit. Second, and relatedly, there are calls for a focus on mitigating bias in AI systems and particularly in the datasets that are used to develop the underlying algorithmic model. Ethical concerns around mitigating bias also link to the notion of increasing fairness (of opportunity) in AI systems. A third building block is controllability and human oversight in (different stages of) AI deployment (e.g. in the context of autonomous driving, but also in the context of the use of AI in government services). Another ethics focus in the context of AI design and deployment, fourth, is a concern for designing AI systems that protect users by way of being "robust" against external manipulation. Related to that, lastly, are suggestions for rigorous testing of AI systems prior to deployment, as well as concerns about the maintenance and repair of AI systems.

1.5 GOVERNANCE APPROACHES

Governance concerns related to ethical AI are suggested across the international AI ethics landscape. These methods vary widely from nation to nation, and from strategy to strategy. One set of methods targets the AI industry, as well as the professional community of computer scientists specifically. Here, codes of conduct are suggested, as well as ethics frameworks for practical application in the industry, ethical training for AI practitioners, and as industry standards, ethics certifications, and declarations. Another popular method to achieve "ethical AI" is the introduction of (independent) expert groups. This may include ethics review boards or similar structures such as ethics committees, ethics working groups or workshops between technology experts, policymakers, stakeholders, and researchers. A major theme in many, but not all, national AI strategies is a call for regulation and guiding legal principles with regard to AI. Many AI strategies remain unclear as to legal specifics and focus on outlining that a legislative response is needed, rather than what it could look like. However, certain legal themes clearly emerge. One of them is the question of whether AI (typically in the form of robots) should be treated as legal persons in order to create AI accountability.[47] Another major theme is the issue of the data rights of citizens, for which discussions around the GDPR serve as a good example. The third significant theme that emerges in the context of AI governance is to focus on regulating AI in an industry-specific way and, as part of that, require sector-specific regulators to develop sufficient knowledge of AI as it applies to their industry.

Here, *standardisation* efforts related to AI increasingly play a role in considering how AI technologies can be best governed on an international level.[48] Standards may refer to technical and institutional aspects of AI innovation and deployment, whereby the former may refer to the robustness of AI systems and/or their security levels, and the latter may refer to design protocols that include "ethics." Industry bodies can play an important role in developing these standards. For example, the IEEE (see above) released the "Standard for Personal Data Artificial Intelligence (AI) Agent" (P7006[49]) in March 2017 and has also launched the "IEEE Global Initiative on Ethics of Autonomous and Intelligent Systems," which will also comprise an "Ethics Certification Programme for Autonomous and Intelligent Systems."[50] But also national governing bodies are working on AI standards. Relatedly, the International Organization for Standardization (ISO) is also currently working on AI standards,[51] while in the US the National Institute of Standards and Technology (NIST) has been tasked to "create a plan for Federal engagement in the development of technical standards and related tools in support of reliable, robust, and trustworthy systems that use AI technologies."[52] The potential reach of standards is wide as it may, eventually, also include standards for data collection and consent, AI model development, algorithm maintenance, and algorithm auditing.[53]

The field of tension between AI innovation and regulation that governments find themselves in, and in which "ethics" is deployed to both boost local AI industries and protect citizens from AI harm can be understood a little better by building on what Mazzucato[54] called "the entrepreneurial state" and what Verhulst and Sloane[55] framed as "AI Localism." The concept of the entrepreneurial state outlines that government investment plays a fundamental role in the economic success of private companies, especially in the context of groundbreaking technological *innovation* (especially in the US). It makes the case that it is key for state actors to not just regulate technologies ex-ante, but to strategically invest in "moonshots" and co-create and influence markets that way. "AI Localism"[56] is a new concept that suggests that there is an emerging field of *locally* driven innovation in AI regulation and governance.[57] This is mostly led by cities and fills a void in the policy realm that is left by national AI strategies sitting in the field of tension between investment in innovation and the need for the mitigation of AI harm. The work that ethics do in national AI strategies, then, is linking macro-concerns emerging government investments into technological innovation (the "entrepreneurial state") and local mitigation strategies for AI harm.

1.6 THE LIMITS AND POTENTIALS OF ETHICS IN NATIONAL AI STRATEGIES

Despite the work "ethics" do in linking macro and micro concerns related to AI innovation and regulation, there are a number of issues that remain. These predominantly pertain to a bigger set of concerns related to the dominance of ethics in the international discourse and policy landscape about AI.

1.6.1 AI Ethics Limits: Five Issues

1. A strategic lack of clarity about "AI" and "ethics" remains. Many national AI strategies neither define "AI" nor "ethics" (notable exceptions are India, Japan, Germany, and, to a lesser degree, the European Commission). This leads to problematic confusions between AGI and narrow AI (see section above), as well as "machine learning," "deep learning," "automated systems," and so on. This vagueness can be seen as a strategy deployed to keep the pool of fundable (AI) innovations as big as possible. But it also prevents more productive conversations about the abilities and limits of such technologies.[58] This may affect the ways in which political leaders and policymakers build technological knowledge and the capacity to regulate big tech companies more effectively. We see a similar pattern with "ethics." A more detailed understanding of how "ethics" is actually enacted in AI design practice (which is mostly in terms of moral machines and ethics frameworks, see above) is absent in the strategy documents. Another issue is that "ethics" may also be used as a placeholder for concerns related to "safety," "privacy" or "bias." But these terms do not mean the same thing. And even the same term can mean different things in different contexts. For example, "bias" in machine learning refers to data systematically diverging from the population it looks to represent, while in law, it refers to the predisposition of a decision-maker against or in favour of a party.

2. AI ethics has no legal implications.[59] In other words, "ethics" is not enforceable by law.[60] A commitment to "ethics" is a gesture of goodwill, and has been shown to not affect the considerations of technology designers.[61] Furthermore, the focus on "ethics" somewhat circumnavigates bigger questions around legal frameworks and policies that may need to be put in place to prevent AI harm (which has been described as a form of "ethics-washing").[62] This shows that the

build-up of legal frameworks that can effectively govern AI development and deployment, whether on a national or transnational level, appears to be an issue that is treated separately from national AI strategies. It is therefore unsurprising that large tech companies have embraced "AI ethics" as a way of being able to continue with "business as usual."[63]

3. Ethics is both abstract and context-specific. This study has shown that it is virtually impossible to talk about ethics without considering the culture- and context-specific meaning of "ethics." This comes across clearly in the national AI strategy documents. For example, the German national AI strategy frames ethics through a focus on data and privacy, whereas the US has a focus on ethics in the context of weapons and the military, or Finland has a focus on the public sector. AI ethics is, therefore, emergent, contextual, cultural. This is rarely acknowledged in the strategy documents themselves, however. "Ethics" is framed in terms of moral philosophy and as something universal that is based on somewhat innate moral values that bind together society. Not only does this privilege a Western canon of ontologies, but it also lacks a more firm grounding in universal frameworks that may be enforceable (such as human rights).[64] It also misses the fact that values and ethics, whether in AI or other technological systems, change over time.

4. The focus on AI ethics affects the global politics of knowledge production. National AI strategies can have large-scale effects on national and international funding landscapes for research, innovation and education and thus play a major role in the politics of knowledge production and power. This creates a certain global vocabulary that becomes dominant (e.g. "AI" instead of "automated systems," "ethics" instead of "human rights" or "bias" instead of "injustice"), and that creates a global hierarchy of concerns. As part of this mechanism, certain kinds of knowledges and practices (e.g. ethics education for computer scientists) take precedent over others (e.g. participatory design and community engagement projects in AI) and receive public or private funding. This can manifest existing power relations, or create new imbalances.

5. The dominance of ethics can invite techno-solutionism. The idea that the social implications and concerns of AI can be boiled down

to moral principles can invite the idea that these principles can be coded into a machine to create "moral machines,"[65] which has been called the "technological approach to AI ethics."[66] This discussion is already prevalent in the discourse that is adjacent to the policy-making realms. It suggests that there can be a technical solution to a social problem.[67] This take on AI ethics could reduce the perceived need for regulation and social reform to address the underlying problem of AI harm, which is historic patterns of inequality and oppression.

1.6.2 AI Ethics Potentials: Ten Cues

Against that backdrop, there are ten cues that can be taken in order to expand the potential of AI ethics in national AI strategies and develop more holistic approaches for addressing and mitigating the potential harms of AI for society.

1. Clearer definitions and more precise terminologies are needed in order to advance the discourse around AI and society without falling into the trap of techno-solutionism. This is particularly true for terminologies around the technological capabilities and limits of AI. Here, technologists and policymakers, but also journalists and educators, have a responsibility to contribute to a solid public understanding of the inner workings of AI technology and the way in which it is deployed in society and with what consequences. This also applies to notions of "bias," "privacy," "security," "fairness," and so on.

2. Shifts in the framing of ethics need to occur to address the issue of ethics being narrowed down to moral machines or ethics frameworks. What is helpful in this regard is specifying ethics along the lines of research ethics, which includes protocols for obtaining participant consent, voluntary participation, and the possibility of withdrawing, as well as a view for the principle of self-determination. Such a reframing does not only shift focus onto the practice of AI design and innovation, but it also highlights the significance of due process.

3. Social sciences need to be integrated more decidedly in research and innovation framings around AI and society, and this must be reflected in funding strategies. They remain underrepresented in

national AI strategies and AI policy bodies that are forming, or have been formed (such as the EC High Level Working Group on Artificial Intelligence). Focusing on combining technical expertise with the expertise of cognitive scientists, behavioural economists and moral philosophers is insufficient and ignores the fact that ethics is a social construct, and the idea of what is right or wrong is an emergent social practice.

4. Specific and flexible legal frameworks and strategies must be developed to holistically address potential AI harm; these cannot be external to strategic approaches to AI on a national level. As part of that, human rights need to become central to questions around how AI may affect society.[68] Human rights questions are already a global issue with well-established frameworks and enforcement mechanisms that can serve as a connection point to (global) issues that emerge in the context of AI design and deployment.

5. Industry- or sector-specific regulation must become a focus of potential AI regulation (here, industry standards may be a useful point of departure). Data and AI applications cannot unproblematically be transferred from one context into the next. For example, healthcare data cannot unproblematically be used for automated risk assessment. However, not only do risks differ, but also needs. For example, the manufacturing industry has different data and AI needs than the service industries. Generalising these issues under "AI" broadly runs the risk of failing to assess industry- or sector-specific needs and requirements when it comes to data collection, data management and the application of AI systems.

6. The notions of inequality and (in)justice must become an integral part of discussions and strategies around AI, especially on governmental and international levels. These discussions must build on a full picture of how technological advancement is permeated by structural inequalities and how this is conditioned on histories of power imbalances as well as (global) oppression and exploitation. Inequalities are not confined to traditional notions of wealth, class, gender or racial inequalities, they are overlapping, complex and intersectional.[69] Against the backdrop of the climate crisis, the notion of inequality and (in)justice must also centre on the environmental consequences[70] and the labour conditions of AI-related manufacturing.

7. Decision makers and practitioners must build up socio-technical and historical literacy related to AI and other automated decision-making technologies. This means that in order to assess the disparate social and ecological impacts of AI systems, policymakers, regulators, and practitioners must be able to understand the political genealogy of these systems. For example, in order to understand the disparate impact of surveillance technology on communities of colour, decision makers need to build up "racial literacy."[71]

8. Decentralised technology innovation and community empowerment must become integral to how technological progress and AI innovation are framed on a high level. Framing AI as central to future prosperity and national security while allowing AI innovation to be centralised in large companies is antithetical to the idea of a democratic order. Strategic approaches to AI must commit to providing communities with the skills, literacy and resources they need to be self-determined in the age of AI, rather than being controlled, coerced, and profiled. This can also serve as an opportunity to develop context-specific and therefore more effective AI applications.

9. Cross-national learning and exchange on the political and civic level is vital and should be encouraged and enhanced in strategic approaches to AI. Currently, large tech companies mediate much of the international exchange on AI through their globally deployed products, but also through global research sponsorship and making their technical expertise available to policymakers. But it is crucial to build on the expertise of those using, or having to use, AI systems, especially on a large scale (such as in the healthcare system).[72] Here international exchange can prevent using the wrong technology for a certain need.

10. AI must be reframed as a gateway or tool for addressing urgent socio-ecological problems, rather than as inevitably determining our collective future. Despite the disruptive rhetoric that is cultivated in many of the national AI strategies, AI is likely to generate gradual rather than abrupt change,[73] alongside rather than instead of humans.[74] Against that backdrop, we may see a receding of the AI hype soon, and we must ask ourselves: what remains? AI prompts us to re-evaluate "big" questions relating to (global) power, democracy

and inequality and to what it means to be a living thing on this earth. Ultimately, the biggest thing AI can do for us is forcing us to keep asking these questions.

1.7 CONCLUSION

This chapter has assessed the work that "ethics" do in AI strategies. To do so, it has defined national AI strategies and located them in a field of tension between fostering AI innovation and mitigating potential AI harm. It has then analysed the complicated political work that "ethics" do in and through national AI strategies, outlining risk mitigation, design and deployment concerns, and governance approaches as the three main areas of concern. It has then suggested that this political work of ethics in the context of AI risk mitigation, AI design and deployment, and AI governance can best be understood as an active link between Mazzucato's[75] notion of the "entrepreneurial state"—i.e. federal investment strategies in "moonshot" technologies that co-create markets—and Verhulst and Sloane's[76] idea of "AI Localism"—i.e. city-led innovation in AI governance and regulation. To make full use of this dynamic, the chapter listed five limiting factors of over-emphasising "ethics" in national AI strategies and outlined ten cues that can help develop a more holistic approach for framing the relationship between AI and society, especially in the context of justice.

NOTES

1. OECD, 2018.
2. Lee, 2018.
3. Although these are publicly traded companies, it is very difficult to generate detailed knowledge about the actual investment into AI because this investment is spread across the whole organisation of the company. For example, AI may take up a substantial part of research and development (R&D) expense, but it may also form a major part of acquisitions (such as the capital-intense acquisition of successful AI start-ups), or even philanthropy (such as university sponsorship).
4. Statista, 2019.
5. Slush and Orrick, 2018.
6. These are just a few, and the most significant, examples of national investment into AI, not every national government is focused on increasing AI investment.
7. Here, it is useful to build on the following definition of "algorithm": "An algorithm is a set of instructions for how a computer should accomplish a particular task. Algorithms are used by many organizations to make

decisions and allocate resources based on large datasets. Algorithms are most often compared to recipes, which take a specific set of ingredients and transform them through a series of explainable steps into a predictable output. Combining calculation, processing, and reasoning, algorithms can be exceptionally complex, encoding for thousands of variables across millions of data points." Caplan, R., Donovan, J., Hanson, L., Matthews, J., "Algorithmic accountability: A primer," 2018. https://datasociety.net/output/algorithmic-accountability-a-primer/.

8. We could also argue that the rise of design as means for organizing society (Sloane, 2019) as well as the swelling of "surveillance capitalism" (Zuboff, 2019) played their part in creating the current focus on AI systems.

9. Harnett, 2018.

10. Esteva et al., 2017.

11. Sokol, 2018.

12. Buolamwini and Gebru, 2018; Sharman, 2018; Wilson, Hoffman and Morgenstern, 2019.

13. Finlayson et al., 2019.

14. Eykolt et al., 2018.

15. 2018.

16. 2018.

17. 2016.

18. 2017.

19. 2018.

20. 2019.

21. 2016.

22. The following resources served as baseline for the search: "Building an AI World—Cifar Report on National and Regional AI Strategies" (Dutton, Barron and Boskovic, 2018); Future of Life Institute List of "National and International AI Strategies" (Future of Life Institute, 2019); Medium "An Overview of National AI Strategies" (Dutton, 2018); "The European AI Landscape—Workshop Report" (European Commission, 2018a). The following strategies were part of the sample: Europe: European Commission, Finland, UK, France, Sweden; Asia: China, India, Japan, Singapore, South Korea, Taiwan, UAE; Oceania: Australia; North America: U.S.A, Canada; Central and South America: none; Africa: none.

Because of the limited scope of this study, AI governance frameworks that are being developed or published by supranational frameworks, such as the OECD, the World Economic Forum, or the UN are excluded (for an OECD analysis of the use of AI in the public sector, see "Hello, World: Artificial Intelligence and its use in the Public Sector," 2019). Also excluded are "ethics codes" published by large professional organisations. Most notable in this context are the Institute of Electrical and Electronics Engineers (IEEE) and the Association for Computing Machinery (ACM). The IEEE does have an official Code of Ethics (IEEE, 2019a), but has also, more recently, published a "global treatise" on "Ethically Aligned Design: A Vision for Prioritizing

Human Well-being with Autonomous and Intelligent Systems" (IEEE, 2019b). Similarly, the ACM updated its Code of Ethics and Professional Conduct in 2018 (ACM, 2018).

23. With the exception of the "Beijing AI Principles" which were released in May 2019 and added subsequently to the analysis due to China's significance in the international AI arena.

24. 2020.

25. AI engineers are among the highest paid jobs in the US (Castellanos, 2019).

26. Mizroch, 2019.

27. Ravi and Nagaraj, 2018.

28. Mari, 2019.

29. Data Science Nigeria, 2019.

30. AIMS, 2019.

31. Crawford and Joler, 2018; Frankel, Chavez and Ribas, 2016.

32. Lee, 2018.

33. Tiku, 2019.

34. Schechner, 2018.

35. Gunia, 2019.

36. Jee, 2019.

37. BBC, 2017.

38. Stark, 2019.

39. U.S. Congress, 2019.

40. It must be noted that governments, and government agencies, can and do use AI technologies for oppression. For example, there is evidence that mass surveillance is used in China to oppress the Uighur population (Baynes, 2019).

41. These are risks that are explicitly related to ethics. They do not include broader AI risks and areas of concern that are articulated and addressed in national AI strategies, such as national security and economic competitiveness (including [mass] unemployment that may be cause by automation).

42. The general risk that is articulated in this context, however, is the one of being left behind economically and being vulnerable in terms of national security (including through cyberattacks, interference into the democratic process, and less advantaged military technology—see section above).

43. The issue of autonomous weapons, or "killer robots," has been a major feature in the general debate around automated decision making system (see, e.g. Suchman, Irani and Ansaro, 2018).

44. The theme of privacy is not new or unique to AI. Technology researchers have discussed privacy, and the politics related to it, for a long time (e.g. Nissenbaum, 2010). We may also add at this point that the question what constitutes personal and thus sensitive data remains a contested one, especially in the context of data anonymity and the power of inferences that can be drawn through AI systems. Much of the power of AI technology rests on the ability of detecting patterns in big data that then form the basis for prediction in individual contexts. This depends on inferring an individual and personal data profile against the backdrop of the larger pattern. Therefore, even though "big" data is anonymised, it creates patterns that

can only accrue relevance in the context of personal and individual context (e.g. whether or not an individual is likely to pay back a loan). This is the reason why some scholars have argued that an exclusive focus on data privacy, such as in the context of the European Union's General Data Protection Regulation (GDPR), only provides partial protection to data subjects (Wachter, Mittelstadt and Russell, 2018).

45. Some documents were explicitly grounded in broader *principles*, such as trust or trustworthiness (which, for example, is key to the EU's take on AI, whereby Finland focused more on experimentation).

46. This is a technical understanding of the "black box," but there are scholars who extend the idea of the black box into the organisational realm. Frank Pasquale (2015), for example, argues that algorithmic decision-making is "black boxed," which means that while we may know what goes into the computer for processing and what the outcome is, there are currently no external auditing systems or regulations for assessing what happens to the data during processing.

47. see Bryson, Diamantis and Grant, 2017.

48. see specifically Cihon, 2019.

49. The P7006 standard "describes the technical elements required to create and grant access to a personalized Artificial Intelligence (AI) that will comprise inputs, learning, ethics, rules and values controlled by individuals" (IEEE, 2017).

50. IEEE, 2018.

51. ISO, 2019; see also Cihon, 2019.

52. Federal Register, 2019.

53. see also Caplan et al., 2018.

54. 2018.

55. 2020.

56. Verhulst and Sloane, 2020.

57. For example, cities have moved to ban certain AI applications, such as facial recognition technology, or have implemented data collaboratives, or have invested into local responsible AI research and high-potential tech ecosystems, or have been the locus of citizen-led engagements with governance questions around AI technology.

58. see Marcus, 2018, on similar issues in the context of "deep learning."

59. Although it has to be underlined that ethics and the law interact (Hildebrandt, 2018), not least because ethical considerations and discourses affect law-making.

60. Chadwick, 2018.

61. McNamara, Smith and Murphy-Hill, 2018.

62. Wagner, 2018.

63. Sloane, 2019.

64. The exception, perhaps, is China, where ethics are broadly understood in terms of a "work ethic." This, however, does not negate but rather underline the point that "ethics" are context- and culture-specific. We might also

want to add the way in which the Chinese government approaches AI in general is well in line with the tradition of large-scale planning (Webster et al., 2017).

65. Wallach and Allen, 2009.
66. Sloane, 2019. Here, the baseline is to work morality into machines through codifying values (Anderson and Leigh Anderson, 2011; Yu et al., 2018). This stream of work by a perceived need to equip artificial agents with a "capacity for moral decision making" when they work towards achieving goals (Noothigattu et al., 2018; Moniz Pereira and Saptawijaya, 2016). Related technology-focused approaches include "fairness" enhancement and "bias" mitigation in algorithmic technologies (Mitchell, Portash and Barocas, 2018; Barocas, Hardt and Narayanan, 2018). Related approaches include the idea of AI intelligibility (see e.g. House of Lords, 2018), AI accountability (Caplan et al., 2018) and algorithm auditing (Courtland, 2018).
67. Greene, Hoffman and Stark, 2019.
68. see also Risse, 2018; Latonero, 2018.
69. Costanza-Chock, 2018; Sloane, 2018.
70. Strubell, Ganesh and McCallum, 2019.
71. see Daniels, Nkonde and Mir, 2019.
72. see Allen, 2018.
73. Brooks, 2019; Chatham House, 2018.
74. Elish and Mateescu, 2019.
75. 2018.
76. 2020.

REFERENCES

ACM. "ACM code of ethics and professional conduct." 2018. https://www.acm.org/code-of-ethics.

Allen, A. "Lost in translation: Epic goes to Denmark." *Politico*, 2018. https://www.politico.com/story/2019/06/06/epic-denmark-health-1510223.

Anderson, M., Anderson, S. L. (Eds.). *Machine Ethics*. Cambridge: Cambridge University Press, 2011.

Anyoha, R. *The History of Artificial Intelligence*. Harvard University, The School of Arts and Sciences, 2017. http://sitn.hms.harvard.edu/flash/2017/history-artificial-intelligence/.

Barocas, S., Hardt, M., Narayanan, A. *Fairness and Machine Learning*. fairmlbook.org, 2018. http://www.fairmlbook.org.

Baynes, C. "Chinese 'Muslim tracker' surveillance system monitoring movements of 2.5m people in Xinjiang." *The Independent*, 2019. https://www.independent.co.uk/news/world/asia/china-uighur-muslim-crackdown-xinjiang-surveillance-tracking-sensenets-a8786076.html.

BBC. "Germany passes stringent hate speech law." 2017. https://www.bbc.com/news/av/technology-40444357/germany-passes-stringent-hate-speech-law.

Berryhill, J., Kok Heang, K., Clogher, R., McBride, K. "Hello, world: Artificial intelligence and its use in the public sector." *OECD*, November 2019. https:// oecd-opsi.org/projects/ai/.

Bolukbasi, T., Chang, K., Zou, J. Y., Saligrama, V., Kalai, A. T. "Man is to computer programmer as woman is to homemaker? Debiasing word embeddings." In *Advances in Neural Information Processing Systems*, 4349–4357, 2016. arXiv:1607.06520v1.

Bostrom, N. *Superintelligence. Paths, Dangers, Strategies.* Oxford: Oxford University Press, 2016.

Bradley, C., Wingfield, R., Metzger, M. "National artificial intelligence strategies and human rights: A review." Global Partners Digital, Global Digital Policy Incubator at the Stanford Cyber Policy Center, April 2020. https://cyber.fsi .stanford.edu/gdpi/content/national-artificial-intelligence-strategies-and -human-rights-review.

Brooks, R. "A better lesson." Blog, 2019. https://rodneybrooks.com/a-better -lesson/.

Broussard, M. *Artificial Unintelligence: How Computers Misunderstand the World.* Cambridge: MIT Press, 2018.

Bryson, J. J., Diamantis, M. E., Grant, T. D. "Of, for, and by the people: The legal lacuna of synthetic persons." *Artificial Intelligence and Law* 25, no. 3 (2017), 273–291. https://doi.org/10.1007/s10506-017-9214-9.

Buolamwini, J., Gebru, T. "Gender shades: Intersectional accuracy disparities in commercial gender classification." In *Proceedings of Machine Learning Research*, 81, 1–15. Conference on Fairness, Accountability, and Transparency, 2018. http:// proceedings.mlr.press/v81/buolamwini18a/buolamwini18a.pdf.

Caplan, R., Donovan, J., Hanson, L., Matthews, J. "Algorithmic accountability: A primer." 2018. https://datasociety.net/output/algorithmic-accountability -a-primer/.

Castellanos, S. "AI engineer jobs ranked among the best in the U.S." *Wall Street Journal Pro Artificial Intelligence*, 2019. https://www.wsj.com/articles/ai-engi neer-jobs-ranked-among-the-best-in-the-u-s-11552945632?mod=djemAIPro.

Cave, S., Dihal, K. "Ancient dreams of intelligent machines: 3,000 years of robots." 2018559 (2018), 473–475. https://doi.org/10.1038/d41586-018-05773-y.

Central Committee of the Communist Party of China. "The 13th five-year plan for economic and social development of the People's Republic of China (2016–2020)." 2016. http://en.ndrc.gov.cn/newsrelease/201612/P0201612076 45765233498.pdf.

Cerulus, L. "Macron: France to invest nearly €1.5B for AI until 2022." *Politico*, 2018. https://www.politico.eu/article/macron-france-to-invest-nearly-e1-5 -billion-for-ai-until-2022/.

Chadwick, P. "To regulate AI we need new laws, not just a code of ethics." *The Guardian*, 2018. https://www.theguardian.com/commentisfree/2018/oct/28 /regulate-ai-new-laws-code-of-ethics-technology-power.

Chatham House. "Artificial intelligence and international affairs: Disruption anticipated." 2018. https://www.chathamhouse.org/publication/artificial -intelligence-and-international-affairs?utm_source=Chatham%20House

&utm_medium=email&utm_campaign=9533492_New%20Publication
%3A%20Artificial%20Intelligence%20and%20International%20Affairs
&dm_i=1S3M,5OC38,RGOFXN,M30PS,1.

CIFAR. "Pan-Canadian artificial intelligence strategy." 2017. https://www.cifar
.ca/ai/pan-canadian-artificial-intelligence-strategy.

Cihon, P. "Technical report: Standards for AI governance: International standards
to enable global coordination in AI research & development." Oxford Internet
Institute, 2019. https://www.fhi.ox.ac.uk/standards-technical-report/.

Clark, G. "Government should lead AI certification: Finkel." *Government News*,
2018. https://www.governmentnews.com.au/government-should-lead-ai
-certification-finkel/.

Costanza-Chock, S. "Design justice: Towards an intersectional feminist framework for design theory and practice." *Proceedings of the Design Research
Society*, 2018. https://papers.ssrn.com/sol3/papers.cfm?abstract_id
=3189696.

Courtland, R. "Bias detectives: The researchers striving to make algorithms fair."
Nature 558 (2018), 357–360. https://doi.org/10.1038/d41586-018-05469-3.

Crawford, K., Joler, V. "Anatomy of an AI system." 2018. https://anatomyof.ai/.

Daniels, J., Nkonde, M., Mir, D. "Advancing racial literacy in tech." 2019. https://
racialliteracy.tech/.

Delcker, J. "Germany's €3B plan to become an AI powerhouse." *Politico*, 2018. https://
www.politico.eu/article/germanys-plan-to-become-an-ai-powerhouse/.

Dutton, T. "An overview of national AI strategies." *Medium AI + Politics*, 2018.
https://medium.com/politics-ai/an-overview-of-national-ai-strategies
-2a70ec6edfd.

Dutton, T., Barron, B., Boskovic, G. "Building an AI world: Report on national
and regional AI strategies." CIFAR, 2018. https://www.cifar.ca/docs/default
-source/ai-society/buildinganaiworld_eng.pdf?sfvrsn=fb18d129_4.

Elish, M. C., Mateescu, A. "AI in context: The labor of integrating new technologies." Data & Society, 2019. https://datasociety.net/output/ai-in-context/.

Esteva, A., Kuprel, B., Novoa, R. A., Ko, J., Swetter, S. M., Blau, H. M., Thrun,
S. "Dermatologist-level classification of skin cancer with deep neural networks." *Nature* 542 (2017), 115–118. https://doi.org/10.1038/nature21056.

Eubanks, V. *Automating Inequality: How High-Tech Tools Profile, Police, and
Punish the Poor.* New York: St Martin's Press, 2018.

European Commission. "The European artificial intelligence landscape." 2018.
https://ec.europa.eu/digital-single-market/en/news/european-artificial
-intelligence-landscape.

Finlayson, S. G., Bowers, J. D., Ito, J., Zittrain, J. L., Beam, A. L., Kohane, I. S.
"Adversarial attacks on medical machine learning." *Science* 363, no. 6433
(2019), 1287–1289. doi: 10.1126/science.aaw4399.

Frankel, T. C., Chavez, M. R., Ribas, J. "The cobalt pipeline. Tracing the path
from deadly hand-dug mines in Congo to consumers' phones and laptops."
The Washington Post, 2016. https://www.washingtonpost.com/graphics/
business/batteries/congo-cobalt-mining-for-lithium-ion-battery/?noredi-
rect=on.

Future of Life Institute. "National and international AI strategies." 2019. https://futureoflife.org/national-international-ai-strategies/?cn-reloaded=1.

Greene, D., Hoffmann, A. L., Stark, L. "Better, nicer, clearer, fairer: A critical assessment of the movement for ethical artificial intelligence and machine learning." Hawaii International Conference on System Sciences (HICSS), Maui, HI, 2019.

Gunia, A. U. K. "Authorities propose making social media executives personally responsible for harmful content." *Time Magazine*, 2019. https://time.com/5565843/united-kingdom-social-media-regulations/.

Harnett, K. "To build truly intelligent machines, teach them cause and effect." *Quanta Magazine*, 2018. https://www.quantamagazine.org/to-build-truly-intelligent-machines-teach-them-cause-and-effect-20180515/.

Hicks, M. *Programmed Inequality. How Britain Discarded Women Technologists and Lost Its Edge in Computing.* Cambridge: MIT Press, 2017.

Hildebrandt, M. *Law for Computer Scientists.* Oxford University Press, 2018, forthcoming. Pre-print for comment. https://lawforcomputerscientists.pubpub.org/.

House of Lords. "AI in the UK: Ready, willing and able?" 2018. https://publications.parliament.uk/pa/ld201719/ldselect/ldai/100/10002.htm.

IEEE. "P7006—Standard for personal data artificial intelligence (AI) agent." 2017. https://standards.ieee.org/project/7006.html.

IEEE. "IEEE launches ethics certification program for autonomous and intelligent systems." 2018. https://standards.ieee.org/news/2018/ieee-launches-ecpais.html.

IEEE. "IEEE code of ethics." 2019a. https://www.ieee.org/about/corporate/governance/p7-8.html.

IEEE. "Ethically aligned design, First edition." 2019b. https://ethicsinaction.ieee.org/.

Jee, C. "Australia's new law threatens jail if social-media firms don't remove violent content." *MIT Technology Review*, 2019. https://www.technologyreview.com/f/613268/australias-new-law-threatens-jail-if-social-media-firms-dont-remove-violent/.

Keyes, O. "The misgendering machines: Trans/HCI implications of automatic gender recognition." *Proceedings of the ACM on Human-Computer Interaction* 2 (2018). CSCW, Article 88. https://doi.org/10.1145/3274357.

Knight, W., Hao, K. "Never mind killer robots—here are six real AI dangers to watch out for in 2019." *MIT Technology Review*, 2019. https://www.technologyreview.com/s/612689/never-mind-killer-robotshere-are-six-real-ai-dangers-to-watch-out-for-in-2019/.

Latonero, M. "Governing artificial intelligence. Upholding human rights & dignity." Data and Society, 2018. https://datasociety.net/output/governing-artificial-intelligence/.

Lee, D. "Meeting the Kenyans powering Silicon Valley's artificial intelligence." *BBC News*, 2018. https://www.bbc.com/news/av/technology-46072113/meeting-the-kenyans-powering-silicon-valley-s-artificial-intelligence.

Lee, K.-F. *AI Superpowers: China, Silicon Valley, and the New World Order.* Boston, MA: Houghton Mifflin Harcourt, 2018.

Lung, N. "Singapore announces initiatives on AI governance and ethics." *OpenGov Asia,* 2019. https://www.opengovasia.com/singapore-announces-initiatives-on-ai-governance-and-ethics/.

Marcus, G. "Deep learning: A critical appraisal." 2018. arXiv pre-print. https://arxiv.org/abs/1801.00631.

Mari, A. "IBM to launch AI research center in Brazil." *Brazil Tech,* 2019. https://www.zdnet.com/article/ibm-to-launch-ai-research-center-in-brazil/.

Mazzucato, M. *The Entrepreneurial State. Debunking Public vs. Private Sector Myths.* 2nd ed. Penguin, 2018.

McNamara, A., Smith, J., Murphy-Hill, E. "Does ACM's code of ethics change ethical decision making in software development?" In *Proceedings of the 26th ACM Joint European Software Engineering Conference and Symposium on the Foundations of Software Engineering (ESEC/FSE '18),* 4–9 November 2018. https://doi.org/10.1145/3236024.3264833.

Metz, C. "As China marches forward on A.I., the White House is silent." *The New York Times,* 2018. https://www.nytimes.com/2018/02/12/technology/china-trump-artificial-intelligence.html?auth=login-email&login=email.

Mitchell, S., Portash, E., Barocas, S. "Prediction-based decisions and fairness: A catalogue of choices, assumptions, and definitions." 2018. arXiv pre-print, arXiv:1811.07867v1.

Mizroch, A. "In Israel, a stand out year for artificial intelligence technologies." *Forbes,* 2019. https://www.forbes.com/sites/startupnationcentral/2019/03/11/in-israel-a-stand-out-year-for-artificial-intelligence-technologies/#6dfde09030a8.

Moniz Pereira, L., Saptawijaya, A. *Programming Machine Ethics.* Springer International Publishing, 2016.

Mozur, P. "Beijing wants A.I. to be made in China by 2030." *The New York Times,* 2017. https://www.nytimes.com/2017/07/20/business/china-artificial-intelligence.html.

Nissenbaum, H. *Privacy in Context: Technology, Policy, and the Integrity of Social Life.* Stanford: Stanford Law Books., 2010.

Noble, S. U. *Algorithms of Oppression: How Search Engines Reinforce Racism.* New York: NYU Press, 2018.

Noothigattu, R., Bouneffouf, D., Mattei, N., Chandra, R., Madan, P., Varshney, K., Campbell, M., Singh, M., Rossi, F. "Interpretable multi-objective reinforcement learning through policy orchestration." 2018. arXiv pre-print, arXiv:1809.08343v1.

OECD. "Private equity investment in artificial intelligence." 2018. https://www.oecd.org/going-digital/ai/private-equity-investment-in-artificial-intelligence.pdf.

O'Neil, C. *Weapons of Math Destruction: How Big Data Increases Inequality and Threatens Democracy.* London: Penguin Books, 2016.

Pasquale, F. *The Black Box Society. The Secret Algorithms that Control Money and Information.* Cambridge, MA: Harvard University Press, 2015.

Pearce, R. "Budget 2018: Government seeks to boost Australian AI capabilities." *Computerworld*, 2018. https://www.computerworld.com.au/article/640926/budget-2018-government-seeks-boost-australian-ai-capabilities/.

Ravi, S., Nagaraj, P. "Harnessing the future of AI in India." Brookings Institution, 2018. https://www.brookings.edu/research/harnessing-the-future-of-ai-in-india/.

Risse, M. "Human rights and artificial intelligence: An urgently needed agenda." Carr Center for Human Rights Policy, Harvard Kennedy School, 2018. https://carrcenter.hks.harvard.edu/files/cchr/files/humanrightsai_designed.pdf.

Schechner, S. "Facebook faces potential $1.63 billion fine in Europe over data breach." *The Wall Street Journal*, 2018. https://www.wsj.com/articles/facebook-faces-potential-1-63-billion-fine-in-europe-over-data-breach-1538330906.

Sharman, J. "Metropolitan police's facial recognition technology 98% inaccurate, figures show." *The Independent*, 2018. https://www.independent.co.uk/news/uk/home-news/met-police-facial-recognition-success-south-wales-trial-home-office-false-positive-a8345036.html.

Sloane, M. "Making artificial intelligence socially just: Why the current focus on ethics is not enough." *LSE British Politics and Policy Blog*, 2018. https://blogs.lse.ac.uk/politicsandpolicy/artificial-intelligence-and-society-ethics/.

Sloane, M. "Inequality is the name of the game: Thoughts on the emerging field of technology, ethics and social justice." In *Proceedings of the Weizenbaum Conference 2019 "Challenges of Digital Inequality—Digital Education, Digital Work, Digital Life"*, 2019. https://doi.org/10.34669/wi.cp/2.9.

Slush, O. "The state of European tech." 2018. https://2018.stateofeuropeantech.com/chapter/state-european-tech-2018/article/executive-summary/.

Sokol, J. "Why artificial intelligence like AlphaZero has trouble with the real world." *Quanta Magazine*, 2018. https://www.quantamagazine.org/why-alphazeros-artificial-intelligence-has-trouble-with-the-real-world-20180221/.

Spencer, M. "Artificial intelligence hype is real." *Forbes Magazine*, 2019. https://www.forbes.com/sites/cognitiveworld/2019/02/25/artificial-intelligence-hype-is-real/#7b11243425fa.

Stark, L. "Facial recognition is the plutonium of AI." *XRDS* 25, no. 3 (2019), 50–55. https://doi.org/10.1145/3313129.

Statista. "Artificial intelligence (AI) funding investment in the United States from 2011 to 2019." 2019. https://www.statista.com/statistics/672712/ai-funding-united-states/.

Strubell, E., Ganesh, A., McCallum, A. "Energy and policy considerations for deep learning in NLP." In *57th Annual Meeting of the Association for Computational Linguistics (ACL)*, Florence, Italy. July 2019. arXiv pre-print. https://arxiv.org/abs/1906.02243.

Suchman, L., Irani, L., Ansaro, P. "Google's march to the business of war must be stopped." *The Guardian Opinion*, 2018. https://www.theguardian.com/commentisfree/2018/may/16/google-business-war-project-maven.

Tiku, N. "The EU hits Google with a third billion-dollar fine. So what?" *Wired Magazine*, 2019. https://www.wired.com/story/eu-hits-google-third-billion-dollar-fine-so-what/.

US Congress. "Algorithmic accountability act of 2019." 2019. https://www.congress.gov/116/bills/hr2231/BILLS-116hr2231ih.pdf.

US National Security Commission on Artificial Intelligence. "Mitigating economic impacts of the COVID-19 pandemic and preserving US strategic competitiveness in artificial intelligence," *White Paper Series on Pandemic Response and Preparedness, No. 2.* May 2020. https://drive.google.com/file/d/1vSRRfqV6S4xGoMxueC-CMG0tYYTGa1Ly/view.

US Department of Defense. "Summary of the 2018 Department of Defense artificial intelligence strategy: Harnessing AI to advance our security and prosperity." 2019. https://media.defense.gov/2019/Feb/12/2002088963/-1/-1/1/SUMMARY-OF-DOD-AI-STRATEGY.PDF.

Verhulst, S., Sloane, M. "Realizing the potential of AI localism." *Project Syndicate*, 7 February 2020. https://www.project-syndicate.org/commentary/local-regulation-of-artificial-intelligence-uses-by-stefaan-g-verhulst-1-and-mona-sloane-2020-02?barrier=accesspaylog.

Wachter, S., Mittelstadt, B., Russell, C. "Counterfactual explanations without opening the black box: Automated decisions and the GDPR." *Harvard Journal of Law & Technology* 31, no. 2 (2018). https://papers.ssrn.com/sol3/papers.cfm?abstract_id=3063289.

Wagner, B. "Ethics as an escape from regulation: From ethics-washing to ethics-shopping?" In *Being Profiling. Cogitas Ergo Sum*, edited by M. Hildebrandt. Amsterdam, Netherlands: Amsterdam University Press, 2018.

Wallach, W., Allen, C. *Moral Machines: Teaching Robots Right from Wrong.* Oxford: Oxford University Press, 2009.

Webster, G., Creemers, R., Triolo, P., Kania, E. "China's plan to 'Lead' in AI: Purpose, prospects, and problems." *New America*, 2017. https://www.newamerica.org/cybersecurity-initiative/blog/chinas-plan-lead-ai-purpose-prospects-and-problems/.

Wilson, B., Hoffman, J., Morgenstern, J. "Predictive inequity in object detection." 2019. arXiv pre-print. https://arxiv.org/abs/1902.11097.

Yu, H., Shen, Z., Miao, C., Leung, C., Lesser, V. R., Yang, Q. "Building ethics into artificial intelligence." In *Proceedings of the Twenty-Seventh International Joint Conference on Artificial Intelligence (IJCAI-18)*, 5527–5533, 2018.

Zuboff, S. *The Age of Surveillance Capitalism: The Fight for a Human Future at the New Frontier of Power.* New York: PublicAffairs, 2019.

CHAPTER 2

Governance of Artificial Intelligence

Emerging International Trends and Policy Frames

Inga Ulnicane, William Knight, Tonii Leach,
Bernd Carsten Stahl, and Winter-Gladys Wanjiku

CONTENTS

Only if we acknowledge technology's power to shape our hearts
and minds, and our collective beliefs and behaviours, will the
discourses of governance shift from fatalistic determinism to the
emancipation of self-determination.[1]

DOI: 10.1201/9780429446726-2

2.1 INTRODUCTION: WHY FOCUS ON AI POLICY AND GOVERNANCE?

Recent advances in machine learning and data analytics have led to high public policy activity addressing artificial intelligence (AI) around the world. Since 2016, national governments, international organisations, civil society organisations, think tanks, and consultancies have launched their AI strategies and reports. Countries and regions from the United States and China to the European Union, France, the United Kingdom, and others have declared their ambitions to be leaders in AI. How to explain this recent political and policy interest in AI?

While the development of AI goes back to the 1950s, major advances in the availability of data and computing power have only recently taken place.[2] This has led to the increasing use of AI over a wide range of areas, from political campaigns and labour markets to health, education, and the military, to name just a few. New technological opportunities and related scandals (e.g. the Cambridge Analytica case) have stirred debates among policymakers, politicians, experts, and stakeholders about the positive and negative effects of AI on politics, economics, labour markets, fairness, privacy, and other key societal issues.[3]

Public policy and governance can play a major role in ensuring beneficial and avoiding harmful developments of AI. [4] While recently AI development has been primarily driven by large global private companies and their profit motives, emerging policy developments suggest that national governments and international organisations, in collaboration with a broad range of stakeholders, are preparing governance frameworks for AI. A wide range of policy and governance tools, including hard and soft legislation and regulation, investments, retraining programmes, awareness, and other measures have been suggested to facilitate the development and use of AI in a socially desirable manner towards ends such as accountability, fairness, and inclusion.

The fast-developing policies and politics of AI have, so far, been studied mostly from an ethical and philosophical viewpoint but less so from the perspective of policy and governance, which can play an important role in shaping technology development and use according to societal interests and values. To address this gap, this chapter aims to reflect on some of the emerging international AI policy trends and ideas. It addresses the two main research questions: What is driving fast-developing AI policies around the world? And what are the main frames of the emerging AI policies? Thus, this chapter aims to contribute to AI research by providing insights into policy dynamics and content. Using concepts and insights from the social studies of emerging sciences and technologies, such as the performative function of hypes and expectations, as well as collaboration and competition dynamics in emerging fields, helps to make sense of emerging AI policies, politics, and governance to contextualise recent AI policies and governance in a longer-term development of emerging technologies and to critically reflect on them.

This chapter proceeds as follows: Section 2.2 introduces a conceptual framework to study emerging sciences and technologies and their governance; Section 2.3 reviews the recent literature on AI governance; Section 2.4 outlines emerging international AI policy trends; Section 2.5 presents three AI policy frames; finally, Section 2.6 summarises the main insights.

2.2 EMERGING SCIENCES AND TECHNOLOGIES AND THEIR GOVERNANCE: HYPE, EXPECTATIONS, AND UNCERTAINTIES

To make sense of the current discussions about AI governance and policy, it is helpful to situate them in the context of social studies of science and technology. These studies address a number of conceptual questions that are highly relevant for reflecting on recent developments in AI policy and governance, including questions such as—What is technology? What are the characteristics of emerging sciences and technologies? What is governance? And what are the specific features of governance of emerging technologies?

According to Eric Schatzberg, technology is an odd concept with multiple meanings.[5] Traditional understandings of technology associating it with hardware need to be revisited in the digital age. According to a popular policy definition that covers digital technologies but is rather business oriented,

> Technology refers to the state of knowledge on how to convert resources into outputs. This includes the practical use and application to business processes or products of technical methods, systems, devices, skills and practices.[6]

To make sense of the diverse understandings of technology, it is helpful to consider a distinction that Schatzberg makes between the cultural and instrumental approach to technology, whereas the cultural approach "view[s] technology as a creative expression of human culture," while the instrumental approach insists that technology "is a mere instrument that serves ends defined by others."[7] He believes that a shift from an instrumental to cultural understanding would "help humans to exert more conscious control over their technological futures."[8]

Co-creation of society and technology, the social embedding of technology and its political nature are some of the key themes addressed in the social studies of science and technology. Sheila Jasanoff reminds us that "technological choices, are, as well, intrinsically political: they order society, distribute benefits and burdens, and channel power,"[9] while Langdon Winner suggests that "we should try to imagine and seek to build technical regimes compatible with freedom, social justice, and other key political ends."[10] The societal embedding of technologies is highlighted by concepts such as "socio-technical systems," which refer to

> the fact that individual technical artefacts or innovations are not operating in isolation. On the contrary, the functioning of technical artefacts and innovations is highly dependent on specific and complex ensembles of elements in which they are embedded. It is not the individual artefact or innovation as such that has an effect, but it is interplay with and embedding in other technical and non-technical elements in society and economy.[11]

Emerging technologies are characterised by a number of distinct features. According to Daniele Rotolo and colleagues,[12] the five key attributes of an emerging technology are radical novelty, relatively fast growth, coherence, prominent impact, and uncertainty and ambiguity. They define an emerging technology as:

> a radically novel and relatively fast-growing technology characterised by a certain degree of coherence persisting over time and with the potential to exert a considerable impact on the socioeconomic domain(s), which is observed in terms of the composition of actors, institutions and patterns of interactions among those, along with the associated knowledge production processes. Its most prominent impact, however, lies in the future, and so in the emergence phase is still somewhat uncertain and ambiguous.[13]

Additionally, researchers in the social studies of science and technology[14] have suggested that newly emerging fields experience very active collaborative dynamics. Robert Merton[15] distinguishes the "hot fields" of emerging sciences from the "cold fields," where the former has a high rate of significant discoveries with implications well beyond the borders of the speciality. "Hot fields" are highly competitive, and they attract larger proportions of talented scientists interested in working on challenging problems. According to Merton, intertwined cognitive and social processes of intense interaction and rivalry in a new scientific field lead to the rapid growth of knowledge and scientific innovation.

Furthermore, emerging technologies are characterised by hypes and expectations, which also have a performative function.[16] The performative approach is

> not interested in hypes as more or less accurate forecasts, but as collectively pursued explorations of the future that affect activities in the present. While the early and high-rising expectations that characterise hype hardly ever materialise precisely as foreseen, they structure and shape the materialisations that eventually occur.[17]

Hypes are closely related to expectations, as "hypes are constituted by expectations at different levels"[18] and expectations shape emerging technologies. Expectations are not always positive, suggesting breakthroughs, hopes, and advancements, as they can also be negative, mentioning potential problems that will have to be solved. According to Harro Van Lente and colleagues,[19] both positive as well as negative expectations

> guide the activities of innovative actors by setting agendas; they provide legitimacy and thus help to attract financing and enrol actors; and they, while often spread through spoken and written words, may materialise in experiments and prototypes.

Importantly for policy and governance, "when more and more actors share similar expectations, the promises inherent to these expectations are gradually translated into requirements, guidelines, and specifications regarding the new technology."[20]

Due to their specific characteristics, such as radical novelty and prominent impact, governance is of particular importance for emerging technologies. Similar to the concept of technology discussed above, the concept of governance has multiple meanings. According to Vasudha Chhotray and Gerry Stoker, "governance is about the rules of collective decision-making in settings where there is a plurality of actors or organisations and where no formal control systems can dictate the terms of the relationship between these actors and organisations."[21] In this definition, governance includes formal as well as informal rules (formal arrangements and informal practices, conventions, and customs); decisions made by a collective of individuals involving issues of mutual influence and control; and a broad understanding of decision-making which can be strategic but can also be contained in the everyday implementation practice of a system or organisation. Moreover, according to Chhotray and Stoker, "[t]he characteristic forms of social interaction in governance rely on negotiation, signals, communication and hegemonic influence rather than direct oversight and supervision."[22] Additionally, according to them, governance "is about coordination and decision-making in the context of a plurality of views and interests. Conflict and dissent provide essential ingredients to a governance process."[23] For them, "governance is practice"[24] and "the purposes of governance then demand to be understood analytically and empirically as a set of practices rather than through the lens of a 'wish-list' of principles to be followed."[25]

In relation to socio-technical systems, Susana Borras and Jakob Edler[26] define governance "as the mechanisms whereby societal actors and state actors interact and coordinate to regulate issues of societal concern." This understanding of governance highlights that the state increasingly coordinates its activities with a wide range of actors, including from the private sector, civil society, and expert communities. Changing ideas about the role of the state in the governance of technologies is also captured in concepts such as "the entrepreneurial state"[27] that emphasises the importance of public sector investing and taking risks to co-shape technological development towards societal goals known in recent policy discussions as Grand Challenges[28] or missions in areas of the United Nations' Sustainable Development Goals, such as environment and climate change.[29]

Governance of emerging sciences and technologies faces special challenges due to uncertainties around their future developments, societal benefits, and risks.[30] To address the specific needs of emerging sciences and technologies, Stefan Kuhlmann and colleagues[31] suggested the concept of "tentative governance" "when public and private interventions are designed as a dynamic process that is prudent and preliminary rather than assertive and persistent. Tentative governance typically aims at creating spaces for probing and learning instead of stipulating definitive targets."[32]

As opposed to more definitive modes of governance, tentative governance maintains flexibility and is open to experimentation, learning, and reflexivity. While uncertainty is a typical characteristic for all sciences and technologies, and thus their governance can benefit from including elements of tentativeness, uncertainties are particularly pronounced in the case of emerging sciences and technologies, and therefore tentative governance is of special importance here. Kuhlmann and colleagues emphasise that

> the added value generated by the tentative governance concept resides, first and foremost, in making clear that in the context of innovation studies governance needs to be appropriately conceptualised in order to avoid unrealistic assumptions about the steering of innovation in a desired way or direction.[33]

According to them, elements of tentativeness can be found in a number of existing social science approaches such as reflexive governance, anticipatory governance, experimentalist governance, constructive technology assessment, and responsible research and innovation (for more on responsible research and innovation, see Section 2.3).

Insights from the literature on emerging technologies and their governance are highly relevant for understanding recent and ongoing developments in the field of AI. Based on these insights, it can be expected that AI will be characterised by dynamic collaboration and competition, the influence of uncertainty, performative function of hype and positive as well as negative expectations. This chapter will examine these features in the context of policy and governance.

2.3 LITERATURE REVIEW OF AI GOVERNANCE: ETHICS, RESPONSIBILITY AND POLICY

In AI debates and research, the term "governance" is used in multiple ways. In AI policy documents, "governance" is mentioned in the context of government, regulation, and ethics without hardly ever defining the term.[34] Similarly, in research on AI, the term "governance" often remains unspecified and is used in many different ways. It is used in the literature on ethical and legal aspects of AI,[35] which is part of AI ethics research.[36] It is also used to examine the use of AI in the public sector and emerging international cooperation. Moreover, it is closely related to discussions about AI policy. This section provides some illustrative examples of the ways that the term "governance" is used in the social studies of AI.

Research on the ethical aspects of AI governance focuses on issues such as fairness, transparency, privacy, and accountability, as well as responses to large-scale discrimination and disappearance of jobs due to AI-based automation.[37] To address these issues, researchers have suggested a number of frameworks and roadmaps for the ethical governance of AI. Alan Winfield and Marina Jirotka define ethical governance as

> a set of processes, procedures, cultures and values designed to ensure the highest standards of behaviour. Ethical governance thus goes beyond simply good (i.e. effective) governance, in that it inculcates ethical behaviours in both individual designers and the organisations in which they work. Normative ethical governance is seen as an important pillar of responsible research and innovation.[38]

Thus, studies of (ethical) AI governance draw on established approaches such as responsible research and innovation, which in recent years has been widely used in science and technology studies, practice and policy.[39] According to one influential definition, "responsible innovation means taking care of the future through collective stewardship of science and innovation in the present"[40] and is based on four dimensions of anticipation, reflexivity, inclusion, and responsiveness. Virginia Dignum, who applies the RRI approach to AI, defines Responsible AI as "the development of intelligent systems according to fundamental human principles and values."[41] According to her, "responsibility is about ensuring that results are beneficial for many instead of a source of revenue for a few."[42]

Winfield and Jirotka[43] suggest a roadmap for ethical governance of robotics and AI, which they see as essential for building public trust. Their roadmap includes ethics, standards, regulation, RRI, and public engagement. By bringing these elements together, they aim to address what they see as a gap between principles and practice. To facilitate translating ethical principles into the practice of effective and transparent ethical governance, Winfield and Jirotka[44] propose the following five pillars: first, publish an ethical code of conduct; second, provide ethics and responsible innovation training; third, practice responsible innovation, including the engagement of wider stakeholders within a framework of anticipatory governance that includes an ethical risk assessment of new products; fourth, be transparent about ethical governance; and fifth, really value ethical governance as one of the core values rather than just a smokescreen.

Another research stream uses the term "governance" to examine the impact of AI on decision-making in public administration.[45] The concept of governance is also used to analyse emerging international AI initiatives and to develop proposals for their future development,[46] as well as to discuss prospects for global cooperation.[47] Some studies have analysed governance and policy aspects of specific AI applications such as autonomous vehicles.[48]

Governance issues are addressed in the literature on AI policy. A number of studies have examined national AI strategies and other policy documents. Some have analysed initial AI policy documents starting from 2016 (see Section 2.4 below) from ethical[49] and expertise[50] perspectives. National strategies of the Nordic countries—Sweden, Finland, Norway and Denmark—as digital frontrunners have been analysed and compared according to the cultural values of trust, transparency, and openness[51] as well as ethical principles[52] and influence of the EU AI policy.[53] Studies of AI policy documents have examined framing of socio-technical future visions in German AI policy documents and media,[54] national varieties of AI discourses in British, German, and Dutch policies,[55] and the shaping of China's AI policy initiatives.[56] The framing of governance, [57] as well as concerns and proposed solutions,[58] in AI policy documents have also been studied.

Several publications provide recommendations for AI policy, outlining key challenges,[59] setting out actionable principles to implement ethics guidelines,[60] and trying to bridge the gap between near-term and long-term AI concerns.[61] A number of publications on AI highlight the need for policies and regulations that would mitigate risks and direct AI development and use towards public benefit.[62]

To summarise, this section demonstrates that the concept of governance has been used in AI research in multiple ways, referring to ethical and legal aspects, responsible innovation, use of AI in the public sector, international AI initiatives, and policy documents. While so far the social studies of AI have had a strong focus on ethics (even when using the terms of policy and governance), this chapter will proceed to examine political, policy, and governance issues, which have so far received less attention.

2.4 FAST-DEVELOPING POLICY FOR AI: INTERNATIONAL TRENDS AND DRIVERS

Since 2016, national governments, international organisations, think tanks, civil societies, and consultancies around the world have regularly launched new AI policy documents.[63] While almost all of these documents mention AI in the title, there is no agreed definition of AI. [64] Policy documents typically use AI as an umbrella term that includes machine learning, algorithms, autonomous systems, and other related terms. According to the definition used in the European Commission's 2018 communication on AI in Europe, AI

> refers to systems that display intelligent behaviour by analysing their environment and taking actions—with some degree of autonomy—to achieve specific goals. AI-based systems can be purely software-based, acting in the virtual world (e.g. voice assistants, image analysis software, search engines, speech and face recognition systems), or AI can be embedded in hardware devices (e.g. advanced robots, autonomous cars, drones or Internet of Things applications).[65]

Early AI policy documents were published by the US Executive Office of the President, UK House of Commons and European Parliament. These documents analyse ethical, social, and economic topics but have been criticised for coming "short of providing an overarching political vision and long-term strategy for the development of a 'good AI society,'"[66] and for occasionally relying on the opinions of public figures such as Elon Musk and Stephen Hawking, rather than on AI experts.[67] In subsequent years, the launch of these documents has been followed by intensified AI policy-making around the world.

According to the Organisation for Economic Co-operation and Development (OECD), in early 2020 "around the world, at least 50 countries (including the European Union) have developed, or are in the process of developing, a national AI strategy."[68] These data also demonstrate that the development of AI strategies is unevenly distributed around the world. Most of the existing strategies have been launched in Europe, North America, and major Asian powerhouses such as China, India, Japan, and South Korea, with very little activity in Africa, Latin America, and large parts of Asia. These uneven developments around the world present limitations and potential challenges with AI policy and governance developments being concentrated in the most developed parts of the world.

Similar uneven international developments can be observed in a related field of AI ethics. A recent review of AI ethics guidelines analysed 84 documents; most of them were released in the US (21), within the EU (19), followed by the UK (13) and Japan (4).[69] Several studies indicate considerable convergence among the documents.[70] In their review of six ethical AI frameworks,[71] Luciano Floridi and colleagues[72] synthesise 47 principles found in these frameworks into five principles: beneficence, non-maleficence, autonomy, justice, and explicability. While the first four of these principles have been used in bioethics, the fifth—explicability—is added specifically for AI. Other studies suggest that in addition to similarities among these frameworks, there are also important differences. The above-mentioned analysis of 84 ethics guidelines by Anna Jobin and colleagues[73] reveals

> a global convergence emerging around five ethical principles (transparency, justice and fairness, non-maleficence, responsibility and privacy), with substantive divergence in relation to how these principles are interpreted, why they are deemed important, what issue, domain or actors they pertain to and how they should be implemented.[74]

The examination of 112 documents by Daniel Schiff and colleagues found meaningful differences across documents prepared by public, private, and non-governmental organisations, highlighting that "as compared to documents from private entities, NGO, and public sector documents reflect more ethical breadth in the number of topics covered, are more engaged with law and regulation, and are generated through a process that are more participatory."[75]

The important question is—what is driving this intensive policy development in AI in the most developed parts of the world? While major policy initiatives have also been launched in cases of other emerging technologies, such as nanotechnology and life sciences, the political and policy attention devoted to AI around the world since late 2016 is unprecedented. AI has some important differences from previous technologies. If nanotechnology and life sciences raised questions about their effects on human health and economy, then AI applications and effects go far beyond that and include major impacts on the political system, labour market, and welfare state. The idea that machine intelligence can supersede human intelligence has captured the collective imagination in cases such as the AlphaGo computer programme beating the Go world champion.[76] Additionally, scandals such as the misuse of social media data for influencing democratic processes by the company Cambridge Analytica have added urgency to the calls for public authorities to regulate the use of AI, machine learning and big data analytics. Thus, the intense political and policy attention paid to AI is largely a result of the broad and diverse effects of AI on numerous areas of human activity.

Another driving force behind the recent development of AI policies has been international organisations such as the World Economic Forum (WEF) and the OECD that have put AI on the agenda of political leaders. In the context of WEF, focus on AI has been part of discussions about the so-called Fourth Industrial Revolution. The concept of the Fourth Industrial Revolution has been promoted by the founder and executive chairman of the WEF, Klaus Schwab, who claims that since 2000 the world has been experiencing the Fourth Industrial Revolution, which is characterised by a fusion of new technologies across physical, digital, and biological domains.[77] According to Schwab, the Fourth Industrial Revolution follows the first one, that from 1760 to 1840 took place due to railroads, steam engines, and mechanical production; the second industrial revolution was from the late 19th century to early 20th century characterised by mass production, electricity, and assembly lines; and finally, the third industrial revolution that from the 1960s onwards took place with the development of computer/digital revolution, semiconductors, personal computing, and the internet. AI is one of the technologies that plays a key role in the discussions about the Fourth Industrial Revolution and associated governance and policy.

Furthermore, the OECD, which has long played a key role in developing ideas for science, technology, and innovation policy,[78] has become a major international forum for expertise and dialogue on AI policy. The OECD AI principles include recommendations for policymakers to invest in AI research and development, foster a digital ecosystem for AI, shape an enabling policy environment for AI, build human capacity, and prepare for labour market transformation, as well as cooperate internationally for trustworthy AI.[79] The OECD AI Policy Observatory is a platform that provides information, data, and multi-disciplinary analysis of AI.[80] The OECD Network of Experts on AI (ONE AI) is a multi-disciplinary and multi-stakeholder community that contributes policy, technical, and business expert input to inform OECD analysis and recommendations.[81]

There have also been other international fora emerging to discuss AI policy, for example, since 2017 the United Nations' International Telecommunication Union has been organising annual AI for Good summits to facilitate global and inclusive dialogue on AI. Moreover, there is a lot of policy learning [82] taking place across countries and organisations.

For example, when the European Commission was preparing its AI policy documents, it reviewed AI strategies from major economic powers: the US, China, Japan, Germany, United Arab Emirates, and the UK.[83] Similarly, recommendations for US national strategy are accompanied by a map of AI national strategies around the world.[84] Furthermore, the European Commission's 2018 document on the European perspective on AI undertakes a detailed analysis of the global AI landscape and the EU's vision and performance in a comparative context.[85] An interesting development in comparing AI policies and performance across countries and regions is the emergence of a number of global AI rankings such as the Global AI Index,[86] Government AI Readiness Index,[87] and AI Index.[88] These rankings compare national AI strategies, investments, publications and a range of other indicators.

Thus, a broad range of AI applications in interaction with global political debates and international policy learning facilitate and reinforce fast-developing AI policies. AI policy developments, however, are unevenly distributed around the world. In the case of fast-developing AI policy in the most developed parts of the world, we can observe the performative function that hype and expectations play[89] (see Section 2.2 above) in shaping not only emerging technology, but also policy. Perceptions of hype and high expectations towards AI help to mobilise policymakers and stakeholders, create a sense of urgency, and guide activities and decisions in policymaking, as will be further demonstrated in the next section.

2.5 EMERGING AI POLICY FRAMES: REVOLUTION, GLOBAL RACE, AND BALANCING BENEFITS, RISKS, AND RESPONSIBILITIES

What are the key ideas, aims, and objectives of AI policy documents that have been launched in recent years? To study the content and ideas of AI policy documents, this chapter draws on the approach of policy framing.[90] Policy framing is a productive way to get insights into policy ideas and understanding because in frames, "facts, values, theories, and interests are integrated."[91] According to Martin Rein and Donal Schön,

> framing is a way of selecting, organising, interpreting, and making sense of a complex reality to provide guideposts for knowing, analysing, persuading, and acting. A frame is a perspective from which an amorphous, ill-defined, problematic situation can be made sense of and acted on.[92]

The policy frames here are derived from reviewing policy documents [93] and political debates on AI. Three key frames can be distinguished: first, AI as a revolutionary, transformative, and disruptive technology; second, closely interconnected global competition and collaboration in the field of AI; and third, a three-pillar approach of facilitating benefits, managing risks, and ensuring responsibilities are met.

The first policy frame that presents AI as a revolutionary, transformative, and disruptive technology highlights promising as well as troublesome aspects of AI. An example of this frame can be seen in the US national AI research and development strategic plan that introduces AI as "a transformative technology that holds promise for tremendous societal and economic benefit. AI has the potential to revolutionise how we live, work, learn, discover, and communicate."[94] Similarly, the EU communication on AI frames AI as "one of the most strategic industries of the 21st century" and states that "like the steam engine or electricity in the past, AI is transforming our world, our society and our industry."[95] As can be seen in this quote, AI is often compared to previous transformative and disruptive technologies as well as industrial and digital revolutions, highlighting similarities as well as differences.

Some policy documents highlight the unique character of AI, describing it as "the most transformative force in the twenty-first century. Its scale, speed, and complexity are unprecedented, disrupting every industry and sector across the globe."[96] On the other hand, documents often emphasise similarities between AI and other technologies and revolutions in terms of presenting opportunities, challenges, and changes. Among the opportunities presented by AI, policy discourse mentions its potential to contribute to achieving the United Nations' Sustainable Development Goals and tackling grand societal challenges "from treating chronic diseases to reducing fatality rates in traffic accidents to fighting climate change or anticipating cybersecurity."[97] At the same time, it is indicated that, as with other revolutions, transformations, and disruptions, AI will change employment and labour markets as well as other fields. Similar to previous transformative and disruptive technologies, AI is expected to bring risks and challenges. This can be seen in the European Commission's statement that "as with any transformative technology, some AI applications may raise new ethical and legal questions, for example, related to liability or potentially biased decision-making."[98]

Comparisons of AI with industrial and digital revolutions can also be seen in the media and academic literature.[99] The discourse of technological revolution is not new. Langdon Winner has pointed out that proclamations of computer and other "revolutions" have been present since the 1960s.[100] In conclusion to his critical examination of the use of the term "revolution" to talk about information technologies, Winner points out that "calling such changes 'revolutionary,' we tacitly acknowledge that these are matters that require reflection, possibly even strong public action to ensure that the outcomes are desirable."[101]

To summarise, the first policy frame highlights that AI is associated with major and far-reaching changes and is often seen as an important element of the Fourth Industrial Revolution discussed in the previous section. National governments and international organisations emphasise very positive expectations towards AI but also mention some problematic aspects. As discussed in Section 2.2, positive expectations, which can be expressed in superlatives, constitute hypes in emerging fields that (irrespective of how accurate they are) affect and guide activities in the present, including agenda-setting and financing. This can be seen in policy documents where statements about revolutionary changes brought by AI are immediately followed with mentions of actions taken by governments:

> AI promises to revolutionise the way all of us go about our daily lives, impacting important sectors, including transport, health, education, defence, and finance. Governments across the world are working to understand the consequences of AI in order to create policy frameworks and regulations that harness its economic and social opportunities while also mitigating its potential risks.[102]

Moreover, the perceived transnational reach of the AI revolution leads to calls for global action and cooperation, as can be seen in this quote:

> AI, the driver of this technological revolution, transcends conventional geographical boundaries and, hence, if we wish to address the heart of the issue, the solutions must be at an international scale.[103]

Thus, strong positive expectations and hype surrounding emerging technology create a sense of urgency for global competition and collaboration, which can be seen in the following second AI policy frame.

The second policy frame focuses on emerging global competition and collaboration in the field of AI. Many countries and organisations have declared their ambitions to be leaders in AI. The 2016 US document "Preparing for the Future of Artificial Intelligence" declared that "the United States, a leader in AI R&D, can continue to play a key role in global research coordination."[104] In summer 2017, China's State Council called for China to become "the world's primary AI innovation center" by 2030.[105] In September 2017, the Russian President announced that the future belongs to AI and "whoever leads in AI will rule the world."[106] In early 2018, speaking at the WEF in Davos, the then UK prime minister announced that "we are establishing the UK as a world leader in Artificial Intelligence."[107] In March 2018, while presenting a national AI strategy, the French President announced the plan to turn his country into a world leader for AI research and innovation.[108] In April 2018, the communication on AI for Europe stated the EU aim "to become a leader in AI revolution, in its own way and based on its values."[109] The December 2018 document on the European perspective on AI depicts the EU's global position as follows:

> There is strong global competition on AI among the USA, China and Europe. The USA leads for now, but China is catching up fast and aims to lead by 2030. For the EU, it is not so much a question of winning or losing the race but of finding a way of embracing the opportunities offered by AI in a way that is human-centred, ethical, secure, and true to our core values.[110]

Discourses around the global leadership in AI have led to comparing AI development to a new space race.[111] Such international competitiveness discourses can help to mobilise political support and resources, but they have also been criticised, for example, in Paul Krugman's 1994 essay "Competitiveness: A Dangerous Obsession" because according to him they lead to bad policies, drawing resources and attention to the "attractive" competitiveness discourse rather than major economic and social problems.[112] An example here would be a well-known "the moon and the ghetto" problem,[113] when some popular areas and hyped technologies such as a space race get much more political attention and resources than more complex social problems of the ghetto. This problem has been pointed out by Jack Stilgoe, who reminds us that "if we overinvest our hopes in new technologies, we underinvest in other necessary but less glamorous areas, including education, public health, infrastructure and maintenance."[114]

Moreover, discourse on international competitiveness in AI depicts technological development as a zero-sum game when one country wins and others lose. Public policy and governance, however, can ensure that global AI development is a positive-sum game increasing benefits for all. Furthermore, the framing of relations between countries in the field of AI development is characterised not only by competition but also by cooperation. An example here are the European countries that in April 2018 signed a declaration to cooperate on AI.[115] Emerging international cooperation initiatives in AI[116] include the Global Partnership on AI (GPAI) launched in 2020. The GPAI, whose Secretariat is hosted at the OECD, currently brings together 18 countries and the EU "to support and guide the responsible adoption of AI that is grounded in human rights, inclusion, diversity, innovation, economic growth, and societal benefit, while seeking to address the UN Sustainable Development Goals."[117] Proposals for international cooperation in the field of AI include suggestions to use technology diplomacy "to help all interested parties develop a shared understanding and coordinate efforts to utilise AI for the benefit of humanity."[118]

Furthermore, competition and cooperation are closely related. Suggestions for the US leadership include calls for building strategic partnerships around the world.[119] Similarly, at the time when the French President announced his plan to turn France into a world leader for AI, he also proposed to set up a group akin to the Intergovernmental Panel on Climate Change for AI.[120] Thus, interactions among countries in AI development can be framed as "a competitive cooperation," a notion coined by Merton[121] to describe relationships in the scientific community where scientists at the same time compete for priority of discovery as well as cooperate to exchange ideas and knowledge. While social studies of science have focused on the intense interaction and competition in emerging fields in science and technology (see Section 2.2 above), here we can see that these dynamics apply not only to the science and technology community, but to the realm of public policy as well. Heightened focus on cooperation and competition among countries in AI development raises traditional questions about who is included and who is excluded, and how the benefits are distributed.

The third emerging frame focuses on the role of policy in balancing benefits, risks, and responsibilities in the development and use of AI as a revolutionary, transformative, and disruptive technology, as indicated in the first frame discussed above. This third AI policy frame typically consists of the three pillars where the first is about realising opportunities, the second deals with mitigating risks and negative outcomes, and the third is about ensuring the responsible and ethical development of AI. While some countries and organisations might prioritise one of these three pillars, elements of them can be found in many documents. For example, the focus of the US 2016 Strategic Plan includes long-term investments in AI research, security and safety of AI, standards and benchmarks, as well as ethical, legal, and societal implications of AI.[122]

The three pillars are present in the EU 2018 communication on AI for Europe. In this document, the first pillar is called "boosting the EU's technological and industrial capacity and AI uptake across economy."[123] It includes actions on stepping up investments, strengthening research and innovation from the lab to the market, supporting AI research excellence centres across Europe, bringing AI to all small businesses and potential users, supporting testing and experimentation, attracting private investments, and making more data available. Here we can see some elements of the previously discussed tentative governance approach to emerging technologies (discussed in Section 2.2 above) when due to uncertainties, governance is open to experimentation. The second pillar focuses on preparing for socioeconomic changes such as job replacement by providing retraining. The third pillar, "ensuring an appropriate ethical and legal framework"[124] includes the preparation of AI ethics guidelines, action to ensure safety and liability, as well as empowering individuals to make the most of AI. While ethics guidelines and regulations are often mentioned next to each other, giving the impression that both are closely related, closer reading and examination reveals more enthusiasm about and progress in launching ethics guidelines, while issues of regulation are met with more caution or even resistance.[125]

This third policy frame aims to present a balanced approach to new technologies where not only positive but also negative expectations towards emerging technology are considered, and mechanisms are suggested to address them. For example, it is not only about investing more in AI as a promising technology but also planning retraining programmes to deal with job losses due to automation. Moreover, focus on ethical, legal, and societal implications and the need for standards, legislation, and ethical frameworks represent an intention to mitigate risks and solve problems. An important question for future research is how this suggested balanced approach is implemented in practice.

Thus, the three emerging AI policy frames demonstrate the performative function of hypes and expectations in the case of an emerging technology. Irrespective of their accuracy, positive and negative expectations towards AI influence emerging policies, political agendas, and resource allocation. Furthermore, policies are affected by actual and perceived competition and collaboration that can have both positive (e.g. mobilisation of resources) as well as problematic (e.g. driving resources from social policies to hyped technologies) consequences.

2.6 CONCLUSIONS: KEY INSIGHTS AND FUTURE RESEARCH QUESTIONS

This chapter provides an overview of emerging trends and frames of AI policy, which since 2016 has been quickly developing around the world. While the beginning of AI development can be traced back at least to the 1950s, only recently has this technology attracted significant policy attention due to major technological advances that have enabled a wide range of applications. Thus, AI today has many characteristics of an emerging technology along with associated uncertainties, collaboration and competition dynamics, and performative function of hype as well as the positive and negative expectations that influence policymaking in this area.

Fast-developing AI policy, along with many strategies and other policy documents launched in recent years, is unprecedented in technology policy. This can be explained by a wide range of AI applications that go beyond typical emerging technology issues about impact on safety and economic growth, and also affect the political system, labour market, and welfare state. Scandals such as the Cambridge Analytica case have added urgency to policy action in this area. Moreover, questions about machines achieving or superseding human intelligence have a special resonance within collective and individual imaginations. Furthermore, international assemblies such as the World Economic Forum and the OECD have drawn additional attention to policies for AI and facilitated cross-national learning in this area. AI policy developments, however, are unevenly distributed around the world and are concentrated in the most developed regions.

This chapter identifies three main AI policy frames. These include first, framing AI as a revolutionary, transformative and disruptive technology; second, closely interconnected global competition and collaboration in the field of AI; and third, a three-pillar approach of realising opportunities, mitigating risks and ensuring responsibilities are met. As suggested by the social studies of emerging technologies, which highlight the performative function of hypes and expectations, these emerging policy frames can have positive as well as problematic effects on resource allocation and political prioritisation. Thus, AI policy analysis can benefit from critical engagement, which questions resource re-allocation based on hypes, competitiveness discourse, and representation of international AI development as a global race where one country wins, and others lose. Moreover, while at the moment AI policies are mostly developed and implemented at the national and EU level, the need for international collaboration is recognised, and international cooperation initiatives are emerging.

ACKNOWLEDGEMENTS

This chapter has benefited from feedback on presentations of earlier drafts at a number of international conferences, including the 2018 Regulating Robotics and AI conference at the European University Institute in Florence (Italy), the EASST 2018 conference in Lancaster (UK), the 2019 Singapore Public Policy Network meeting, the 2019 ISA Annual Convention in Toronto (Canada), and the UACES 2019 conference in Lisbon (Portugal). This work was supported by the European Union's Horizon 2020 Framework Programme for Research and Innovation under the Specific Grant Agreements No. 720270 (HBP SGA1), No. 785907 (HBP SGA2) and No. 945539 (HBP SGA3).

NOTES

1. Jasanoff, Sheila. *The ethics of invention: Technology and the human future.* New York: W.W. Norton & Company, 2016, 267.
2. See e.g. Coeckelbergh, Mark. *AI ethics.* Cambridge: The MIT Press, 2020; Dignum, Virginia. *Responsible artificial intelligence. How to develop and use AI in a responsible way.* Cham: Springer, 2019; Marcus, Gary, and Ernest Davis. *Rebooting AI: Building artificial intelligence we can trust.* New York: Pantheon Books, 2019.
3. See e.g. Bartoletti, Ivana. *An artificial revolution: On power, politics and AI.* Southampton: Indigo Press, 2020; Noble, Safiya Umoja. *Algorithms of oppression: How search engines reinforce racism.* New York: NYU Press, 2018; O'Neil, Cathy. *Weapons of math destruction: How big data increases inequality and threatens democracy.* London: Penguin Books, 2016; Zuboff, Shoshana. *The age of surveillance capitalism: The fight for a human future at the new frontier of power.* London: Profile Books, 2019.
4. Ulnicane, Inga, Knight, William, Leach, Tonii, Stahl, Bernd Carsten and Winter-Gladys Wanjiku. "Framing governance for a contested emerging technology: Insights from AI policy." *Policy and Society* 40, no.2 (2021): 158–177. https://doi.org/10.1080/14494035.2020.1855800; Ulnicane, Inga, Eke, Damian Okaibedi, Knight, William, Ogoh, George and Bernd Carsten

Stahl. "Good governance as a response to discontents? Déjà vu, or lessons for AI from other emerging technologies." *Interdisciplinary Science Reviews* 46, no. 1–2 (2021): 71–93. https://doi.org/10.1080/03080188.2020.1840220; Ulnicane, Inga "Artificial Intelligence in the European Union: Policy, ethics, and regulation." In *Routledge Handbook of European Integrations*, edited by Thomas Hoerber, Ignazio Cabras, and Gabriel Weber, 254-269. Abingdon: Routledge, 2022.

5. Schatzberg, Eric. *Technology: Critical history of a concept.* Chicago: The University of Chicago Press, 2018.
6. OECD/Eurostat. *Oslo manual 2018: Guidelines for collecting, reporting and using data on innovation.* 4th edition. The Measurement of Scientific, Technological and Innovation Activities. Paris: OECD Publishing/Luxembourg: Eurostat, 2018, 254. https://doi.org/10.1787/9789264304604-en
7. Schatzberg. *Technology: Critical history of a concept,* 5.
8. Schatzberg. *Technology: Critical history of a concept,* 15.
9. Jasanoff. *The ethics of invention: Technology and the human future,* 243.
10. Winner, Langdon. *The whale and the reactor. A search for limits in an age of high technology.* Second edition. Chicago: The University of Chicago Press, 2020, 55.
11. Borras, Susana, and Jakob Edler, eds. *The governance of socio-technical systems: Explaining change.* Cheltenham: Edward Elgar, 2014, 1.
12. Rotolo, Daniele, Hicks, Diana and Ben R. Martin. "What is an emerging technology?" *Research Policy* 44, no. 10 (2015): 1827–1843. https://doi.org/10.1016/j.respol.2015.06.006
13. Rotolo, Hicks and Martin. "What is an emerging technology?," 1828.
14. E.g. Crane, Diana. *Invisible colleges. Diffusion of knowledge in scientific communities.* Chicago, IL: The University of Chicago Press, 1972; Mulkay, Mike J. *The social process of innovation. A study in the sociology of science.* London: Macmillan, 1972.
15. Merton, Robert. "Behaviour patterns of scientists." In *The sociology of science. Theoretical and empirical investigations,* edited by Robert Merton and Norman Storer, 325–342. Chicago: University of Chicago Press, 1973 [1968]: 331.
16. E.g. Van Lente, Harro, Spitters, Charlotte and Alexander Peine. "Comparing technological hype cycles: Towards a theory." *Technological Forecasting and Social Change* 80, no. 8 (2013): 1615–1628. https://doi.org/10.1016/j.techfore.2012.12.004
17. Van Lente, Spitters and Peine. "Comparing technological hype cycles: Towards a theory," 1616.
18. Van Lente, Spitters and Peine. "Comparing technological hype cycles: Towards a theory," 1616.
19. Van Lente, Spitters and Peine. "Comparing technological hype cycles: Towards a theory," 1616.
20. Van Lente, Spitters and Peine. "Comparing technological hype cycles: Towards a theory," 1616.
21. Chhotray, Vasudha and Gerry Stoker. *Governance theory and practice. A cross-disciplinary approach.* London: Palgrave Macmillan, 2009, 3.

22. Chhotray and Stoker. *Governance theory and practice. A cross-disciplinary approach*, 4.
23. Chhotray and Stoker. *Governance theory and practice. A cross-disciplinary approach*, 6.
24. Chhotray and Stoker. *Governance theory and practice. A cross-disciplinary approach*, 6.
25. Chhotray and Stoker. *Governance theory and practice. A cross-disciplinary approach*, 5.
26. Borras and Edler. *The governance of socio-technical systems: Explaining change*, 13–14.
27. Mazzucato, Mariana. *The entrepreneurial state. Debunking public vs. private sector myths*. London: Anthem Press, 2013.
28. See e.g. Ulnicane, Inga. "'Grand challenges' concept: A return of the 'big ideas' in science, technology and innovation policy?" *International Journal of Foresight and Innovation Policy* 11, no. 1–3 (2016): 5–21. https://doi.org/10.1504/IJFIP.2016.078378
29. Mazzucato, Mariana. *Mission economy: A moonshot guide to changing capitalism*. London: Allen Lane, 2021.
30. Kuhlmann, Stefan, Stegmaier, Peter and Kornelia Konrad. "The tentative governance of emerging science and technology—A conceptual introduction." *Research Policy* 48, no. 5 (2019): 1091–1097. https://doi.org/10.1016/j.respol.2019.01.006
31. Kuhlmann, Stegmaier and Konrad. "The tentative governance of emerging science and technology—A conceptual introduction."
32. Kuhlmann, Stegmaier and Konrad. "The tentative governance of emerging science and technology—A conceptual introduction," 1091.
33. Kuhlmann, Stegmaier and Konrad. "The tentative governance of emerging science and technology—A conceptual introduction," 1096.
34. Ulnicane, Eke, Knight, Ogoh and Stahl. "Good governance as a response to discontents? Déjà vu, or lessons for AI from other emerging technologies," 34.
35. E.g. Cath, Corinne. "Governing artificial intelligence: Ethical, legal and technical opportunities and challenges." *Philosophical Transactions A* 376 (2018): 1–8. https://doi.org/10.1098/rsta.2018.0080; Winfield, Alan F.T. and Marina Jirotka. "Ethical governance is essential to building trust in robotics and artificial intelligence systems." *Philosophical Transactions A* 376 (2018): 1–13. https://doi.org/10.1098/rsta.2018.0085
36. E.g. Cath, Corinne, Sandra Wachter, Brent Mittelstadt, Mariarosaria Taddeo and Luciano Floridi. "Artificial intelligence and the 'Good Society': The US, EU, and UK approach." *Science and Engineering Ethics* 24 (2018): 505–528. https://doi.org/10.1007/s11948-017-9901-7; Jobin, Anna, Ienca, Marcello and Effy Vayena. "The global landscape of AI ethics guidelines." *Nature Machine Intelligence* 1 (2019): 389–399. https://doi.org/10.1038/s42256-019-0088-2; Floridi, Luciano, Cowls, Josh, Beltrametti, Monica et al. "AI4People – An ethical framework for a good AI society: Opportunities, risks, principles, and recommendations." *Minds & Machines* 28 (2018): 689–707. https://doi.org/10.1007/s11023-018-9482-5.

37. Cath. "Governing artificial intelligence: Ethical, legal and technical opportunities and challenges."
38. Winfield and Jirotka. "Ethical governance is essential to building trust in robotics and artificial intelligence systems," 2.
39. de Saille, Stevienna. "Innovating innovation policy: The emergence of 'responsible research and innovation.'" *Journal of Responsible Innovation* 2, no. 2 (2015): 152–168.
40. Stilgoe, Jack, Owen, Richard and Phil Macnaghten. "Developing a framework for responsible innovation." *Research Policy* 42, no. 9 (2013): 1570.
41. Dignum. *Responsible artificial intelligence. How to develop and use AI in a responsible way.* Cham: Springer, 2019, 6.
42. Dignum. *Responsible artificial intelligence. How to develop and use AI in a responsible way.* Cham: Springer, 2019, 6.
43. Winfield and Jirotka. "Ethical governance is essential to building trust in robotics and artificial intelligence systems."
44. Winfield and Jirotka. "Ethical governance is essential to building trust in robotics and artificial intelligence systems."
45. See e.g. Kuziemski, Maciej and Gianluca Misuraca. "AI governance in the public sector: Three tales from the frontiers of automated decision-making in democratic settings." *Telecommunications Policy* 44, no. 6 (2020): 1–13. https://doi.org/10.1016/j.telpol.2020.101976; Young, Matthew M., Bullock, Justin B. and Jesse D. Lecy. "Artificial discretion as a tool of governance: A framework for understanding the impact of artificial intelligence on public administration." *Perspectives on Public Management and Governance* 2, no. 4 (2019): 301–313. https://doi.org/10.1093/ppmgov/gvz014
46. See e.g. Cihon, Peter, Maas, Matthijs M. and Luke Kemp. "Fragmentation and the future: Investigating architectures for international AI governance." *Global Policy* 11, no. 5 (2020): 545–556. https://doi.org/10.1111/1758-5899.12890
47. Ala-Pietilä, Pekka and Nathalie A. Smuha. "A framework for global cooperation on artificial intelligence and its governance." In *Reflections on artificial intelligence for humanity*, edited by Bertrand Braunschweig and Malik Ghallab, 237–265. Cham: Springer, 2021.
48. Taeihagh, Araz and Hazel Si Min Lim. "Governing autonomous vehicles: Emerging responses for safety, liability, privacy, cybersecurity, and industry risks." *Transport Reviews* 39, no. 1 (2019): 103–128. https://doi.org/10.1080/01441647.2018.1494640
49. See e.g. Cath, Wachter, Mittelstadt, Taddeo and Floridi. "Artificial intelligence and the 'Good Society': The US, EU, and UK approach."
50. See e.g. Galanos, Vassilis. "Exploring expanding expertise: Artificial intelligence as an existential threat and the role of prestigious commentators, 2014–2018." *Technology Analysis & Strategic Management* 31, no. 4 (2019): 421–432. https://doi.org/10.1080/09537325.2018.1518521
51. Robinson, Stephen Cory. "Trust, transparency, and openness: How inclusion of cultural values shapes Nordic national public policy strategies for artificial intelligence (AI)." *Technology in Society* 63 (2020): 101421. https://doi.org/10.1016/j.techsoc.2020.101421

52. Dexe, Jacob and Ulrik Franke. "Nordic lights? National AI policies for doing well by doing good." *Journal of Cyber Policy* (2020): 1–18. https://doi .org/10.1080/23738871.2020.1856160

53. af Malmborg, Frans and Jarle Trondal. "Discursive framing and organizational venues: Mechanisms of artificial intelligence policy adoption." *International Review of Administrative Sciences* (2021). https://doi.org/10 .1177/00208523211007533

54. Köstler, Lea and Ringo Ossewaarde. "The making of AI society: AI futures frames in German political and media discourses." *AI & Society* (2021): 1–15. https://doi.org/10.1007/s00146-021-01161-9

55. Ossewaarde, Marinus and Erdener Gulenc. "National varieties of artificial intelligence discourses: Myth, utopianism, and solutionism in West European policy expectations." *Computer* 53, no. 11 (2020): 53–61. https:// doi.org/10.1109/MC.2020.2992290

56. Roberts, Huw, Josh Cowls, Jessica Morley, Mariarosaria Taddeo, Vincent Wang and Luciano Floridi. "The Chinese approach to artificial intelligence: An analysis of policy, ethics, and regulation." *AI & SOCIETY* 36, no. 1 (2021): 59–77. https://doi.org/10.1007/s00146-020-00992-2

57. Ulnicane, Knight, Leach, Stahl and Wanjiku. "Framing governance for a contested emerging technology: Insights from AI policy."

58. Ulnicane, Eke, Knight, Ogoh and Stahl. "Good governance as a response to discontents? Déjà vu, or lessons for AI from other emerging technologies."

59. Calo, Ryan. "Artificial intelligence policy: A primer and roadmap." *UC Davis Law Review* 51, no. 2 (2017): 399–435. https://doi.org/10.2139/ssrn.3015350

60. Stix, Charlotte. "Actionable principles for artificial intelligence policy: Three pathways." *Science and Engineering Ethics* 27, no. 1 (2021): 1–17. https://doi .org/10.1007/s11948-020-00277-3

61. Stix, Charlotte and Matthijs M. Maas. "Bridging the gap: The case for an 'Incompletely Theorized Agreement' on AI policy." *AI and Ethics* (2021): 1–11. https://doi.org/10.1007/s43681-020-00037-w

62. See e.g. Broussard, Meredith. *Artificial unintelligence: How computers misunderstand the world.* Cambridge: The MIT Press, 2018; Dwivedi, Yogesh K., Hughes, Laurie, Ismagilova, Elvira, Aarts, Gert, Coombs, Crispin, Crick, Tom, Duan, Yanqing, et al. "Artificial intelligence (AI): Multidisciplinary perspectives on emerging challenges, opportunities, and agenda for research, practice and policy." *International Journal of Information Management* 57 (2019). https://doi.org/10.1016/j.ijinfomgt.2019 .08.002; Stilgoe, Jack. *Who's driving innovation? New technologies and the collaborative state.* Cham: Palgrave Macmillan, 2020.

63. For an overview, see e.g. OECD. *Artificial intelligence in society.* Paris: OECD Publishing, 2019. https://doi.org/10.1787/eedfee77-en

64. See e.g. Ulnicane, Knight, Leach, Stahl and Wanjiku. "Framing governance for a contested emerging technology: Insights from AI policy."

65. European Commission. *Artificial intelligence for Europe.* Communication COM(2018) 237. Brussels: European Commission, 2018, 1.

66. Cath, Wachter, Mittelstadt, Taddeo and Floridi, "Artificial intelligence and the 'Good Society': The US, EU, and UK approach," 505.

67. Galanos, "Exploring expanding expertise: Artificial intelligence as an existential threat and the role of prestigious commentators, 2014–2018."
68. AI Strategies and Public Sector Components. https://oecd-opsi.org/projects/ai/strategies/ (Last accessed 15 February 2020).
69. Jobin, Ienca and Vayena, "The global landscape of AI ethics guidelines."
70. See e.g. Coeckelbergh, *AI ethics*; Vesnic-Alujevic, Lucia, Nascimento, Susana and Alexandre Pólvora. "Societal and ethical impacts of artificial intelligence: Critical notes on European policy frameworks." *Telecommunications Policy* 44, no. 6 (2020): 1–14. https://doi.org/10.1016/j.telpol.2020.101961
71. These are: first, the Asilomar AI principles, second, the Montreal declaration for responsible AI, third, the general principles offered in the second version of Ethically Aligned Design, fourth, the Statement on Artificial Intelligence, Robotics and "Autonomous" Systems from the European Commission' European Group on Ethics in Science and New Technologies, fifth, the five overarching principles for an AI code form the UK House of Lords report AI in the UK: ready, willing and able? and sixth, the tenets of the Partnership on AI.
72. Floridi, Cowls, Beltrametti, et al. "AI4People—An ethical framework for a good AI society: Opportunities, risks, principles, and recommendations."
73. Jobin, Ienca and Vayena, "The global landscape of AI ethics guidelines."
74. Jobin, Ienca and Vayena, "The global landscape of AI ethics guidelines," 389.
75. Schiff, Daniel, Borenstein, Jason, Biddle, Justin and Kelly Laas. "AI ethics in the public, private, and NGO sectors: A review of a global document collection." *IEEE Transactions on Technology and Society* 2, no. 1 (2021): 31. https://doi.org/10.1109/TTS.2021.3052127
76. See e.g. Lee, Kai-Fu. *AI superpowers: China, silicon valley, and the new world order.* Boston: Houghton Mifflin Harcourt, 2018.
77. Schwab, Klaus. *The fourth industrial revolution.* New York: Penguin, 2017.
78. Henriques, Luisa and Philippe Larédo. "Policy-making in science policy: The 'OECD model' unveiled." *Research Policy* 42, no. 3 (2013): 801–816. https://doi.org/10.1016/j.respol.2012.09.004
79. The OECD AI Principles. https://www.oecd.ai/ai-principles (Last accessed 19 April 2021).
80. The OECD AI Policy Observatory. https://www.oecd.ai/ (Last accessed 19 April 2021).
81. The OECD Network of Experts on AI (ONE AI). https://www.oecd.ai/network-of-experts (Last accessed 19 April 2021).
82. Dolowitz, David P. and David Marsh. "Learning from abroad: The role of policy transfer in contemporary policy-making." *Governance: An International Journal of Policy and Administration* 13, no. 1 (2000): 5–24. https://doi.org/10.1111/0952-1895.00121
83. European Commission. *AI policy seminar: Towards and EU strategic plan for AI. Digital transformation monitor.* Brussels, 29 November 2017.
84. Carter, William A., Kinnucan, Emma and Josh Elliot. *A national machine intelligence strategy for the United States.* Washington, DC: Center for Strategic & International Studies, 2018, 19.

85. European Commission. *Artificial intelligence: A European perspective.* Luxembourg: Publications Office of the European Union, 2018.
86. The Global AI Index. https://www.tortoisemedia.com/intelligence/global -ai/ (last accessed 15 April 2021).
87. The Government AI Readiness Index. https://www.oxfordinsights.com/ government-ai-readiness-index-2020 (Last accessed 15 April 2021).
88. The AI Index. https://aiindex.stanford.edu/ (Last accessed 15 April 2021).
89. Van Lente, Spitters and Peine. "Comparing technological hype cycles: Towards a theory."
90. Rein, Martin and Donald Schön. "Reframing policy discourse." In *The argumentative turn in policy analysis and planning,* edited by Frank Fischer and John Forester, 145–166. London: UCL Press, 1993.
91. Rein and Schön. "Reframing policy discourse," 145.
92. Rein and Schön. "Reframing policy discourse," 146.
93. More on AI policy documents see here See e.g. Ulnicane, Knight, Leach, Stahl and Wanjiku. "Framing governance for a contested emerging technology: Insights from AI policy."
94. Executive Office of the President. *The national artificial intelligence research and development strategic plan.* Washington, DC: National Science and Technology Council, 2016, 3.
95. European Commission. *Artificial intelligence for Europe,* 1.
96. BIC/APPGAI (Big Innovation Centre/All-Party Parliamentary Group on Artificial Intelligence). *International Perspective and Exemplars.* 30 October 2017, 10.
97. European Commission. *Artificial intelligence for Europe,* 1.
98. European Commission. *Artificial intelligence for Europe,* 2.
99. See e.g. Makridakis, Spyros. "The forthcoming artificial intelligence (AI) revolution: Its impact on society and firms." *Futures* 90 (2017): 46–60. https://doi.org/10.1016/j.futures.2017.03.006
100. Winner, *The whale and the reactor. A search for limits in an age of high technology,* 98.
101. Winner, *The whale and the reactor. A search for limits in an age of high technology,* 117.
102. BIC/APPGAI (Big Innovation Centre/All-Party Parliamentary Group on Artificial Intelligence). *International Perspective and Exemplars,* 4.
103. BIC/APPGAI (Big Innovation Centre/All-Party Parliamentary Group on Artificial Intelligence). *International Perspective and Exemplars,* 19.
104. Executive Office of the President. *Preparing for the future of artificial intelligence.* Washington, DC: National Science and Technology Council Committee on Technology, 2016.
105. Larson, Christina. "China's massive investment in artificial intelligence has an insidious downside." *Science* 8 (2018). https://doi.org/10.1126/science.aat2458
106. RT. "'Whoever leads in AI will rule the world': Putin to Russian children on Knowledge Day." 1 September 2017. https://www.rt.com/news/401731-ai -rule-world-putin/ (Last accessed 16 February 2020).

107. WEF. "Theresa May's Davos address in full." 25 January 2018. https://www
.weforum.org/agenda/2018/01/theresa-may-davos-address/ (Last accessed
16 February 2020).

108. Rabesandratana, Tania. "Emmanuel Macron wants France to become a
leader in AI and avoid 'dystopia.'" *Science* 30 (March 2018). https://doi.org
/10.1126/science.aat7491

109. European Commission. *Artificial intelligence for Europe*, 19.

110. European Commission. *Artificial intelligence: A European perspective*, 12–13.

111. E.g. Allen, John and Amir Husain. "The next space race is artificial intelligence." *Foreign Affairs*, 3 November 2017; Horowitz, Michael, Kania,
Elsa B., Allen, Gregory C. and Paul Scharre. *Strategic competition in and
era of artificial intelligence*. Washington, DC: Centre for a New American
Security, 25 July 2018.

112. Krugman, Paul. "Competitiveness: A dangerous obsession." *Foreign Affairs*
73, no. 2 (1994): 28–44.

113. Nelson, R. Richard. *The Moon and the Ghetto. An essay on public policy
analysis*. New York: W.W. Norton & Company, 1977.

114. Stilgoe, *Who's driving innovation? New technologies and the collaborative
state*, 51.

115. Information from the European Commission. https://ec.europa.eu/digital
-single-market/en/news/eu-member-states-sign-cooperate-artificial-intel-
ligence (Last accessed 16 April 2019).

116. See e.g. Cihon, Maas and Kemp. "Fragmentation and the future:
Investigating architectures for international AI governance."

117. The Global Partnership on Artificial Intelligence. https://gpai.ai/ (Last
accessed 20 April 2021).

118. Feijóo, Claudio, Kwon, Youngsun, Bauer, Johannes M., Bohlin, Erik, Howell,
Bronwyn, Jain, Rekha, Potgieter, Petrus, Vu, Khuong, Whalley, Jason, and
Jun Xia. "Harnessing artificial intelligence (AI) to increase wellbeing for all:
The case for a new technology diplomacy." *Telecommunications Policy* 44,
no. 6 (2020): 2. https://doi.org/10.1016/j.telpol.2020.101988

119. Carter, Kinnucan and Elliot. *A national machine intelligence strategy for the
United State*, 42–45.

120. Rabesandratana. "Emmanuel Macron wants France to become a leader in
AI and avoid 'dystopia.'"

121. Merton, Robert. "The normative structure of science." In *The sociology of
science. Theoretical and empirical investigations*, edited by Robert Merton
and Norman Storer, 267–278. Chicago, IL: The University of Chicago Press,
1973 [1942].

122. Executive Office of the President. *The national artificial intelligence research
and development strategic plan*.

123. European Commission. *Artificial intelligence for Europe*, 5.

124. European Commission. *Artificial intelligence for Europe*, 13.

125. Ulnicane, Eke, Knight, Ogoh and Stahl. "Good governance as a response to
discontents? Déjà vu, or lessons for AI from other emerging technologies."

CHAPTER 3

Multilateralism and Artificial Intelligence

What Role for the United Nations?

Eugenio V. Garcia

CONTENTS

3.1 INTRODUCTION

Applications of artificial intelligence (AI) in business, government and everyday life have been developing at a breakneck pace, fuelled by powerful computing hardware, abundant data and online training of machine learning algorithms. International relations, global security and diplomacy are likely to be profoundly affected as well, and many anticipate that such ground-breaking technological developments will be capable of, inter alia, reshaping the character of warfare in the 21st century.[1]

The level of AI readiness by governments and companies will have a dramatic effect on competitiveness and will probably become a critical factor in investments and economic growth. AI-driven industry automation in developed countries of labour-intensive jobs could arguably displace the traditional comparative advantages of developing countries,

DOI: 10.1201/9780429446726-3

such as cheap workforce and raw materials. A widening gap in prosperity and wealth would mostly affect those countries unable to develop digital skills and infrastructure to reap the rewards of AI opportunities in productivity and innovation.[2] If not long ago, global inequality was gauged in terms of *have* and *have-not* countries, a new divide could be emerging between *AI-ready* and *not-AI-ready*.[3]

As a general-purpose technology with multiple capabilities, AI can pose challenges that need to be prevented or mitigated by pooling resources and expertise in defining agreed parameters to safely develop its full potential.[4] AI governance is likely to gain traction over the next years, and the United Nations (UN), the most representative and wide-ranging multilateral organisation in global politics, will eventually get further involved in providing space for international cooperation and facilitating negotiations on how to deal with controversies surrounding AI policymaking. With its unmatched range and universality, the UN can offer a neutral, nonpartisan, multilateral platform for intergovernmental discussions on AI in several domains. Some remain sceptical of any substantive agreement among the major players, envisioning scenarios of inter-State jostling, rivalry redux, AI "arms race" and "decoupling," which could seriously undermine multilateralism.[5] It is not difficult to foresee, nonetheless, that the absence of collaborative forms of governance, combined with mistrust towards the multilateral system, will render it more cumbersome for the international community to cope with today's large-scale challenges.[6]

A broad definition of AI policymaking strategy has been proposed as "a research field that analyses the policymaking process and draws implications for policy design, advocacy, organisational strategy, and AI governance as a whole."[7] Compared with the growing number of studies addressing AI risk in domestic policy, there is much less research on foreign policy and international governance. This chapter will discuss possible strategic approaches for the UN to overcome obstacles and promote more engagement on this matter at the global level. What are the next concrete steps the UN should take on AI policy? Should Member States support any sort of AI oversight mechanism? Is there political will or a minimum consensus to do so? If not, are there any alternatives?

3.2 THE INTERNATIONAL GOVERNANCE OF AI: A FRAGMENTED LANDSCAPE

Concerns about the impact of disruptive technologies in society, particularly AI, can be roughly divided into two basic categories: a) long-term trajectories that could lead to artificial general intelligence (AGI) being created with human-level cognitive capabilities and the possibility of reaching a critical threshold through recursive self-improvement to achieve superintelligence, thus potentially posing an existential risk to humanity;[8] and b) near-term AI policy regarding safety measures, technical standards, performance metrics, norms, policies, institutions, and other governance tools deemed necessary in view of the all-encompassing legal, ethical, and societal implications of this technology, including codes of conduct, regimes, or other normative instruments to be adopted at the international level.[9]

The fundamental question to be asked is how the UN can successfully articulate both categories and be realistically proactive going forward, despite considerable scepticism about its ability to deliver in such a complex and unchartered domain. It would be advisable for the organisation to start addressing near-term AI policy concerns in the first instance. Progress achieved in this area could later help prepare future discussions on long-term risks, but the opposite is much less palatable for the Member States in the present circumstances. Besides, more focused conversations could be easily derailed or glossed over if competing with speculative anxieties addressed to a different audience.

One does not need to wait for ideal, Goldilocks conditions to frame the problem in the search for a desirable outcome in a reasonable timespan. Experts have been wrestling with policy dilemmas so that AI governance can work for all societies.[10] To many, a do-nothing policy is hardly an option.[11] In a normative vacuum, governments and private companies, chasing after strategic advantage and profit, may push even harder for rapid AI development regardless of considerations based upon law, ethics, safety, or security. Driven by a logic of "AI race," perceived hostility would increase distrust among States, and more investments could be channelled to defence budgets, possibly turning confrontation into a self-fulfilling prophecy.

Responsible governance strategies could help prevent or minimise the impact of more disturbing scenarios. Norms and other regulatory approaches to mitigate risks are possible responses to unintended consequences of AI technologies. Certainly, incentivising predictability by means of norm-setting is not just a question of inducing good behaviour by States or protecting the weak from the powerful. Rather, it is a matter of building commonly accepted rules for all and minimum standards to avert, for instance, strategic uncertainty, undesirable escalations, and unforeseen crises spinning out of control. Facing the danger of unsafe AI systems without proper oversight, demands will grow stronger to set in motion international cooperation to avoid mutual harm.[12] From a military perspective, if left without proper human control, smart machines running wild on a mass scale would be a commander's worst nightmare. Their destabilising fallout could increase turbulence rather than provide more security to States.[13]

When it comes to laws, norms, and regulations, the AI landscape today is fraught with fragmentation at all levels. It is worth asking the question of whether a fragmented international governance of AI could be effective or, not being the case, there is a need for a centralised international organisation. It has been argued that the risk of creating a slow and brittle institution speaks against it, but a well-designed centralised regime covering a set of coherent issues could be "beneficial."[14] Although fragmentation is likely to persist for the time being, if States fail to coordinate their responses and adopt international standards, as Turner put it, then regulation for AI can become "Balkanised, with each territory setting its own mutually incompatible rules." Norms, therefore, should be seen as an enabler of predictable and orderly interactions reducing uncertainty in everyone's interest.[15]

Despite the relative lack of clarity on the way forward, it should be expected that AI governance will sometimes go global and require more international coordination.[16] Research and policy proposals on this topic are beginning to shed light upon the likelihood of international cooperation on transformative AI-related issues, incentives needed for the parties to reach meaningful agreements, proper conditions for compliance, and costs of defection or unilateral, non-cooperative measures.[17] Proposals range from informal mechanisms in narrowly-focused domains to much more ambitious, institutionalised forums, such as the establishment of an international regulatory agency, to be named, for example, the International Artificial Intelligence Organisation (IAIO) aimed at setting standards and benchmarks across areas to be regulated. However, even the proponents of such broad-spectrum organisation concede that reaching a workable international consensus on this idea seems rather a remote possibility in the short term.[18]

Another proposition aims at creating a new body modelled on the UN Intergovernmental Panel on Climate Change (IPCC) to give policymakers technical, neutral assessments, subject to review by States, underlining the opportunities, implications, and potential risks of AI, always through evidence-based research by the tech and scientific communities.[19] Miailhe made a case for an Intergovernmental Panel on Artificial Intelligence (IPAI) to gather a large interdisciplinary group of experts with a mandate to collect, organise, and analyse up-to-date information.[20] As emerging technologies become more and more sophisticated, sound technical advice will be in high demand if intergovernmental negotiations are to be launched to tackle these thorny issues.

Civil society organisations have been putting forward numerous proposals on principles and AI ethical frameworks, including the landmark 2017 Asilomar AI principles championed by the Future of Life Institute.[21] A recent paper surveyed dozens of contributions around the world on normative guidance in ethical and rights-based approaches to principles for AI.[22] Linking government and business networks, the World Economic Forum (WEF) has been bolstering public–private partnerships on the Fourth Industrial Revolution and the future of technology governance (e.g. by suggesting an "AI regulator for the 21st century").[23] Also worth recalling is the Partnership on AI, established by leading companies to study and formulate best practices, and the Future Society's Global Data Commons.[24] Another work in progress relates to the outcome of the International Congress for the Governance of Artificial Intelligence (ICGAI), to be held in May 2021 in Prague, and its focus upon initial steps towards putting in place international mechanisms for an "agile governance" of AI.[25]

Motivations for adopting AI policy and ethics documents by governments, the private sector, and civil society are manifold: genuine social responsibility, search for competitive advantage, signalling leadership, seeking to influence narratives on what should be done, marketing tool for business corporations to promote their brand or to pre-empt restrictive laws. Ethics boards are indeed a welcome development for the industry, but self-regulation is not a panacea since "the interests of companies are rarely fully aligned with the interests of society as a whole."[26] On the positive side, even if these initiatives lack enforcement authority, new ideas on principles, institutions, mechanisms, or informal settings may contribute to the debate through cross-pollination and act as building blocks for more ambitious projects when the momentum for it arises.

Better coordination can often occur among like-minded States, such as in the European Union, and cross-regional groups or organisations with a widely shared agenda (but a restricted membership), such as the G7, the Organisation for Economic Cooperation Development (OECD) or, to a lesser degree, the G20.[27] There is non-negligible activity within these groups on AI principles and policy design. The G7 leaders, for example, agreed upon the Charlevoix Common Vision for the Future of Artificial Intelligence, in June 2018, outlining commitments to inter alia promote human-centric AI and its commercial adoption, generate public trust, support lifelong learning, and respect privacy and data protection frameworks in AI design and implementation.[28]

Some countries are taking action at the bilateral and regional levels, in a move that could accelerate the transition from private stakeholder initiatives to governmental policymaking at the global level. In December 2018, Canada and France bilaterally proposed a Global Partnership for AI (GPAI) to "support and guide the responsible adoption of AI that is human-centric and grounded in human rights, inclusion, diversity, innovation and economic growth." Their ultimate goal was to create a standing forum, involving governments, the industry, and academia, to monitor and debate the policy implications of AI globally.[29] Other countries were invited to join, and the proposal was later discussed within the G7. In June 2020, a group of 14 States and the EU officially launched the enlarged GPAI initiative, pledging their support to responsible AI development in a manner consistent with "human rights, fundamental freedoms, and our shared democratic values."[30]

With the net advantage of several fully functioning institutional structures, Europe has been moving faster than other regions. In June 2018, The European Commission created a High-Level Expert Group on Artificial Intelligence (AI HLEG) to support the implementation of the European Strategy on AI, including recommendations on future-related policy development and ethical, legal, and societal issues related to this technology. In addition to guidelines on AI and data protection, the Council of Europe set up in 2019 an Ad Hoc Committee on Artificial Intelligence (CAHAI) to conduct consultations on a legal framework for the development, design, and application of AI, based on the Council's standards on human rights, democracy, and the rule of law. Also, the European Commission has been preparing to introduce AI legislation in civilian applications and will want its new regulatory framework to have a long-reaching global effect, akin to the General Data Protection Regulation, which was adopted in 2016 to enable rules on privacy and transfer of personal data.[31]

In May 2019, the OECD adopted recommendations to promote and implement far-reaching AI principles, the first-ever intergovernmental standard of its kind. Governments signed up to actively cooperate and work together to advance these principles by encouraging international, cross-sectoral, and open multi-stakeholder initiatives on a consensual basis. The recommendations included two substantive sections: 1) Principles for responsible stewardship of trustworthy AI: i) inclusive growth, sustainable development and well-being; ii) human-centred values and fairness; iii) transparency and explainability; iv) robustness, security, and safety; and v) accountability; and 2) National policies and international cooperation for trustworthy AI: i) investing in AI research and development; ii) fostering a digital ecosystem for AI; iii) shaping an enabling policy environment for AI; iv) building human capacity and preparing for labour market transformation; and v) international cooperation for trustworthy AI.[32] In February 2020, the OECD.AI Policy Observatory was launched as a platform to "shape and share" AI policies across the globe, so as to provide policymakers with reliable guidance on the implementation of AI principles in real-world situations.[33]

Thanks to the countless lists of AI principles laid out over the last few years, as Newman argued, a sort of "normative core" is emerging, but much remains to be done in terms of translating these guidelines into practice. Hence the importance of intergovernmental initiatives that can function as a hub for AI governance, allow for international coordination in implementing shared principles, and serve as a counterpoint to "AI nationalism."[34] These steps, however, have been heavily concentrated upon a few States, notably Western developed countries. Some major players, such as China and Russia, are often absent from these circles of like-minded States, with the notable exception of the G20, which in June 2019 endorsed in Japan non-binding AI principles explicitly drawing from the OECD recommendations.[35] Even more striking is the fact that the Global South is underrepresented in this debate, with many areas of Africa, Asia, Latin America, and the Caribbean completely away from this vital conversation. Taking as a yardstick, for instance, the number of AI national strategies adopted at the domestic level, the overwhelming majority comes from high-income countries.[36]

At the global level, there is wide convergence on general ideas, but little agreement on the details of exactly how they should be interpreted, prioritised, or implemented. Moving from soft law to hard regulation will be a tough nut to crack, especially when the goal is to frame a regulatory policy before the technology is fully understood and developed. In matters pertaining to power, wealth, and security among States, the continuation of self-help, beggar-thy-neighbour policies may increase incentives for national trajectories that reinforce great-power competition and thwart attempts at galvanising multilateral efforts. Greater inter-stakeholder cooperation is sorely needed to mutually align different AI ethics agendas in key areas, such as transparency, accountability, fairness, privacy, and responsibility. Multilateralism cannot provide all the answers, but its long-established architecture for broad representation and diplomatic bargain can be a readily available alternative to work out a much-needed compromise where conflict seems to prevail. Can the UN come to the rescue?

3.3 WHAT THE UNITED NATIONS HAS BEEN DOING, COULD IT DO MORE?

In his address to the General Assembly in September 2018, UN Secretary-General António Guterres warned that "multilateralism is under fire precisely when we need it most." He highlighted two "epochal challenges" in particular: climate change, which is of course of great concern, but not the subject of this chapter; and risks associated with advances in technology, from mass economic unemployment to cybercrime and malicious use of digital tools.[37] Guterres cautioned against the weaponisation of AI and the possibility of a dangerous arms race, including the development of lethal autonomous weapons systems, going so far as to contend that "the prospect of machines with the discretion and power to take human life is morally repugnant." Less oversight over these weapons, he added, could severely compromise efforts to contain threats, prevent escalation, and ensure compliance with international humanitarian law and human rights law. The Secretary-General urged Member States "to use the United Nations as a platform to draw global attention to these crucial matters and to nurture a digital future that is safe and beneficial for all."[38]

An electrical engineer himself by background, Guterres was the leading force behind the High-Level Panel on Digital Cooperation, which I will discuss in the next section. Back in 2018, he had launched his own Strategy on New Technologies, with the objective of defining how the UN system will support the use of these technologies to accelerate the achievement of the 2030 Sustainable Development Agenda and to facilitate their alignment with the values enshrined in the UN Charter, the Universal Declaration of Human Rights, and the norms and standards of international law.[39] In the following year, the UN Chief Executives Board for Coordination adopted guidelines for a system-wide strategic approach for supporting capacity development on AI.[40] By the same token, 50 UN entities jointly designed in 2020 a Data Strategy as a "comprehensive playbook based on global best practice" to improve coordination on building the data, digital, technology and innovation capabilities the UN needs to succeed in the 21st century. The announcement of the Data Strategy by the Secretary-General was somewhat obscured in the news by the COVID-19 pandemic, but its long-term vision will remain a reference for the organisation for the next years.[41] Guterres also gives his backing to UN Global Pulse, a hands-on initiative established in 2009 to harness the power of big data, increasingly working in recent years to develop AI tools for development, humanitarian action, and peace. Its staff work through a network of innovation labs, which operate in New York, Jakarta, and Kampala.[42]

The main downsides of a scattered environment of policies and programmes are duplication of efforts, overlap, and inter-bureaucratic feuding among UN agencies to occupy niches and exert leadership. Most of the UN initiatives on new technologies are focused upon the implementation of the Sustainable Development Goals (SDGs), such as the annual Science, Technology, and Innovation Forum of the Economic and Social Council (ECOSOC). On the AI front, the flagship UN event for global dialogue with the wider public is the AI for Good Global Summit, hosted every year in Geneva by the International Telecommunications Union (ITU), in partnership with other UN agencies, the XPrize Foundation (organisation offering incentivise prize competitions), and the Association for Computing Machinery (ACM).[43]

The UN Educational, Scientific, and Cultural Organisation (UNESCO) have been promoting a humanistic approach on ethics, policy, and capacity-building in response to emerging challenges related to AI, including philosophical reflections on what it means to be human in the face of disruptive technologies. Playing a key role in this regard, the World Commission on the Ethics of Scientific Knowledge and Technology (COMEST), an advisory body created in 1998 to give policy advice for decision-makers, pioneered workshops and roundtables leading up to the publication of a report on robotics ethics, with a view to positioning UNESCO as a valuable instrument for intellectual exchanges on this matter.[44] Furthermore, the first International Research Centre of Artificial Intelligence (IRCAI), under the auspices of UNESCO, shall have its seat in Slovenia, aiming to provide a coordination point, funding route, and exploitation accelerator for approaches to the SDGs that make use of AI.[45]

More recently, an Ad Hoc Expert Group of 24 members was tasked by UNESCO to produce, in a two-year process, the first draft of a global standard-setting instrument on ethics of AI. In a preliminary study released in July 2019, it was stressed that AI is not confined to a tangible location, which makes regulation of AI technology more challenging nationally and internationally. Due to their transnational character, durable solutions need to be found at the global level. A normative instrument on the ethics of AI should serve as a means of mainstreaming universal values into AI systems, which must be compatible with internationally agreed human rights and standards, and be aligned to a human-centred vision.[46] Some experts believe that UNESCO's contribution, within its mandate, could be complementary to other initiatives underway, such as by the OECD, but with a focus upon aspects that are generally neglected: culture, education, science, and communication. The definitive format of this normative document (either a declaration, recommendation, or a convention to be approved by the Member States) will be decided by UNESCO's General Conference by the end of 2021. However, a non-binding recommendation on basic principles has been considered so far more flexible and better suited to the complexity of the ethical questions raised by AI.

Following internal consultations and virtual meetings, the Ad Hoc Expert Group made available online, in May 2020, a "zero draft" of its outcome document to invite commentaries by the public. In addition to values and principles drawn from or inspired by the consensus achieved in the 80+ published frameworks related to AI ethics, areas of policy action were given special attention: promoting diversity and inclusiveness; addressing labour market changes and the social, economic, cultural, and environmental impact of AI; fostering education, awareness, international cooperation, governance mechanisms, and AI ethics research and development; and ensuring the trustworthiness of AI systems, responsibility, accountability, and privacy.[47] The experts of the Group are especially worried about the need for a multidisciplinary, holistic approach, with due regard to human rights. They mostly agree that the UN has a significant role to play, akin to a "beacon," empowering people and increasing participation by all sectors of society.[48]

Also important, the UN Interregional Crime and Justice Research Institute (UNICRI) established in 2017 a Centre for Artificial Intelligence and Robotics in The Hague, with the aim of disseminating information, undertaking training activities, and promoting public awareness. Directed by Irakli Beridze, the Centre has been active in cybercrime, law enforcement (in partnership with Interpol), criminal justice, counterterrorism, and malicious use of AI from the perspective of its mandate. In 2018, the website "AI & Global Governance" of the Centre for Policy

Research of the United Nations University (UNU) began to publish online cross-disciplinary insights and "inform existing debates from the lens of multilateralism," as a tool for Member States, multilateral agencies, funds, programmes, and other partners.[49] Other noteworthy activities include the following: research on AI-related technologies conducted by the UN Institute for Disarmament Research (UNIDIR); the UN Innovation Network, connecting a collaborative community within the UN system; the Innovation Cell of the UN Department of Political and Peacebuilding Affairs (DPPA), aimed at incubating and leveraging use cases in peace and security; as well as a myriad of projects developed by UN agencies to apply AI in their daily practice in the field.[50]

At this stage, a distinction must be made between civilian AI applications and their deployment for military purposes. Civilian and military uses will presumably follow different multilateral tracks on the road to future international norms. Finding common ground on AI-enabled military capabilities will be no easy task. Amid growing polarisation and frictions on various hotspots, the international security environment does not seem conducive to sweeping global agreements in a very short time.[51] In disarmament and arms control, unilateralism and dissent among major players render political commitments more troublesome and undermine attempts at negotiating multilateral solutions. UN-sponsored processes on security and stability in cyberspace are another example of remarkable difficulties in making meaningful headway.[52]

In international security, one of the most pivotal AI-related multilateral discussions has been taking place in the open-ended Group of Governmental Experts (GGE) on emerging technologies in lethal autonomous weapons systems, under the UN Convention on Certain Conventional Weapons (CCW). These painstaking deliberations in Geneva are revealing of opportunities and predicaments encountered along the way. As decisions must be made by consensus, diverging views hamper swift progress. Meetings move around lengthy debates on methodology, definitions, and whether States should negotiate principles or constraints (if any) on fully autonomous weapons. Military powers that are actively pursuing ways to mobilise AI capabilities have been opposing the introduction of any restrictions on these technologies. Other countries support a pre-emptive ban on the grounds that "killer robots" will not be able to comply with international humanitarian law and maintain human responsibility for the use of force.[53] No agreement has been reached so far on proposals for a legally binding instrument to ensure "meaningful human control" over such weapons. The GGE will continue to hold meetings until 2021.[54]

Admittedly, such diplomatic talks are sensitive to political susceptibilities and need to receive continued reassurance to prevent pushbacks. The UN Secretary-General has a principled position against lethal autonomous weapons systems, but creating another track at this moment will probably meet resistance from some Member States. In the 11 guiding principles agreed by the GGE in 2019, the delegations reaffirmed that "the CCW offers an appropriate framework for dealing with the issue," within the context of the objectives and purposes of the CCW, "which seeks to strike a balance between military necessity and humanitarian considerations."[55] Alternatively, the UN leadership can push for international cooperation for the peaceful uses of responsible AI or some other language discouraging its militarisation. Yet, if these principles were openly championed by the organisation, Member States could read them in terms of political implications and their likely impact in governmental AI policymaking, a scenario which may end up raising questions regarding their convenience and suitability. All in all, any outcome on autonomous weapons is presently dependent upon the timeframe of the GGE.

In the meantime, there would still be political space for States to address international regulation of *civilian AI applications* and how to ensure that guardrails and governance tools will be in place sooner rather than later. To begin with, ongoing initiatives, such as those mentioned in the previous section, could be utilised as stepping-stones to persuade leaders in the field to move forward and create the conditions for a credible UN multilateral process in the long run. Accordingly, one way for the UN to have a more prominent role is to seek ways to make the transition from civil society and private sector initiatives to governmental policymaking at two levels of implementation: domestic and international.

At the domestic level, one should expect more calls for national legislation on civilian and commercial AI applications in many countries. Hard regulation on standards and certifications may face opposition in some quarters. In the end, if and when such norms are ever adopted, in most cases national governments will have the power to enforce them. The UN can facilitate the debate by sharing knowledge and best practices whenever possible, but national choices will ultimately belong to each State concerned.

At the international level, it is still too early to predict whether there will be room to move from voluntary or confidence-building measures to legally binding instruments anytime soon. Higher stakes, economic interests, and political considerations may increase the probability that diverging views and other factors might come into play to stall breakthroughs in the international governance of AI. Yet, the contributions of the OECD, European Union, and other groups could perhaps give the UN leverage to call for discussions that are truly global in scope and representation. The UN would be in a privileged position to secure an inclusive platform for cooperation with the participation of multiple stakeholders in the AI community of business, research, and development. The next section will assess current perspectives for concrete action in this domain.

3.4 THE HIGH-LEVEL PANEL ON DIGITAL COOPERATION AND THE WAY AHEAD

The High-Level Panel (HLP) on Digital Cooperation was established by the UN Secretary-General in 2017 to look into proposals to build trust and cooperation between Member States and other stakeholders, the private sector, research centres, civil society, and academia. In its report, released in June 2019, the HLP envisaged potential roles for the UN to add value in the digital transformation: as a convener; providing a space for debating values and norms; generating standard-setting; holding multi-stakeholder or bilateral initiatives on specific issues; developing the capacity of Member States; ranking, mapping, and measuring cybersecurity; and making available arbitration and dispute-resolution mechanisms.[56]

The HLP report put forward several recommendations, such as inviting stakeholders to commit to a "Declaration of Digital Interdependence," creating regional and global digital help desks, and adopting in 2020 a "Global Commitment for Digital Cooperation" to consolidate in a single political document shared values, principles, understandings, and objectives regarding the governance of cyberspace. Also, in recommendation 3C, it did not shy away from making principled statements of ethical significance, the stipulation that "life and death decisions should not be delegated to machines" being a case in point.[57]

Recommendation 3C, the most relevant guidance for AI governance contained in the HLP report, called for engineering and ethical standards to be developed through multi-stakeholder and multilateral approaches. No indication was given, however, on how multilateral mechanisms could be put in motion to implement this recommendation. Risks can be mitigated by means of norm-setting, agreed rules and standards, and responsible governance strategies to promote safe and beneficial AI. But for the UN to effectively encourage implementation, a strategic approach is required to avoid the expected pitfalls when powerful technologies meet international politics.

One of the submissions to the HLP, presented by experts from Oxford and Cambridge, maintained that the international governance of AI should be anchored to a regime under the UN meeting the following criteria: being "inclusive (of multiple stakeholders), anticipatory (of fast-progressing AI technologies and impacts), responsive (to the rapidly evolving technology and its uses), and reflexive (critically reviews and updates its policy principles)." It could be centred around a dedicated, legitimate, and well-resourced regime, possibly taking numerous forms: a UN specialised agency (such as the World Health Organisation), a related organisation to the UN (such as the World Trade Organisation), or a subsidiary body to the General Assembly (such as the UN Environment Programme). This regime should fulfil the objectives of coordination, comprehensive coverage, cooperation over competition, and collective benefit. They recommended, among its key components, the creation of a coordinator to develop a system-wide AI engagement strategy to catalyse efforts, multilateral treaties, and arrangements to govern AI; an Intergovernmental Panel to provide an authoritative voice on the state and trends of AI technologies; and a "UN AI Research Organisation (UNAIRO)" to focus upon building AI tools "in the public interest," as well as conducting basic research on improving these techniques in a safe, careful, and responsible environment.[58]

For these ideas to become operational, Member States must be on board. Within an adversarial context permeated by political quarrels, clashing views, and other stumbling blocks, too many layers and institutions tend to be more expensive and slow coordination in an already fragmented ecosystem. Even if new structures could be brought together under an umbrella body, budgetary constraints, which have been causing chronic financial stress to the UN, would trigger opposition by many Member States. Streamlined, low-cost arrangements would be preferable to perform a coordinating role, building upon existing institutions and initiatives in the UN system.

Digitalisation and AI will definitely stay on the international agenda in the foreseeable future. The HLP report endorsed "multi-stakeholderism" to get a more diverse spectrum of participants involved in governance in the digital sphere. One of the options was to revamp the Internet Governance Forum in order to advance the concept of an IGF+ model, open to all stakeholders and institutionally connected to the UN system.[59] As Kaljurand pointed out, the IGF+ would comprise of five bodies: 1) an advisory group appointed by Secretary-General; 2) a cooperation accelerator; 3) a policy incubator to propose norms and policies; 4) an observatory and help desk to give advice on drafting legislation or tackling crisis situations; and 5) a trust fund linked to the Executive Office of the Secretary-General "to reflect its interdisciplinary and system-wide approach."[60]

Cross-references with the cyber domain are indeed relevant for AI governance, to the extent that digital technologies increasingly intersect with machine learning and other AI-enabled techniques.[61] Moving from "internet governance" to "digital cooperation" has already been, in a way, a conceptual enlargement of the terrain the UN would seek to chart. Could this broadening of the intended scope backfire? It is clear by now that the IGF+ model is the option of choice on the table, since the IGF "already has a UN mandate, an institutional form of sorts, and governmental and stakeholder support."[62] Some questions remain though: would the UN ultimately embrace AI and cyberspace in a single undertaking as far as governance is concerned? Would this avoid duplication, institutional fatigue, or more bureaucratic layers that can prove inefficient? Or, contrariwise, are these two domains of interest utterly different or too complex to be treated as a unified field?

Against this background, the 75th anniversary of the UN in 2020 was expected to be a key milestone for a relaunching of the organisation. The theme is chosen for the commemorations ("The future we want, the UN we need: reaffirming our collective commitment to multilateralism") set the tone and invited Member States to acknowledge and seriously examine those technologies most likely to have a decisive impact on our lives, linking these concerns with the need for a revitalised multilateral system. It was a timely opportunity to counter frequent criticism of flaws attributed to the UN, but preparations were severely affected by the COVID-19 pandemic and the ensuing interruption of the regular day-to-day work at the UN Headquarters in New York. Consequently, in-person meetings were cancelled, others postponed, and projects put on hold. With a staggering death toll, the pandemic demonstrated tragically that cross-border issues respect no political boundaries and call for collective action to manage its most dramatic consequences.[63]

Despite the adversities, after consultations with champions and key constituents,[64] as a follow-up of the HLP on Digital Cooperation, the Secretary-General released a roadmap, in June 2020, in which the UN's willingness to be a convener and platform for multi-stakeholder policy dialogue was again reiterated. A number of recommendations were outlined on universal connectivity, digital public goods, human rights, digital inclusion, surveillance technologies (facial recognition), online harassment and violence, trust, security and stability, and for strengthening the IGF. Guterres will appoint an Envoy on Technology in 2021 to advise the senior leadership of the organisation on key technological trends and serve as an advocate and focal point for digital cooperation (a "first port of call" for the broader UN system).[65]

Concerning recommendation 3C specifically, the roadmap highlighted three outstanding challenges: a) lack of representation and inclusiveness in AI global discussions; b) inadequate overall coordination of AI-related initiatives, "in a way that is easily accessible to other countries outside the existing groupings"; and c) the need to build capacity and AI expertise, particularly in the public sector, "to bring national oversight or governance to the use of such technologies." On the way forward, in order to address issues raised around "inclusion, coordination, and capacity-building," the Secretary-General declared his intention to establish a multi-stakeholder *advisory body* on global AI cooperation to provide guidance that is "trustworthy, human-rights based, safe and sustainable, and promotes peace."[66]

The roadmap echoed two common-sense perceptions: a) that the UN is willing to have a more proactive role in AI governance; and b) that it has also been cautious and refraining from taking measures that are premature without substantial support from the UN membership.[67] As an intergovernmental organisation relying upon decisions by Member States, the UN itself has limited power, considering above all the fact that "national governments are reluctant to impede innovation in an emerging technology by pre-emptory regulation in an era of intense international competition," as Marchant noted.[68]

A desirable prerequisite is to keep the major players engaged, so that AI governance can be instrumental in providing safety, security, and stability to safeguard workable international regulatory regimes. Governments pursuing nationalist agendas and large corporations concerned with profitability may resist too invasive multilateral processes.[69] Many States, nonetheless, attach great value to the UN as a broker to bridge differences among the membership. The informal core group on exponential technological change has gathered 50+ Member States since 2017 to address tech issues in the UN and its links to the SDGs. Following the HLP report, the group decided to transition to a new expanded configuration to go beyond the 2030 Agenda and include in the discussion all three pillars of the UN: peace and security, human rights, and development. As a result, the first meeting of the new Group of Friends on Digital Technologies took place in November 2019, in New York, co-chaired by the Permanent Representatives of Finland, Mexico, and Singapore, to exchange views on its programme of work for 2020 and explore the interlinkages between digital technologies and the three pillars, including cooperation and governance in cross-cutting issues. Again, COVID-19 disrupted the original plans, and the effectiveness of the Group of Friends is still to be tested.[70]

At this juncture, even though some proposals may require more time for maturation, others could be implemented in a more straightforward manner, without the need for a fully-fledged, previous commitment from States on the preconditions for establishing new criteria, benchmarks, and rules at the global level. Consultative and non-binding international settings, strictly on a voluntary basis, mindful of the principle of "do no harm," could be feasible if initially focused upon information gathering, independent analyses, and recommendations geared at prevention instead of regulation per se.

Traditional, institutionally based intergovernmental diplomacy seems too slow and time-consuming if compared with the astounding pace of technological innovation. There is currently a "governance gap," as AI technology has been evolving much faster than international law's ability to keep up. This quandary partially explains why "an amorphous and constantly evolving set of informal soft law governance mechanisms" are coming in to fill the void.[71] Informal, ad-hoc, plurilateral initiatives spurred by like-minded countries ("coalitions of the willing") may at times bring about added value in governance, but they usually lack universal appeal and raise suspicion of their agendas in the eyes of States left outside these groups.

Trying to be too ambitious from the very beginning may lead to a dead-end and risk backlash. A better solution to escape short-term paralysis is for the UN, with the authority and legitimacy conferred to it by Member States, to offer a collective space, open to all, to encourage cooperation and advance recommendations.[72] Besides mobilising leading experts and exchanging information, the new AI advisory body announced in the Secretary-General's roadmap can collect evidence to reduce both misinformation and fear by the general public about AI risks, so that myth, hype, and misunderstandings are dissipated and duly separated from the body of technical knowledge available so far.[73] Although not mandated to engage in normative deliberations, the invited experts could promote best practices and start discussing standardisation and compliance in search for commonalities, which can over time generate critical mass to expand their work to other areas as appropriate.

There is a long way before the conditions are ripe for the adoption of international rules on audit and certification schemes applicable to AI technologies. Advisory bodies, such as the one the Secretary-General decided to establish, can be conceived as a first step in that direction. Taking advantage of expertise and knowledge produced in the UN system, priority should be given to close coordination with UNESCO's Ad Hoc Expert Group. An informal coalition could be built to articulate the more forthcoming Member States in a building-block strategy towards a multilateral process, under the auspices of the UN, in a place and timeframe yet to be determined. If successful, this incremental approach could hopefully enjoy increasing support and become a precursor for advancing institution-building in this area. It may eventually give rise to a comprehensive, IPCC-modelled Intergovernmental Panel on Artificial Intelligence, or another permanent structure that can respond to the demands and expectations of our time.

3.5 CONCLUSION

On closer inspection, AI governance is not just about regulation or imposing restrictions, but encouraging prevention, horizon scanning, and foresight as well. It may take more time than expected for the international community to start moving in earnest towards consequential measures on AI policymaking. Effective multilateralism essentially means that international issues should ideally be addressed in good faith by all interested parties, following procedures commonly agreed upon, upholding the rule of law, fairness, and both geographical and gender balance, in order to reach political solutions that can accommodate all views and concerns as much as possible. Against all the odds, the UN is well-positioned to offer structured machinery for cooperation among Member States and other stakeholders to address the impact of emerging technologies.[74]

Again, these all-important issues concern all societies, and their consideration should not be confined to a few influential actors. The larger AI debate would benefit from the participation of more scholars, politicians, and policymakers of the Global South as a means of "bringing the Rest in."[75] When stakes are too high and entail worldwide externalities, all countries are likely to be affected in one way or another. Dealing with

AI risks in the near- and long-term will require political will, capacity-building, inclusiveness, and more diverse representation in a plurality of settings. With the right amount of support from Member States, the UN can help bridge the gap at the global level and provide a legitimate, representative, and policy-oriented locus for deeper international cooperation on AI matters in the years ahead.

ACKNOWLEDGEMENTS

I thank Maurizio Tinnirello for the invitation and Thomas Campbell, Irakli Beridze, and the anonymous reviewers for their insightful comments on the first draft. The views expressed herein are those of the author.

NOTES

1. C. Brose, "War's sci-fi future: The new revolution in military affairs," *Foreign Affairs* 98, no. 3 (May–June 2019): 122–134; P. Gasser et al., *Assessing the strategic effects of artificial intelligence* (Center for Global Security Research, Lawrence Livermore National Laboratory, and Technology for Global Security, 2018), https://www.tech4gs.org/assessing-the-strategic-effects-of-artificial-intelligence.html; K. F. Lee, *AI superpowers: China, silicon valley, and the new world order* (Boston: Houghton Mifflin Harcourt, 2018); D. Wagner and K. Furst, *AI supremacy: Winning in the era of machine learning* (Scotts Valley: CreateSpace, 2018); K. Payne, "Artificial intelligence: A revolution in strategic affairs?" *Survival* 60, no. 5 (2018): 7–32.
2. *Digital economy report 2019*, UNCTAD, 2019, https://unctad.org/en; J. Manyika and J. Bughin, *The promise and challenge of the age of artificial intelligence* (McKinsey Global Institute, 2018), 4, https://www.mckinsey.com/featured-insights/artificial-intelligence.
3. There are no Latin American, Caribbean, or African countries in the top 20 ranking of government AI readiness. *Government artificial intelligence readiness index 2019* (Oxford Insights and Canada's International Development Research Centre, 2019), https://ai4d.ai/wp-content/uploads/2019/05/ai-gov-readiness-report_v08.pdf.
4. This chapter is not the right place for a discussion on the "definition" of AI, a controversial subject that would require lengthy explanations. Please refer to S. Bringsjord and N. S. Govindarajulu, "Artificial intelligence," *Stanford Encyclopedia of Philosophy*, https://plato.stanford.edu/entries/artificial-intelligence, and R. V. Yampolskiy, ed., *Artificial intelligence, safety and security* (Boca Raton: Chapman and Hall/CRC, 2018).
5. As discussed in a conference organised by the Foresight Institute, "general scepticism prevails about the chances of success for any effort to engage national actors in a conversation about decreased application of AI in the military." A. Duettmann et al., *Artificial general intelligence: Coordination & great powers* (San Francisco: Foresight Institute, White paper, 2018), 6, https://foresight.org

/wp-content/uploads/2018/11/AGI-Coordination-Great-Powers-Report.pdf. See also The AI arms race, *Financial Times*, FT Series, https://www.ft.com/content/21eb5996-89a3-11e8-bf9e-8771d5404543.

6. As one expert put it, "for the three gravest planetary challenges—technology, ecology, and nuclear annihilation—we need an accurate, just, and timely multilateral approach." A. H. Bajrektarevic, "The answer to AI is intergovernmental multilateralism," *New Europe*, 13 March 2020, https://www.neweurope.eu/article/the-answer-to-ai-is-intergovernmental-multilateralism.

7. B. Perry and R. Uuk, "AI governance and the policymaking process: Key considerations for reducing AI risk," *Big Data and Cognitive Computing* 3, no. 2 (June 2019): 3, https://www.mdpi.com/2504-2289/3/2.

8. N. Bostrom, *Superintelligence: Paths, dangers, strategies* (Oxford: Oxford University Press, 2014); C. Chace, *Surviving AI: The promise and peril of artificial intelligence* (San Mateo: Three Cs Publishing, 2015); J. Barrat, *Our final invention: Artificial intelligence and the end of the human era* (New York: St. Martin's Press, 2013); S. D. Baum, *A survey of artificial general intelligence projects for ethics, risk, and policy*, Global Catastrophic Risk Institute, Working Paper 17-1, November 2017, https://papers.ssrn.com/sol3/papers.cfm?abstract_id=3070741.

9. This near- and long-term distinction does not deny the fact that these problems are somehow interconnected and there are also medium-term risks to reckon with. Cf. A. Dafoe, *AI governance: A research agenda* (Future of Humanity Institute, University of Oxford, 2017), https://www.fhi.ox.ac.uk/wp-content/uploads/GovAIAgenda.pdf. A fine overview of international governance arrangements for global catastrophic risks can be found in L. Kemp and C. Rhodes, *The cartography of global catastrophic governance* (Stockholm: Global Challenges Foundation, 2019), https://globalchallenges.org/the-cartography-of-global-catastrophic-governance.

10. For current initiatives, see J. Butcher and I. Beridze, "What is the state of artificial intelligence governance globally?" *The RUSI Journal* 164, no. 5–6 (2019): 88–96, https://doi.org/10.1080/03071847.2019.1694260.

11. P. Engelke, *AI, society, and governance: An introduction* (Washington: The Scowcroft Center for Strategy and Security, March 2020), https://www.atlantic-council.org/wp-content/uploads/2020/03/Final-AI-Policy-Primer-0220.pdf.

12. Danzig stressed this point when referring to pathogens, AI systems, computer viruses, and radiation released by accident: "Agreed reporting systems, shared controls, common contingency plans, norms, and treaties must be pursued as means of moderating our numerous mutual risks." R. Danzig, *Technology roulette: Managing loss of control as many militaries pursue technological superiority* (Washington: CNAS, June 2018), 2, https://www.cnas.org/publications/reports/technology-roulette.

13. Military powers might have little choice but begin discussions over "whether some applications of AI pose unacceptable risks of escalation or loss of control" and take measures to improve safety. P. Scharre, "Killer apps: The real dangers of an AI arms race," *Foreign Affairs* 98, no. 3 (May–June 2019): 135–145.

14. P. Cihon, M. M. Maas, and L. Kemp, "Should artificial intelligence governance be centralised? Design lessons from history," *Proceedings of the AAAI/ACM Conference on AI, Ethics, and Society*, February 2020, 228–234, https://doi.org/10.1145/3375627.3375857. On informal organisations, transgovernmental networks, and transnational public–private partnerships, see K. Abbott and B. Faude, "Choosing low-cost institutions in global governance," *International Theory*, June 2020, https://www.researchgate.net/publication/342109046_Choosing_low-cost_institutions_in_global_governance.

15. J. Turner, *Robot rules: Regulating artificial intelligence* (London: Palgrave Macmillan, 2019), 239–240.

16. It is important to say that in some domain-specific AI applications, a certain degree of coordination has been under way within a few multilateral institutions, such as the International Telecommunications Union (ITU), the International Civil Aviation Organization (ICAO), and the International Maritime Organization (IMO).

17. Dafoe, *AI governance*, 46.

18. O. J. Erdelyi and J. Goldsmith, "Regulating artificial intelligence: Proposal for a global solution," Paper presented at the *AAAI/ACM Conference on Artificial Intelligence, Ethics and Society*, New Orleans, 1–3 February 2018, 6, http://www.aies-conference.com/2018/accepted-papers.

19. The IPCC is the UN body for assessing the science related to climate change, created to provide policymakers with regular scientific assessments and put forward adaptation and mitigation options. Cf. https://www.ipcc.ch.

20. N. Miailhe, "AI & global governance: Why we need an intergovernmental panel for artificial intelligence," *Articles & Insights*, Centre for Policy Research, UNU, 20 December 2018, https://cpr.unu.edu/ai-global-governance-why-we-need-an-intergovernmental-panel-for-artificial-intelligence.html.

21. The Asilomar principles call inter alia for "race avoidance" (teams developing AI systems should actively cooperate to avoid corner-cutting on safety standards); "human values" (AI systems should be designed and operated so as to be compatible with ideals of human dignity, rights, freedoms, and cultural diversity); preventing an "AI arms race" (an arms race in lethal autonomous weapons systems should be avoided); and AI for the "common good" (AI should only be developed in the service of widely shared ethical ideals and for the benefit of all humanity rather than one State or organisation). Future of Life Institute, https://futureoflife.org/ai-principles.

22. J. Fjeld, et al., *Principled artificial intelligence: Mapping consensus in ethical and rights-based approaches to principles for AI* (Cambridge: Berkman Klein Center for Internet & Society at Harvard University, Research Publication, 15 January 2020), http://nrs.harvard.edu/urn-3:HUL.InstRepos:42160420. Also World Economic Forum, *AI governance: A holistic approach to implement ethics into AI* (Geneva: White Paper, January 2019), https://www.weforum.org/whitepapers/ai-governance-a-holistic-approach-to-implement-ethics-into-ai.

23. WEF, Shaping the future of technology governance: artificial intelligence and machine learning, https://www.weforum.org/platforms/shaping-the-future-of-technology-governance-artificial-intelligence-and-machine-learning.

24. The Global Data Commons aims at supporting the achievement of the Sustainable Development Goals and it has been envisioned as a precursor for the AI for SDGs Center (AI4SDG), designed by its proponents to become "an engine for practical experimentation and scaling up of governance models for AI." The Future Society, https://thefuturesociety.org/2019/05/28/ai-for-sdgs-center-ai4sdg. For the Partnership on AI see https://www.partnershiponai.org.

25. One of their proposals is the creation of a multi-stakeholder Global Governance Network for AI (GGN-AI), drawing inspiration from the "governance coordinating committees" first put forward by W. Wallach and G. Marchant, "Toward the agile and comprehensive international governance of AI and robotics," *Proceedings of the IEEE* 107, no. 3 (March 2019), https://ieeexplore.ieee.org/stamp/stamp.jsp?arnumber=8662741.

26. As noted by G. Marcus, *In the global AI agenda* (Cambridge: MIT Technology Review Insights, 26 March 2020), 7, https://mittrinsights.s3.amazonaws.com/AIagenda2020/GlobalAIagenda.pdf.

27. The 2019 Osaka Declaration of the G20 embraced the principle of human-centred AI by recognising that these technologies can help promote inclusive economic growth, bring great benefits to society and empower individuals: "The responsible development and use of AI can be a driving force to help advance the SDGs and to realise a sustainable and inclusive society, mitigating risks to wider societal values." Japan's Ministry of Foreign Affairs, https://www.mofa.go.jp/policy/economy/g20_summit/osaka19/en/documents/final_g20_osaka_leaders_declaration.html.

28. G7 Summit, Canada 2018, "Charlevoix common vision for the future of artificial intelligence," http://www.g7.utoronto.ca/summit/2018charlevoix/ai-commitment.html.

29. Cf. the original document, "Mandate for the international panel on artificial intelligence," Canada and France, https://pm.gc.ca/en/news/backgrounders/2018/12/06/mandate-international-panel-artificial-intelligence.

30. GPAI's 15 founding members are Australia, Canada, France, Germany, India, Italy, Japan, Mexico, New Zealand, Republic of Korea, Singapore, Slovenia, United Kingdom, United States, and the European Union. Drawing from the OECD recommendations on AI policy, four working groups will be created to address the following themes: 1) responsible AI; 2) data governance; 3) the future of work; and 4) innovation and commercialisation. GPAI will be supported by a Secretariat, to be hosted by the OECD, as well as by two "centers of expertise" (in Montreal and Paris). Cf. "Joint Statement from founding members of GPAI," https://www.diplomatie.gouv.fr/en/french-foreign-policy/digital-diplomacy/news/article/launch-of-the-global-partnership-on-artificial-intelligence-by-15-founding.

31. GDPR is a regulation, not a directive, directly binding and applicable, and became a model for many national laws outside the European Union, including Chile, Japan, Brazil, South Korea, Argentina, and Kenya. First meeting of the Ad hoc Committee on Artificial Intelligence (CAHAI), Council of Europe, Strasbourg, 15 November 2019, https://www.coe.int/en/web/human-rights -rule-of-law. See also European Commission's AI HLEG, https://ec.europa.eu /digital-single-market/en/high-level-expert-group-artificial-intelligence.

32. *Recommendation of the Council on Artificial Intelligence* (Paris: OECD/ LEGAL/0449, 21 May 2019), https://legalinstruments.oecd.org/en/instruments/OECD-LEGAL-0449.

33. For further information and additional documents, visit the OECD website at https://oecd.ai.

34. J. C. Newman, *Decision points in AI governance: Three case studies explore efforts to operationalize AI principles* (U.C. Berkeley, Center for Long-Term Cybersecurity, White Paper Series, 2020, 30–40), https://cltc.berkeley.edu /2020/05/05/new-cltc-report-decision-points-in-ai-governance.

35. Emblematic of differences of opinion, the G20 did not extend its support to Section 2 recommendations on "national policies and international cooperation," G20 Ministerial Meeting on Trade and Digital Economy, Tsubuka, 8–9 June 2019, https://www.mofa.go.jp/files/000486596.pdf.

36. Campbell noted that "there are few states with AI national strategies or plans or significant investments in several geographic regions across the globe, including: South America, Central America, Eastern Europe, Central Asia, Southeast Asia, and Africa." T. A. Campbell, *Artificial intelligence: An overview of state initiatives* (UNICRI and FutureGrasp, 2019), cf. Executive Summary, http://www.unicri.it/in_focus/files/Report_AI-An_Overview _of_State_Initiatives_FutureGrasp_7-23-19.pdf.

37. Address of the UN Secretary-General to the 73rd General Assembly, 25 September 2018, https://www.un.org/sg/en/content/sg/speeches/2018-09 -25/address-73rd-general-assembly.

38. See also *Current developments in science and technology and their potential impact on international security and disarmament efforts*, Report of the UN Secretary-General, General Assembly, A/73/177, 17 July 2018, https://www .un.org/disarmament/publications/library/73-ga-sg-report.

39. Among the pledges and commitments to pursue this strategy were the following: deepening the UN's internal capacities and exposure to emerging technologies; increasing understanding, advocacy, and dialogue; supporting dialogue on normative and cooperation frameworks; and enhancing UN system support to government capacity development. Cf. *UN Secretary-General's strategy on new technologies* (New York, September 2018), 3–5, https://www.un.org/en/newtechnologies/images/pdf/SGs-Strategy-on -New-Technologies.pdf.

40. This document, "A United Nations system-wide strategic approach and road map for supporting capacity development on artificial intelligence," put a significant emphasis on capacity-building for developing countries. Geneva, 17 June 2019, https://digitallibrary.un.org/record/3811676.

41. Their goal is to implement a "data action" agenda for a data-driven transformation of the organisation engaging the whole UN system. *Data strategy of the secretary general for action by everyone, everywhere* (New York, May 2020), https://www.un.org/en/content/datastrategy.

42. The UN Global Pulse seeks to utilise AI and digital data to gain a better understanding of changes in human well-being and to "get real-time feedback on how well policy responses are working." Cf. https://www.unglobalpulse.org and *E-analytics guide: Using data and new technology for peacemaking, preventive diplomacy, and peacebuilding*, UN Global Pulse, April 2019, https://www.unglobalpulse.org/document/e-analytics-guide-using-data-and-new-technology-for-peacemaking-preventive-diplomacy-and-peaceuilding.

43. The AI for Good Global Summit brings together speakers from governments, the industry, academia, and civil society to discuss how AI can be used to achieve inter alia results in ending poverty, alleviating hunger, promoting health, and identifying development solutions. *AI for good global summit 2019* (Summit Insights, Geneva, 28–31 May 2019, International Telecommunication Union and XPRIZE Foundation), https://itu.foleon.com/itu/aiforgood2019/home.

44. See in particular *Report of COMEST on robotics ethics* (Paris: UNESCO, 2017), https://unesdoc.unesco.org/ark:/48223/pf0000253952.

45. International Research Centre of Artificial Intelligence (IRCAI), https://ircai.org.

46. *Preliminary study on a possible standard-setting instrument on the ethics of artificial intelligence*, UNESCO General Conference, 40 C/67, 30 July 2019, https://unesdoc.unesco.org/ark:/48223/pf0000369455.

47. *Outcome document*: first version of a draft text of a recommendation on the ethics of artificial intelligence. Ad Hoc Expert Group (AHEG) for the preparation of a draft text of a recommendation on the ethics of artificial intelligence, UNESCO, SHS/BIO/AHEG-AI/2020/4 Rev, 15 May 2020, https://unesdoc.unesco.org/ark:/48223/pf0000373434.

48. Interview with Professor Edson Prestes, member of UNESCO's Ad Hoc Expert Group and member of the UN High-Level Panel on Digital Cooperation, 2 June 2020. The work of the IEEE is an important reference in this area: *Ethically aligned design: A vision for prioritising human well-being with autonomous and intelligent systems* (New York: Institute of Electrical and Electronics Engineers, 2018), https://ethicsinaction.ieee.org.

49. AI & Global Governance, Centre for Policy Research, UNU, https://cpr.unu.edu/tag/artificial-intelligence.

50. *United Nations activities on artificial intelligence* (Geneva: International Telecommunication Union, 2019), https://www.itu.int/dms_pub/itu-s/opb/gen/S-GEN-UNACT-2019-1-PDF-E.pdf.

51. R. Gowan, "Muddling through to 2030: The long decline of international security cooperation," *Articles & insights*, Centre for Policy Research, UNU, 24 October 2018, https://cpr.unu.edu/muddling-through-to-2030-the-long-decline-of-international-security-cooperation.html.

52. C. Ruhl et al., *Cyberspace and geopolitics: Assessing global cybersecurity norm processes at a crossroads* (Washington: Carnegie Endowment for International Peace, Working Paper, February 2020), https://carnegieendowment.org/2020/02/26/cyberspace-and-geopolitics-assessing-global-cybersecurity-norm-processes-at-crossroads-pub-81110.

53. Critics of the ban claimed that this alternative would be "impractical." F. Slijper et al., *State of AI: Artificial intelligence, the military and increasingly autonomous weapons* (Utrecht: PAX, April 2019), https://www.paxvoorvrede.nl/media/files/state-of-artificial-intelligence--pax-report.pdf.

54. Except from a few more active delegations, the number of experts from the Global South taking the floor and making proposals in the GGE is remarkably low. Report of the 2019 session of the Group of Governmental Experts on Emerging Technologies in the Area of Lethal Autonomous Weapons Systems, Geneva, 21 August 2019, CCW/GGE.1/2019/CRP.1/Rev.2, https://www.unog.ch.

55. Report of the 2019 session of the GGE.

56. *The age of digital interdependence: Report of the UN Secretary-General's high-level panel on digital cooperation* (New York, 10 June 2019), 4–5, https://digitalcooperation.org/report.

57. Recommendation 3C reads as follows: "We believe that autonomous intelligent systems should be designed in ways that enable their decisions to be explained and humans to be accountable for their use. Audit and certification schemes should monitor compliance of AI systems with engineering and ethical standards, which should be developed using multi-stakeholder and multilateral approaches. Life and death decisions should not be delegated to machines. We call for enhanced digital cooperation with multiple stakeholders to think through the design and application of these standards and principles such as transparency and non-bias in autonomous intelligent systems in different social settings." Ibid. 38.

58. They suggested an "innovative model of multipartite representation and voting," mirrored in the International Labour Organisation. L. Kemp et al., "UN high-level panel on digital cooperation: A proposal for international AI governance," Submission by Centre for the Study of Existential Risk, University of Cambridge, and Centre for the Governance of AI, Future of Humanity Institute, Oxford University, 2019, https://digitalcooperation.org/responses.

59. The HLP report put forward three potential models for global digital cooperation: a strengthened and enhanced IGF+; a distributed co-governance architecture; and a digital commons architecture.

60. M. Kaljurand, "From IGF to IGF+," in W. Kleinwächter et al., *Towards a global framework for cyber peace and digital cooperation. An agenda for the 2020s* (Berlin: Federal Ministry of Economics and Technology, 2019), 54–56, https://www.hans-bredow-institut.de.

61. See, for instance, Y. Lannquist et al., "The intersection and governance of artificial intelligence and cybersecurity," *The Future Society*, 21 May 2020, https://www.researchgate.net.

62. W. J. Drake, "Considerations on the high-level panel's 'Internet Governance Forum Plus' model," *CircleID*, 4 November 2019, http://www.circleid.com/posts.

63. Turner cogently explained this point: "Given the arbitrary nature of international borders, there is no reason why AI's impacts should be self-contained within the country in which it originates. Instead, much like a wildfire, tsunami or virus, AI's impacts will cross man-made boundaries with impunity. The danger of a country being cross-infected ought to encourage its national leaders to promote international standards as a matter of national self-preservation as much as anything else." Turner, *Robot rules*, 244.

64. The author of this chapter had the honour to join some of these consultations and contribute with inputs in the preparations for the Secretary-General's roadmap. A full list of participants in the round-table discussions is available at www.un.org/en/digital-cooperation-panel.

65. *Roadmap for digital cooperation: Implementation of the recommendations of the independent high-level panel on digital cooperation*, Report of the Secretary-General, New York, 11 June 2020, 15, https://www.un.org/en/content/digital-cooperation-roadmap.

66. According to the roadmap, this advisory body will comprise Member States, relevant UN entities, interested companies, academic institutions, and civil society groups. Ibid. 17–18.

67. As a commentator put it, "much like its role during nuclear non-proliferation discussions, the UN must be able to navigate the social disruptions resulting from ubiquitous AI adoption with finesse." Nicholas Wright, "AI & global governance: Three distinct AI challenges for the UN," *Articles & insights*, Centre for Policy Research, UNU, 7 December 2018, https://cpr.unu.edu/ai-global-governance-three-distinct-ai-challenges-for-the-un.html.

68. For these reasons, he added, "it is safe to say there will be no comprehensive traditional regulation of AI for some time, except perhaps if some disaster occurs that triggers a drastic and no doubt poorly-matched regulatory response." G. Marchant, "'Soft law' governance of artificial intelligence," *AI Pulse*, UCLA School of Law, 25 January 2019, https://aipulse.org/soft-law-governance-of-artificial-intelligence.

69. In the age of global politics, normative guidance for the safe deployment of AI systems would benefit from insights brought by tech-leaders and tech-takers alike. E. Pauwels, "How can multilateralism survive the era of artificial intelligence?," *UN Chronicle* LV, no. 3–4 (December 2018), https://unchronicle.un.org/article/how-can-multilateralism-survive-era-artificial-intelligence.

70. During the first meeting, many delegations pledged their support to the Group of Friends, but a few Member States warned that "duplication" should be avoided and, for this reason, the Group would better wait for the results of ongoing processes in the UN General Assembly, such as the Open-Ended Working Group (OEWG) and the Group of Governmental Experts (GGE) on developments in the field of information and telecommunications in the

context of international security. For more information on these two processes, see UNODA's website: https://www.un.org/disarmament/ict-security. On multilateral frameworks in cybersecurity, see UNIDIR's portal: https://cyberpolicyportal.org/en/multilateral-legislation.

71. R. Hagemann et al., "Soft law for hard problems: The governance of emerging technologies in an uncertain future," *Colorado Technology Law Journal*, 5 February 2018, https://ssrn.com/abstract=3118539.

72. An example along these lines would be the creation of a "Global Foresight Observatory" on the convergence of AI with other emerging technologies, i.e. a multi-stakeholder platform to foster cooperation in technological and political preparedness for responsive innovation. This sort of initiative fits well with what the UN can do even in hard-knock situations. E. Pauwels, *The new geopolitics of converging risks: The UN and prevention in the era of AI*, Centre for Policy Research, UNU, 2 May 2019, 53, https://cpr.unu.edu /the-new-geopolitics-of-converging-risks-the-un-and-prevention-in-the -era-of-ai.html.

73. Many private companies may welcome this approach, since too much emphasis on the "dark side" of the technology does not make justice to the resources being invested in AI for the public good by the industry.

74. Concerning the internal, bureaucratic machinery of the organisation, not being historically an entity readily recognised for innovation, the UN has been taking some steps to incorporate new approaches to technology in its toolkit, as previously noted in this chapter. A sustained effort will be needed to continue and expand this trajectory going forward.

75. A. Acharya and B. Buzan, *The making of global international relations: Origins and evolution of IR at its centenary* (Cambridge: Cambridge University Press, 2019), 302.

CHAPTER 4

Governing the Use of Autonomous Weapon Systems

Alfredo Toro Carnevali

CONTENTS

DOI: 10.1201/9780429446726-4

POPULAR CULTURE LONG AGO introduced the fear that machines would one day take over the world. Films like *2001: Space Odyssey* (1968) by Stanley Kubrick and *Terminator* (1984) by James Cameron showcased intelligent computer systems that rebelled against humans. However, the weapon systems of today are a far cry from *Terminator*'s Skynet. They are examples of the application of narrow AI, which displays a range of cognitive abilities that often allows it to equal or excel the performance of human beings, but only in very specific tasks. They remain unable to apply such capabilities along a range of domains as human intelligence can.[1] AlphaGo is a classic example of narrow AI. This machine was created by DeepMind to play the Chinese game GO, which is much more complex than chess and allows for countless plays. AlphaGo was fed 30 million games and continued to train itself using its 12 neural networks. It then went on to defeat the reigning GO champion with a play that seemed almost inconceivable to humans. However, despite its superhuman abilities in this particular game, AlphaGo cannot play any other game or perform any other task.[2]

Like other examples of narrow AI, Autonomous Weapon Systems (AWS) work by having a human programmer collect and input data into the machine's memory, which the machine can then draw upon to continue to learn and manage its operations. In other words, using the data stored and the instructions pre-programmed by the human controller, the machine is able to select one or more options from a range of possible outcomes. In synthesis, the output selected by the machine will always be the consequence of instructions and data provided by the programmer.[3]

What defines AWS—in particular—is their ability to search for, select and engage a target on their own.[4] Unlike remote-controlled weapons such as drones, AWS could choose a target and attack it without human intervention or supervision.[5] There are currently three types of weapon systems often associated with the term "autonomous weapon systems":[6]

- *Semi-autonomous* weapon systems are those that require a human to direct the weapon system towards a target and attack it. The Predator and Reaper drones are examples.

- *Human supervised autonomous* weapon systems are those that can select a target and decide on a course of action but still rely on the oversight of an operator. Examples of these weapons include Israel's Iron Dome, the United States Navy's Phalanx, and the Aegis combat system.

- *Fully Autonomous* weapon systems are those that can select a target and attack it without any human interaction. Israel's Harpy is a close example. This weapon system can select radars and destroy them within a confined time and space without any human oversight.[7]

According to Paul Scharre, there are examples of potentially fully autonomous weapon systems that date back to the 1980s, but they have only been employed with direct human involvement. Ultimately, he argues, what defines an autonomous weapon system is not its level of sophistication but the level of operational freedom that it is granted by commanders.[8] However, there is little doubt that as weapon systems become smarter there will be an increasing willingness on the part of states to allow them to operate with greater autonomy. After all, AWS could potentially bring to the fore a number of substantive advantages to the world's militaries, including:

a) The ability to operate without a communications link, thus reducing the risk of hacking or jamming on the battlefield.

b) The ability to operate at speeds that far surpass human capacities. AWS can process data at electronic speeds as compared to human's neuromuscular delay of 0.25 seconds.[9] Paul Scharre describes how a simulation of the use of the Aegis defense system showed how a task performed under human control takes just under one minute, compared to half of that time when used semi-autonomously, and just a few heartbeats when given full autonomy.[10]

c) The possibility to reduce costs. AWS would not require an operator to manage each individual unit but could rely on one person to oversee multiple units.[11]

The question remains as to whether these weapon systems can be legally employed in armed conflicts. Many wonder if the use of AWS would comply with the existing framework of International Humanitarian Law (IHL)[12] or if their introduction would require a whole new legal framework. Article 36 of the 1977 Additional Protocol I of the Geneva Convention of 1949, relating to the Protection of Victims of International Armed Conflicts, offers some insight into this matter:

> In the study, development, acquisition or adoption of a new weapon, means or method of warfare, a High Contracting Party is under an

obligation to determine whether its employment would, in some or all circumstances, be prohibited by this Protocol or by any other rule of international law applicable to the High Contracting Party.[13]

In line with Article 36, this next section will look into the technical capability of AWS to effectively comply with the core principles of distinction, proportionality and precautions of attack in armed conflicts as codified in IHL.

4.1 PRINCIPLES OF INTERNATIONAL HUMANITARIAN LAW

4.1.1 The Principle of Distinction

In order to comply with the principle of distinction, AWS would have to be able to distinguish between civilians and combatants and between civilian objects and military objectives. Article 48 of the 1977 Additional Protocol I stipulates, in this regard, that:

> In order to ensure respect for and protection of the civilian population and civilian objects, the parties to the conflict shall at all times distinguish between the civilian population and combatants and between civilian objects and military objectives and accordingly shall direct their operations only against military objectives.[14]

Furthermore, Article 51(b) of the 1977 Additional Protocol I prohibits those attacks which "employ a method or means of combat which cannot be directed at a specific military objective."[15] In other words, an attack that cannot discriminate between military and civilian targets.

So the question is whether AWS can discriminate between civilians and combatants, and between civilian objects and military objectives to such a degree that they can be considered to comply with the principle of distinction better or as well as a trained human combatant? The simple answer is that at their current stage of development, AWS would face a steep challenge in adequately meeting these requirements.

In the first place, AI has historically struggled with perception and image recognition.[16] Second, AWS can be very sensitive to weather conditions and battlefield haze, which degrade their functions and can cause false alarms. Third, AWS can only recognise pre-determined target types based on pre-programmed criteria but are not able to make sense of other elements in their surrounding environment.

Fourth, AWS can only be as good as the data that it receives from the programmer or that they are able to collect. This is a problem because relevant data on combat situations and environments is very scarce. Additionally, regardless of the amount of data, training and tests conducted, every mission will consist of a unique scenario.[17] Paul Scharre explains that even with simulations that test millions of different scenarios, testing all possibilities in an autonomous system is essentially impossible. After all, these tests are constrained by the imagination of the programmer. The reality is that in combat situations, AWS will be exposed to human errors, unforeseen weather conditions and imaginative actions by enemies seeking to exploit its weaknesses. If these situations cannot be predicted by the programmer, they cannot be tested.[18]

In fifth place, finding targets in dense environments where there are abundant signals, background traffic, and potential decoys, can be a particular problem for AWS. For example, it has been found that learning machines can be fooled by adversarial images. These images, which are no more than abstract lines and shapes, have been confidently identified as concrete objects such as a starfish or a cheetah. Furthermore, this behaviour is beyond human comprehension, and thus programmers are mystified as to how to prevent it.[19]

Danks and London bring to the reader's attention that beyond the issue of image classification, the bigger problem with learning machines is that they are essentially black boxes, which exhibit "counterintuitive and unexpected forms of brittleness," that programmers cannot properly understand and/or predict.[20]

A report by the United Nations Institute for Disarmament Research (UNIDIR) on the "Safety, Unintentional Risk and Accidents in the Weaponization of Increasingly Autonomous Technologies," asserts that it is not possible—at this time—to fully understand the behaviour of machine learning systems such as AWS. It further argues that "this poses challenges for attaining the levels of formal verification that are demanded for many software code-based systems, especially for systems performing critical functions on which human lives may rely."[21] In other words, in a combat situation, AWS could fail to discriminate between civilians and combatants or may even decide to kill a civilian or attack a civilian object in contravention of IHL, without the programmer being able to understand why it did so or how to correct the problem.

It appears therefore that at their current stage of technological development, it would be unrealistic to expect AWS to be able to comply with the principle of distinction as well as a trained human combatant. As technology evolves, however, there may be a need to reassess this statement.

4.1.2 The Principles of Proportionality and Precautions in Attack

With regards to the principle of proportionality, Article 51(5)(b) of Additional Protocol I of the Geneva Convention of 1949 states that an attack will be deemed indiscriminate and thus in violation of IHL, if it "may be expected to cause incidental loss of civilian life, injury to civilians, damage to civilian objects, or a combination thereof, which would be excessive in relation to the concrete and direct military advantage anticipated."[22]

With respect to the principle of precautions in attack, Article 57(2)(a) requires those who plan an attack to take all necessary precautions not to launch an attack that "may be expected to cause incidental loss of civilian life, injury to civilians, damage to civilian objects, or a combination thereof, which would be excessive in relation to the concrete and direct military advantage anticipated."[23]

In other words, every time an attack is considered, two elements must be weighed in together: the impact that such an attack would have on the civilian population and the military advantage[24] derived from such an action. The question here is whether AWS can, in selecting a target and deciding on whether to conduct an attack, properly assess the incidental loss of life allowed with respect to a given military advantage.

As Wagner asserts, at the very least, AWS would have to be designed to anticipate all potential decisions in an abstract manner and "be able to determine how many civilian casualties would be acceptable under the circumstances at the time." The system may also have to decide what type of weapon should be used under existing circumstances and whether it would be lawful to use such a weapon in areas where civilians are present in light of the expected military advantage. Furthermore, it would have to reassess the permissibility of an attack every time the circumstances in the ground changed.[25]

Others point out that existing technology may allow AWS to determine how much harm a given attack will inflict on civilians. For example, commanders already use collateral damage simulators to assess the impact of attacks. However, determining military advantage may prove to be more difficult, given that by its very nature, it would require contextual analysis and allow for much greater operational discretion.[26]

Marco Sassoli agrees that assessing anticipated military advantage is essentially a subjective process. He further clarifies that AWS would need clear criteria in order to assess military advantage consistently, and such criteria does not exist. But, rather than closing the window on the possibility that AWS may one day comply with the principles of proportionality and precautions in attack, he sees this as an opportunity for states to agree on how exactly to calculate military advantage.[27]

Suchman adds that the level of situational awareness needed to assess proportionality and take precautions in attacks cannot be fully specified, much less predicted, and therefore cannot be clearly translated into code.[28] Human Rights Watch argues that AI is not capable of high-level reasoning like humans and will never be able to meet the challenge of applying the core principles of IHL on the modern battlefield.[29]

The International Committee of the Red Cross (ICRC) compares the capacities of AWS and humans, asserting that while machines can act quickly within established parameters, their situational awareness and capacity to make decisions is limited. Humans, on the other hand, while having a reduced attention span and a limited ability to respond rapidly, have a much better awareness of their environment and much better decision-making capabilities.[30] The conclusion being that "human understanding, rationality, and judgment exceed any conceivable system of fixed rules or any computational system."[31]

It would appear that in their current stage of technological development, AWS would not be in a position to comply with the principles of proportionality and precautions in attack as well as a trained human combatant. Having already assessed the ability of AWS to conform with the principle of distinction above, it is possible to conclude that they are not in a position to comply with relevant core principles of IHL. As stated before, as AI continues to develop, there may be a need to revisit this statement in the future.

In light of this conclusion, the international community must examine options for a new instrument that would ban, regulate or guide the development and use of AWS. In this regard, three multilateral governance mechanisms shall be considered: a) a ban treaty, b) regulations on the use of AWS and c) a framework convention. These mechanisms will be examined on the basis of the three following criteria:

1) *Clarity*: Understood as the ability to set clear and unambiguous parameters that states can follow in order to fully comply with the principles of distinction, proportionality and precautions in attack.

2) *Feasibility*: Understood as the likelihood that a substantive number of countries, including those with the capacity to develop and use AWS, will engage in negotiations and accept the outcome.

3) *Applicability*: Understood as the ability to set parameters that can and are likely to be implemented in practice.

4.2 A NEW LEGAL FRAMEWORK

4.2.1 A Ban Treaty

In a paper titled, "Precedent for Preemption: The Ban on Blinding Lasers as a Model for a Killer Robots Prohibition: Memorandum to Convention on Conventional Weapons Delegates," Human Rights Watch recommends taking a look at Protocol IV of the Convention on Certain Conventional Weapons (CCW) on the use of blinding lasers as a clear precedent to draft a ban on AWS.[32]

Human Rights Watch explains that the negotiations on blinding lasers were motivated by doubts on whether these weapons could conform to IHL. They also suggest that negotiating parties agreed that a ban on blinding lasers would be the best option precisely because it would cast aside all doubts and offer clarity on their illegality. With a ban, there would be no need for case-by-case assessments and no need to create standardised rules of operation.[33]

4.2.1.1 Clarity

A ban treaty on AWS drafted along the lines of Protocol IV of the CCW would be in sync with Paul Scharre's assertion that those treaties that completely ban a weapon are more successful than those that try to establish complicated rules to control its use.[34] Such a governance mechanism would cast aside all doubts about the legality of this category of weapons and its conformity with IHL. Commentators, however, have questioned the feasibility of adopting such a protocol given the military utility of AWS. Foy, for example, argues that a ban would prevent any violations of IHL but sees such an instrument as unrealistic.[35]

4.2.1.2 Feasibility

Anderson and Waxman believe that a ban would be unlikely. They argue that although calls to ban autonomous weapons may find support among a group of states and non-governmental actors, it will not be acceptable for those that have the capacity to develop and use them in the future.[36] In this respect, Maurizio Tinnirello has shown how major powers are already scrambling to develop sophisticated AI systems.[37]

This argument finds some echo in the discussions that have taken place in the context of the "Group of Governmental Experts on Emerging

Technologies in the Area of Lethal Autonomous Weapon Systems" (GGE LAWS), open to all State and non-State parties to the Convention on Certain Conventional Weapons.[38]

28 of the 125 countries that are parties to the CCW have proposed a full ban on AWS.[39] However, none of them actually seems to have the capacity to develop them. On the other hand, countries like France and Germany that could potentially develop AWS have proposed softer instruments such as a political declaration or a set of transparency and confidence-building measures.[40] The United States has stated that the negotiation of any legal or political instrument is premature.[41] While the Russian Federation has said that universal criteria regulating certain functions of AWS would not be "practical," and has thus called for every State to develop its own standards.[42] Only China, among the major international actors favours stronger regulation.[43]

4.2.1.3 Applicability

Protocol IV of the CCW on blinding lasers is considered "a very successful pre-emptive ban, since no State has ever employed permanently blinding lasers in armed conflict."[44] However, some worry that if a treaty banning AWS were to be established, states may look for loopholes in the agreement. They insist that new weapon systems that provide an important advantage to one side are likely to be adopted by its adversaries, leading to the erosion of existing legal frameworks as was the case with airplanes and submarines.[45]

This argument has a precedent in the Convention on Cluster Munitions.[46] This instrument prohibits states from developing, producing, stockpiling, transferring and using cluster munitions. However, it does not prohibit more recent and technologically advanced types of cluster munitions that have the capability to detect and engage a single target object and contain electronic self-destruct and self-deactivation mechanisms. In this regard, by hurrying to legislate and failing to create flexible review mechanisms a ban may become obsolete or allow for states with more advanced technology to circumvent the agreement.[47] This could pose a great risk to the applicability of the agreement.

4.2.2 Regulatory Framework on the Use of AWS

John Lewis has proposed a new protocol on AWS mirroring Protocol II of the CCW on "Prohibitions or Restrictions on the Use of Mines, Booby-Traps and Other Devices."[48] This protocol regulates but does not ban the use of these weapons. Since once activated they possess the ability to target and kill without human supervision, regulations have focused on deploying them in circumstances that avoid indiscriminate attacks on civilians and civilian objects.

Protocol II of the CCW uses targeting criteria to determine whether the deployment of mines, booby traps and other devices are permissible. Of particular relevance to the case of AWS is Article 3(8) of the Protocol,[49] which deems indiscriminate and prohibits the use of these weapons if:

1. They are not intended to be used against a military objective.

2. They cannot be employed specifically against a military objective.

3. They cannot be used in conformity with the principles of proportionality and precautions in attack.

4.2.2.1 Regulations on Targeting

A potential protocol regulating the use of AWS could consider a set of limited prohibitions along the lines of Protocol II of the CCW that could help guarantee that they are always used in compliance with the principles of distinction, proportionality, and precautions in attack. Those limitations could stipulate, for example, that AWS cannot be used in densely populated areas, that they can only be deployed to remote battlefields where the risk to civilians and civilian objects is minimal or non-existent, and that they can only target military objectives.[50]

On this point, Marco Sassoli has stated that:

> Pending revolutionary technological innovations, this problem may be solved by allowing a weapon system to target autonomously only those categories of objects that are, without question, targetable. It is suggested, therefore, that autonomous weapon systems incapable of distinguishing meaningfully may be used in an environment where no civilians could be endangered.[51]

4.2.2.2 Regulations on Residual Human Control

In addition to regulating potential targets, limits on the autonomy of weapons systems could also be considered. Paul Scharre suggests that humans should be involved in determining whether an attack complies with the principles of distinction, proportionality and precautions in an attack. He believes that they should be informed about the targets, the weapon of choice and the context in which the attack is to take place.[52]

In summary, a potential protocol regulating the use of AWS could establish limitations on targeting and residual human control.

4.2.2.3 Clarity

Limiting potential attacks by AWS to areas where the risk to civilians and civilian objects is minimal or non-existent and keeping a human in the loop could provide a clear mandate to states on how to comply with the principles of distinction, proportionality, and precautionary attacks. Some argue, however, that states may have a hard time agreeing on a set of clear and unambiguous rules on the use of AWS.[53]

4.2.2.4 Feasibility

Some seem to believe that "a more modest attempt to regulate these weapons" may translate into a higher initial buy-in by those countries with a capacity to develop and use them and may even result in a higher rate of compliance with the core principles of IHL.[54] However, others could argue that the discussions of the "Group of Governmental Experts on Emerging Technologies in the Area of Lethal Autonomous Weapon Systems" (GGE LAWS) reveal that countries such as France, Germany, the United States and the Russian Federation are not willing to engage in negotiations of a legally binding instrument of any kind.

4.2.2.5 Applicability

The applicability of the rules set in a protocol will depend on their clarity. Nothing prevents a set of well-defined rules on targeting from being applied to the letter. However, as is the case with a possible ban treaty on AWS, states seeking military gain may look for loopholes in the agreement. And once a new weapon system has been used to the advantage of one side, others are likely to use it as well, eroding the existing legal framework.[55]

Rules on residual human control are likely to encounter some of the same challenges as those on targeting. In addition, though, they may face important operational challenges. Some have expressed doubts on whether it is reasonable to expect a human operator to be able to oversee the operation of several AWS units. Some claim that a human may not have enough time or information to respond to the decisions of the machine.[56] Along the same lines, a report by UNIDIR argues that increasing machine autonomy leads to a greater "cognitive load for humans," which in turn diminishes their situational awareness and their ability to "understand what the system is doing so as to supervise and intervene in time-critical situations."[57]

On a similar note, Marco Sassoli notes that given the speed with which machines process information, humans will be unable to understand and if needed stop or redirect their operation. He further argues that humans will tend to trust the machine and may hesitate to counter its actions. As an example, he cites the case of Iran Air Flight 655, which was shot down by mistake on 3 July 1988 by a surface to air missile launched from the USS Vincennes. This surface to air missile was outfitted with the Aegis combat system and was operating on supervised-autonomous mode. The impact could have been prevented, but the operator made the decision to trust the system[58]. This goes to show that guaranteeing residual human control in practice may turn out to be harder than expected.

4.2.3 A Framework Convention

Another alternative would be to create a framework convention that would set standards and procedures for the employment of AWS. The original agreement would not be substantive; it would simply set in place a number of procedural measures such as creating a small secretariat, convening an annual meeting with participating states and stakeholders, and provisions to negotiate a deal. It could also involve, as is the case with the United Nations Framework Convention on Climate Change, the creation of a technical or scientific committee.

4.2.3.1 Clarity

Since the initial agreement would not be substantive and states would only be agreeing on a timeframe for negotiations, it is not possible to predict whether the deal that emerges from a framework convention, if one does in fact emerge, would create a mandate that is clear and straight forward.

4.2.3.2 Feasibility

According to James Foy, a framework convention would allow states to wait and see how AWS are developed and used before committing to a binding agreement. On this last point, Foy insists that given that AWS are undergoing fast technological development, a framework that allows for consistent and frequent re-examination would be the most appropriate avenue to address the challenge presented by these weapon systems.[59]

An initial "wait and see" approach could potentially, as Foy suggests, guarantee a greater buy-in by countries who are not ready to commit themselves to a binding agreement, including those with the capability to develop AWS. It would also allow for national and regional efforts to draft codes of conduct or Law of Armed Conflict manuals to follow their course, while preserving an international multilateral forum where they can be brought together and organised.[60] National and regional codes of conduct and relevant manuals could also help to inform the negotiating process and temporarily fill the gaps in treaty law.

Despite its apparent benefits, a framework convention—based on the notion of "wait and see"—comes with an important risk: once vested interests have developed the technology at great expense, it may become politically unviable to regulate it.[61] Marchant et al., citing David Collingridge, speak of the quintessential challenge of governing new technologies:

> Prior to the development and deployment of the technology, not enough is known about its potential risks to warrant or guide any restrictions or limitations, whereas once the technology has been developed and deployed, it is often too late to undertake meaningful regulations because the commercial momentum behind the technology is now too strong and entrenched.[62]

Anderson and Waxman add their voices to this concern, arguing that now is the time to consider appropriate governance mechanisms for AWS before their development and use become entrenched and harder to change.[63]

4.2.3.3 Applicability

It is possible to presume that a negotiating process that brings in a substantial number of states, including those with the capacity to develop and use AWS, as well as relevant industry and non-governmental actors, over a long period of time, and with the advice of a technical and scientific committee, may be able to produce an outcome that can be effectively implemented.

CONCLUSION

Based on the previous analysis of the clarity, feasibility and applicability of a ban treaty, regulations on targeting and residual human control and a framework convention, the following preliminary conclusions are offered:

- First, of all the governance mechanisms examined, a ban treaty would guarantee the greatest clarity in adhering to the core principles of IHL mentioned above. At the same time, it would face the greatest challenge in bringing in those states with the ability to develop and use AWS, and therefore ranks low in feasibility.

- Second, of all the mechanisms examined, regulations on residual human control may be the hardest to implement for the operational reasons explained above. This poses not only a challenge to its applicability but also to its ability to effectively contribute to AWS' compliance with the core principles of IHL. Regulations on targeting, on the other hand, may prove to be much more easily implemented, but only after states have agreed on its scope and key definitions.

- Third, of all the mechanisms examined, a framework convention is likely to guarantee greater participation by countries with the ability to develop and use AWS. However, by proposing a longer framework for negotiations, arguably enough for countries to see how AWS are developed and used, it runs the risk of allowing vested interests to set in and prevent an agreement at all. Having said that, an outcome that is inclusive and emerges from a broad, informed, and long consultation process that takes into account the evolving technology in AWS, may rank very high in applicability.

In conclusion, in order to offer clarity, feasibility and applicability, a governance mechanism would need to provide a clear mandate on how to comply with IHL, guarantee that those countries with the capacity to develop and use AWS are engaged and accept a potential negotiated outcome, and that agreements reached can and are likely to be implemented in practice. All the while, taking into account that AWS will continue to evolve technologically at a very fast pace. None of the instruments examined so far in this chapter can offer this package. However, a combination of them could be the solution.

First, set up a framework convention that draws in those countries with the ability to develop and use AWS, as well as relevant experts, interest groups and the broader international community. Second, in the context of the framework convention negotiate and adopt an initial moratorium on the use of AWS in civilian-populated areas. Third, create a technical/scientific committee in order to monitor the use of AWS and assess technological improvements. Fourth, continue to meet regularly to examine the reports of the technical/scientific committee and assess whether the moratorium should be maintained, modified, or lifted. This mechanism could perhaps help steer the process forward and reach the desired outcome, one that meets the standards of clarity, feasibility and applicability.

NOTES

1. Maziar Homayounnejad, "Lethal autonomous weapon systems under the law of armed conflict," PhD dissertation, King's College London, 2019, 48.
2. Paul Scharre, *Army of none: Autonomous weapons and the future of war*, London: WW Norton & Company, 2018, Kindle edition, Chapter 8.
3. Homayounnejad, "Lethal autonomous weapon systems under the law of armed conflict," 46.
4. Scharre, *Army of none*, Chapter 6.
5. International Committee of the Red Cross, "Ethics and autonomous weapon systems: An ethical basis for human control?," Paper presented at the Meeting of the Group of Governmental Experts on Emerging Technologies in the Area of Lethal Autonomous Weapon Systems, Convention on Certain Conventional Weapons, Geneva, 29 March 2018.
6. Gregory P. Noone and Diana C. Noone, "The debate over autonomous weapons systems," *Case Western Reserve Journal of International Law* 47 (2015): 28.
7. From now on, all references to AWS will apply only to the category of fully autonomous weapons.
8. Scharre, *Army of none*, Chapter 3.
9. Homayounnejad, "Lethal autonomous weapon systems under the law of armed conflict," 47.
10. Scharre, *Army of none*, Chapter 10.
11. Homayounnejad, "Lethal autonomous weapon systems under the law of armed conflict," 47.
12. According to the ICRC, International Humanitarian Law is a set of rules which seek to limit the effects of armed conflict for humanitarian reasons. International Committee of the Red Cross, "Advisory service on international humanitarian law," 2019, https://www.icrc.org/en/doc/assets/files/other/what_is_ihl.pdf [last accessed 18 July 2019].
13. Article 36, "Additional protocol I of the Geneva conventions of 1949," https://ihl-databases.icrc.org/ihl/INTRO/470 [last accessed 1 November 2019].
14. Article 48, "Additional protocol I of the Geneva conventions of 1949," https://ihl-databases.icrc.org/ihl/INTRO/470 [last accessed 1 November 2019].
15. Article 51(b), "Additional protocol I of the Geneva conventions of 1949," https://ihldatabases.icrc.org/ihl/INTRO/470 [last accessed 1 November 2019].
16. Scharre, *Army of none*, Chapter 10.

17. Homayounnejad, "Lethal autonomous weapon systems under the law of armed conflict," 76–77.
18. Scharre, *Army of none*, Chapter 9.
19. Ibid., Chapter 11.
20. David Danks and Alex John London, "Regulating autonomous systems: Beyond standards," *IEEE Intelligent Systems* 32, no. 1 (2017): 91.
21. UNIDIR, "Safety, unintentional risk and accidents in the weaponization of increasingly autonomous technologies," 2016, https://www.unidir.org/files/publications/pdfs/safety-unintentional-risk-and-accidents-en-668.pdf [last accessed 1 November 2019].
22. Article 51(5)(b), "Additional protocol I of the Geneva conventions of 1949," https://ihl-databases.icrc.org/ihl/INTRO/470 [last accessed 1 November 2019].
23. Article 57(2)(a), "Additional protocol I of the Geneva conventions of 1949," https://ihl-databases.icrc.org/ihl/INTRO/470 [last accessed 1 November 2019].
24. The advantage anticipated from an attack must be military in nature. See "How the LAW protects in war," ICRC, https://casebook.icrc.org/glossary/military-advantage [last accessed 1 November 2019].
25. Markus Wagner, "Taking humans out of the loop: Implications for international humanitarian law," *Journal of Law Information and Science* 21 (2011): 162.
26. James Foy, "Autonomous weapons systems: Taking the human out of international humanitarian law," *Dalhousie Journal of Legal Studies* 23 (2014): 56.
27. Marco Sassoli, "Autonomous weapons and international humanitarian law: Advantages, open technical questions and legal issues to be clarified," *International Law Studies/Naval War College* 90 (2014): 331.
28. Lucy Alice Suchman, "Situational awareness and adherence to the principle of distinction as a necessary condition for lawful autonomy," 273–283, in *Lethal Autonomous Weapons Systems*. German Federal Foreign Office, Berlin, 2017.
29. Human Rights Watch, "Losing humanity, the case against killer robots," 2012, https://www.hrw.org/report/2012/11/19/losing-humanity/case-against-killer-robots) [last accessed 1 May 2019].
30. International Committee of the Red Cross, "Ethics and autonomous weapon systems: An ethical basis for human control?"
31. Peter Asaro, "On banning autonomous weapon systems: Human rights, automation, and the dehumanization of lethal decision-making," *International Review of the Red Cross* 94, no. 886 (2012): 687–709.
32. Human Rights Watch, "Precedent for preemption: The ban on blinding lasers as a model for a killer robots prohibition: Memorandum to convention on conventional weapons delegates," 2015, https://www.hrw.org/news/2015/11/08/precedent-preemption-ban-blinding-lasers-model-killer-robots-prohibition [last accessed 8 November 2015].
33. Ibid.
34. Scharre, *Army of none*, Chapter 21.

35. Foy, "Autonomous weapons systems," 66.
36. Kenneth Anderson and Matthew Waxman, "Law and ethics for autonomous weapon systems: Why a ban won't work and how the laws of war can," *American University Washington College of Law Research Paper No.* 2013-11 (2013): 21.
37. Maurizio Tinnirello, "Offensive realism and the insecure structure of the international system: Artificial intelligence and global hegemony," in *Artificial Intelligence Safety and Security*, 339–356, Chapman and Hall/CRC, 2018.
38. The GGE LAWS has so far met four times, on November 2017, April and August 2018, and March 2019.
39. Algeria, Argentina, Austria, Bolivia, Brazil, Chile, China, Colombia, Costa Rica, Cuba, Djibouti Ecuador, Egypt, El Salvador, Ghana, Guatemala, Holy See, Iraq, Mexico, Morocco, Nicaragua Pakistan, Panama, Peru, State of Palestine, Uganda, Venezuela and Zimbabwe. See Campaign to Stop Killer Robots, "Country views on killer robots," 2018, https://www.stopkillerro-bots.org/wpcontent/uploads/2018/11/KRC_CountryViews22Nov2018.pdf [last accessed 28 November 2018].
40. Germany, "Security dimension and options," Paper presented at the Meeting of the Group of Governmental Experts on Emerging Technologies in the Area of Lethal Autonomous Weapon Systems, Convention on Certain Conventional Weapons, Geneva, 13 April 2018.
41. Unites States statement delivered by Ian R. McKay, Paper presented at the Meeting of the Group of Governmental Experts on Emerging Technologies in the Area of Lethal Autonomous Weapon, Convention on Certain Conventional Weapons, Geneva, 13 April 2018.
42. Russian Federation, "Russia's approaches to the elaboration of a working definition and basic functions of lethal autonomous weapons systems in the context and purposes and objectives of the convention," Paper presented at the Meeting of the Group of Governmental Experts on Emerging Technologies in the Area of Lethal Autonomous Weapon Systems, Convention on Certain Conventional Weapons, Geneva, 4 April 2018.
43. Campaign to Stop Killer Robots, "Country views on killer robots."
44. Rebecca Crootof, "Why the prohibition on permanently blinding lasers is poor precedent for a ban on autonomous weapon systems," *Lawfare*, https://www.lawfareblog.com/why-prohibition-permanently-blinding-lasers-poor-precedent-ban-autonomous-weapon-systems [last accessed 24 November 2015].
45. Anderson and Waxman, "Law and ethics for autonomous weapon systems," 21.
46. The Convention on Cluster Munitions, https://www.clusterconvention.org/the-convention/convention-text/ [last accessed 1 November 2019].
47. Anderson and Waxman, "Law and ethics for autonomous weapon systems," 21.
48. John Lewis, "The case for regulating fully autonomous weapons," *Yale Law Journal* 124, no. 4 (January–February 2015).

49. Article 3(8) of protocol II of the CCW, https://treaties.un.org/doc/Treaties/1996/05/19960503%2001-38%20AM/Ch_XXVI_02_bp.pdf [last accessed 1 November 2019].
50. John Lewis, "The case for regulating fully autonomous weapons," *Yale Law Journal* 124, no. 4 (January–February 2015): 1324.
51. Marco Sassoli, "Autonomous weapons and international humanitarian law: Advantages, open technical questions and legal issues to be clarified," *International Law Studies/Naval War College* 90 (2014): 327.
52. Paul Scharre has called for his proposal to be considered in the format of a general principle with wide application to other emerging technologies. This paper, however, restricts the conversation to a potential legal protocol on the use of AWS. See Scharre, *Army of none*, Chapter 6.
53. Anderson and Waxman, "Law and ethics for autonomous weapon systems," 21.
54. Lewis, "The case for regulating fully autonomous weapons," 1318.
55. Anderson and Waxman, "Law and ethics for autonomous weapon systems," 21.
56. Danks and London, "Regulating autonomous systems," 90.
57. UNIDIR, "Safety, unintentional risk and accidents in the weaponization of increasingly autonomous technologies."
58. Sassoli, "Autonomous weapons and international humanitarian law," 337.
59. Foy, "Autonomous weapons systems," 69.
60. Codes of conduct offer the benefit of expedience when compared to binding agreements. However, as the number of codes of conduct developed by states and other relevant stakeholders proliferate without order or rank, agreement on common standards becomes harder. See Gary Marchant et al., "International governance of autonomous military robots," *The Columbia Science and Law Review* 12 (2011): 310. Law of Armed Conflict manuals (LOAMs) also offer important benefits, including very detailed and comprehensive guidelines sometimes ranging in the hundreds of pages. See Homayounnejad, "Lethal autonomous weapon systems under the law of armed conflict," 64. However, like codes of conducts, LOAMs can also suffer from a lack of order and rank.
61. Sassoli, "Autonomous weapons and international humanitarian law," 322.
62. See David Collingridge, *The social control of technology* St Martin, New York, 1980, in Marchant et al., "International governance of autonomous military robots," *The Columbia Science and Law Review* 12 (2011): 314.
63. Anderson and Waxman, "Law and ethics for autonomous weapon systems," 9.

CHAPTER 5

Lessons for Artificial Intelligence from Other Global Risks

Seth D. Baum, Robert de Neufville,
Anthony M. Barrett, and Gary Ackerman

CONTENTS

5.1 INTRODUCTION

Those who do not learn from history are doomed to repeat it—or so the saying goes. The progression of artificial intelligence (AI) technology is pushing human society in new directions, but not all of the dynamics are entirely new. Many features of the AI issue have arisen in other contexts. That holds both for AI as it exists today and as it may exist in the future. Likewise, efforts to manage the progression of AI and improve outcomes

DOI: 10.1201/9780429446726-5

for society have much to learn from past experience with other issues that have similar features. A little history can go a long way.

The process of learning from history is broadly similar to the concept of transfer learning in the computer science of AI. Transfer learning refers to the process of saving knowledge gained from solving one problem and then applying it to solving another, different problem.[1] Transfer learning is a significant challenge in AI and a major focus of ongoing computer science research. Humans are in many respects substantially more capable at transfer learning than current AI systems—AI transfer learning is currently grappling with tasks such as recognising different types of features within an image.[2] Nonetheless, even among humans, transfer learning can take dedicated effort, especially for complex tasks such as addressing major global issues.[3]

The focus of this chapter is to present some insights from the study of global risks, especially (but not exclusively) global catastrophic risks. These insights are often of particular relevance for AI catastrophe scenarios, especially (but again not exclusively) long-term runaway AI scenarios in which humanity is unable to control AI, and catastrophe ensues. These AI catastrophe scenarios have several similarities to other global risks, including but not limited to their potential extreme catastrophic severity. In many cases, these other risks have been addressed and studied much more extensively than AI has. The chapter aims to accelerate the study of AI risk by leveraging the substantial body of experience and scholarship on other global risks.

The field of AI is of course not new. It has a rich history over many decades, as is documented in several excellent histories.[4] The idea of a runaway AI catastrophe is also not new—it can be traced to early work in the 1960s[5] and even the 1860s.[6] What is relatively (but again not completely) new is the treatment of AI as a social, risk, and policy issue. Much of this is driven by the considerable recent successes of AI technology and its many applications across society. Some of it is also driven by a specific interest in the more dramatic long-term AI scenarios.[7] Now is a good time for the AI issue to learn from other issues.

There is a vast universe of insight available from other global risks, and one chapter can only survey a small portion of it. The portion presented here is a mix of what the present authors are most familiar with and what we believe is most important for improving AI outcomes. That includes some emphasis on cases from US history, though much of it is of international relevance. Many prior studies have also applied insights from other global risks to specific aspects of the challenge of managing AI.[8] In one similar study, Allen and Chan[9] survey four emerging technologies to derive insights for AI as a US national security issue. The present chapter also surveys multiple sources of lessons, covering four global risks of relevance for improving overall AI outcomes, especially with respect to catastrophic risks.

It should be noted that transferring lessons from one global risk to another is not the only reason to study multiple risks. Another reason is to address important questions that span multiple risks, such as how to prioritise scarce resources across multiple risks and how to address tradeoffs in potential actions that could increase one risk but decrease another. Cross-risk tradeoffs may be of particular relevance to AI due to their potential to affect many sectors of society, including sectors implicated in other global risks. While AI poses certain risks, if it is developed safely and responsibly, it could bring a range of benefits, including reductions in other global risks.[10] Cross-risk allocation and tradeoff decisions provide a compelling reason to study multiple global risks; the potential to transfer lessons across risks provides another. We therefore believe that cross-risk research should be emphasised in programmes to understand and address AI and other global risks.

After an overview of key terms, the chapter proceeds with discussions of four global risks, each embodying a specific theme of relevance to AI. First, biotechnology is a field of emerging technology with numerous important social benefits and also major risks. Second, nuclear weapons are technologies of paramount strategic importance across the international community. Third, global warming is a major risk that derives from profit-seeking activity by some of the largest corporations in the world and widespread consumer use. Fourth, asteroid collision is an extreme global risk that has garnered substantial international scientific and policy attention despite its very low probability. The chapter transfers insights from the histories of these four cases to the study of how to effectively manage AI.

5.2 DEFINITIONS

Before proceeding, it is worth briefly pausing to define some key concepts used in this chapter, especially for the benefit of an interdisciplinary audience. The concepts of AI, risk, and global catastrophic risk all have multifaceted and contested definitions. To a large extent, the substance of this chapter is not sensitive to the particular definition used, but it is nonetheless worth elaborating on the definitions.

A common definition of AI is any artificial agent that can "achieve goals in a wide range of environments."[11] However, this emphasis on goal achievement is contested. For example, Goertzel[12] explores definitions of intelligence rooted in self-organisation and involving more than just the achievement of goals. Also contentious is exactly how wide the range of environments must be for an artificial system to qualify as AI. Indeed, a common observation is that once computers can achieve a task (e.g. defeating humans at chess), then this task is no longer seen as requiring AI, which is a matter of moving the goalposts.[13] An inclusive definition of AI could potentially include, for example, those "intelligent" doors at the supermarket that open when people walk up to them. An exclusive definition could potentially exclude any system that cannot perform the same set of cognitive tasks as the human mind in the same way the human mind would perform them.

For the present chapter, the exact scope of AI is less important than the potential societal consequences of some AI systems (assuming, of course, that these systems qualify as AI). The introduction refers to dramatic long-term AI scenarios, including catastrophic runaway AI. That is shorthand for a hypothesised form of future AI whose intelligence reaches the point where it can outsmart humans and wrest control from humanity. Such AI may undergo a process called recursive self-improvement, in which the AI makes a smarter AI, which makes a smarter AI, *ad infinitum*, potentially resulting in an "intelligence explosion" or "Singularity."[14] The forms of AI involved in this process are often known as strong AI, artificial general intelligence (AGI), or superintelligence. In contrast, current AI is "weak" and narrow, with capabilities only within a relatively narrow portion of intellectual tasks, in contrast with human minds, which can succeed across a relatively wide range of tasks.

It should be stressed that the primary arguments of this chapter do not depend on the exact form of the AI but only on its potential to pose a significant global risk. While a runaway AI presumably could pose a global risk, other forms of AI may as well. Likewise, it should also be noted that a number of analysts have expressed scepticism about runaway AI scenarios.[15] Even if these scenarios can be dismissed, then the lessons in this chapter may be applicable to other AI scenarios.

This raises the question of what qualifies as a risk. To start from the basics, a risk is a "possibility of loss or injury."[16] Risk is commonly quantified as the probability of some loss multiplied by the severity of the loss if it occurs. Attention to global risks such as runaway AI are commonly predicated on the view that the risk of extreme loss can be important even if its probability is low. The exact probability of runaway AI is a controversial matter and not essential for this chapter.

This chapter makes some use of the concept of global catastrophic risk. Global catastrophe has been defined in a variety of ways, including as the death of at least 25% of the human population[17] or as a significant undesirable change in the state of the global human system.[18] Some treatments emphasise the risk of human extinction on the grounds that extinction would entail the loss of all future generations,[19] whereas others argue that sub-extinction catastrophes involving significant permanent harm can be of comparable importance.[20]

The present chapter takes a wider view of global risk. Its focus is on the lessons that can be learned from global risks, not the severity of the global events that the risks entail. The severity is important for the lessons in some cases but not all of them. The chapter includes cases in which there are fruitful lessons even if the lesson is coming from a global risk whose severity does not meet the standards for global catastrophe outlined above. The point here is the insightfulness of the lesson, not the size of the risk.

5.3 BIOTECHNOLOGY

Biotechnology has been defined as "the application of science and technology to living organisms as well as parts, products, and models thereof to alter living or non-living materials for the production of knowledge, goods, and services."[21] Biotechnology is in several respects, a close analogue to AI. Both are classes of emerging technology with many applications that can either decrease or increase global risks. Biotechnology can help counter pandemics, such as by enabling the rapid synthesis of vaccines[22] or using "gene drives" to propagate disease resistance among the population of insect vectors like mosquitoes.[23] Alternatively, biotechnology can exacerbate or even cause pandemics, such as by laboratory accidents that inadvertently release deadly pathogens[24] and by making it easier for dangerous pathogens to be weaponised.[25]

Infectious diseases and AI are also similar in that a small source can readily self-replicate and spread worldwide. Biological pathogens self-replicate within their host organisms (e.g. within human bodies) and can jump from host to host. Similarly, some computer software can self-replicate via "copying" and "pasting" within a computer and via transmission from computer to computer—hence the term "computer virus." Computer viruses may not all involve AI; whether they do may depend on one's definition of AI. Computer security firm Malwarebytes contends that "there are currently no examples of AI-enabled malware in the wild," but the possibility is "realistic" with existing AI techniques or fairly straightforward extensions of them.[26] Such self-replication and propagation would presumably be even more feasible for more advanced forms of AI. (An important exception would be for forms of AI that require specialised hardware to run on.)

These two similarities—both are emerging technologies with diverse applications and potential for propagation via self-replication—make biotechnology a valuable case study for AI. Biotechnology is of further value because it has a relatively extensive history as a societal issue.

One early episode was the 1975 Asilomar Conference on Recombinant DNA Molecules, aimed at assessing and managing risks from recombinant DNA research. The applicability of the 1975 Asilomar Conference to AI governance is explored in detail by Grace.[27] Grace finds that while recombinant DNA turned out to not be as dangerous as some scientists initially feared, the conference nonetheless had some success in getting this portion of the scientific community to take precautions in their research. Specifically, the US National Institutes of Health issued safety guidelines that is required for the researchers it funded, including a moratorium on recombinant DNA. Industry labs also voluntarily opted to comply with the NIH guidelines.

As Grace[28] documents, a major contributor to the success of the 1975 Asilomar Conference was substantial buy-in from the relevant scientific community. A majority of the relevant scientists, including many leaders in the field, indicated concern about the risk. The moratorium was widely—perhaps universally—followed, despite the lack of an enforcement mechanism, especially in industry. It may have helped that in the 1970s, academia already had a culture of political activism regarding issues such as environmental degradation and the Vietnam War. The success was thus due less to institutional requirements and more to communities of people. As Grace[29] puts it, "informal social mechanisms played an overwhelming part in producing a pause in research and triggering further action."

Likewise, social buy-in may be essential for successfully addressing issues in AI. Baum[30] distinguishes between extrinsic measures for addressing AI, which are imposed on AI communities from the outside, and intrinsic measures, which originate from within. AI governance conversations sometimes emphasise extrinsic measures, such as in calls to ban dangerous AI technologies,[31] restrict the development of certain forms of AI to a single lab with United Nations oversight,[32] or install research review boards to assess which AI research can proceed.[33] However, measures such as these may fail if they do not have substantial buy-in from the AI community, especially if the relevant forms of AI are widely pursued. Therefore, it is important to seek buy-in from AI communities, so that any rules or guidelines would be self-enforcing. The 1975 Asilomar Conference is an important case in point.

The prospect of widespread AI community buy-in is of particular relevance to the idea of relinquishing dangerous AI technology proposed by Joy.[34] This proposal has been criticised for requiring universal buy-in among computer scientists, especially in the face of commercial or national security pressures.[35] However, if sufficient buy-in could be achieved, relinquishment might succeed even without substantial institutional pressure; the relinquishment of recombinant DNA is a case in point. Furthermore, several studies have expressed concern that even a global AI institution with enforcement powers could fail to prevent dangerous secret AI projects.[36] Thus, achieving informal community buy-in may be more important than establishing formal governance institutions, though there may nonetheless be a constructive role for both. (The challenge of monitoring AI projects is discussed further in the section on nuclear weapons.)

A more recent and controversial case is the debate over the gain of function (GOF) research on potential pandemic pathogens (PPP). This research manipulates existing pathogens to make them more pathogenic in order to learn more about the pathogen and advance the medical response to outbreaks. The research is controversial due to concerns that the enhanced pathogen could accidentally or intentionally be released from the lab, enter the human population and spread. The enhancements could result in a more severe pandemic than what would occur from the naturally occurring pathogens. An active debate has emerged on the merits of GOF-PPP experiments. Some argue that the benefits exceed the risks, including people involved in the experiments.[37] Others argue the opposite, including people who commonly emphasise security perspectives on biotechnology.[38]

In 2012, GOF-PPP researchers agreed to a voluntary pause on these experiments.[39] Then, in 2014, the US government announced a moratorium on GOF-PPP experiments in order to assess whether the potential public health benefits of the experiments were worth the risks. The US National Science Advisory Board for Biosecurity commissioned a risk-benefit analysis to inform the debate. The ensuing report[40] spans 1,006 pages but does not reach a definitive conclusion on whether the benefits exceed the risks. One proposed explanation for the report's inconclusiveness is that "the areas that separate pro- and anti-GOF advocates fall into areas of judgement and belief, and these differences cannot be adjudicated by risk-benefit analysis."[41] Despite the lingering disagreements and ambiguities, the US lifted the moratorium in 2017.[42]

The controversy surrounding the GOF-PPP case makes it arguably a more relevant case study for AI than the case of recombinant DNA. As with GOF-PPP experiments, experts are divided on the risks and benefits of AI, especially for the prospect and risk of long-term runaway AI. Achieving consensus on an AI moratorium may thus be more difficult, and there may be pressure to end the moratorium even before the risks and potential benefits are conclusively evaluated, and consensus is reached on how best to proceed. Therefore, the GOF-PPP case may be fertile ground for further study on advancing AI debates and reaching clear conclusions and consensus on how to manage potentially dangerous AI research.

An additional line of research on biotechnology worth examining is an assessment of biotechnology stakeholder reactions to efforts to promote responsible research and innovation, or RRI.[43] RRI aims to promote an inclusive and reflective technology research and development process, with one aim being for "societal alignment."[44] However, Kuzma and Roberts[45] find significant reluctance to adopt RRI among biotechnologists. Notably, academic biotechnologists expressed more reluctance than their industry counterparts, due to concerns about intellectual freedom and scepticism about non-expert outsiders imposing unwise restrictions. This finding resembles that of a recent survey of AGI research and development projects, in which academic projects were more likely to articulate intellectual values and industry projects were more likely to articulate values based on benefiting humanity.[46]

While the RRI biotechnology study of Kuzma and Roberts[47] is ongoing, they meanwhile call for a "more practical RRI" in which RRI researchers and advocates are actively engaged with technology projects instead of advocating RRI from the side-lines in research journals and other venues. This would appear to be wise advice for all fields of technology, including AI, and for all paradigms for improving technology development processes and outcomes, including but not limited to RRI.

Grotto[48] reviews the history of the governance of genetically modified organisms (GMOs) in agriculture and derives implications for the potential regulation of AI. Grotto contrasts the treatment of GMOs in Europe, where strict regulations drastically curtailed the use of GMOs, to the US, where a business-friendly regulatory regime led to widespread cultivation of GMOs. Grotto notes that these divergent regulatory environments were not inevitable but instead were linked to historical coincidences such as European concern about food safety derived from the outbreak of mad cow disease in the United Kingdom. Additionally, the initial regulatory decisions have had lasting effects over several decades in both jurisdictions. The same could potentially apply to regulations of AI.

Finally, it is worth noting the difficulties inherent in controlling even the most pernicious forms of biotechnology. The use of biological weapons was outlawed by the Geneva Protocol of 1925, and over 180 states have signed the 1972 Biological and Toxin Weapons Convention that prohibits the acquisition and stockpiling of these weapons. Yet, the fundamentally dual-use nature of biotechnology, where the same technique or equipment could be used for beneficial or harmful ends, enabled several states—most notably the Soviet Union in the 1970s and 1980s—to flout the international bioweapon ban and embark on massive bioweapons programmes. Despite multiple attempts over several decades, the international community has been unable to craft a verification regime for the convention that is both practically enforceable and politically acceptable. This might serve as a negative lesson in the difficulties of exercising international control over technologies—like some forms of AI—that have inherently dual-use applications. For example, image recognition techniques that can enhance public web search engines can also enhance target recognition in weapon systems. This is not the case with respect to nuclear weapons (discussed in the next section), where the underlying technologies are far less dual-use in nature.

5.4 NUCLEAR WEAPONS

Biotechnology is similar to AI as risky, potentially self-propagating, dual-use technologies. However, the vast majority of biotechnology applications (with the few exceptions mentioned above) are in the civilian sector. In contrast, the destructive power of nuclear weapons is emblematic of a military technology with unequivocal and paramount strategic importance on the international stage. Potentially, AI could have similar importance, especially for more advanced forms of AI. Therefore, the extensive history and study of nuclear weapons may be a fruitful source of insights for AI. (Nuclear technology also has civilian applications, though these are not explored given that the attendant dual-use issues are substantially similar to those of biotechnology, which has already been considered.)

A potential distinction between AI and nuclear weapons is that whereas concerns about nuclear weapons often focus on intentional harm to geopolitical adversaries, concerns about AI (especially runaway AI) often focus on accidental harm to everyone.[49] However, this distinction is at most a matter of degree. It is true that countries generally do not aim to attack themselves with their own nuclear weapons, but AI developers also generally do not aim to harm themselves with their own AI systems. Furthermore, nuclear weapons must also be handled with great care to avoid accidental detonation on home soil.[50] Therefore, while nuclear weapons are not a perfect analogue for AI, the similarities may be sufficient to apply lessons from the former to the latter.

One AI topic for which nuclear weapons lessons may be especially salient is the prospect of a race to be the first to build advanced AI. It is sometimes proposed that a sufficiently advanced AI, such as a strong AI or AGI, could confer extreme "winner takes all" advantages to whoever builds it first.[51] This could occur in particular if the AI undergoes a rapid intelligence explosion but remains under the control of its builders, who then may obtain a high degree of power over all global affairs. If control is lost, catastrophe could ensue. A recent survey found no significant evidence of a race to build AGI, and instead found significant cooperation between projects.[52] Meanwhile, there is some competition on other, more modest forms of AI, such as between the US and China[53] and between companies within sectors such as autonomous vehicles.[54] The prospect of an advanced AI race is plausible due to the strategic implications of the technology, and it is also a concern because it could preclude sufficient caution with respect to the safety of the technology.[55]

Several studies propose that the Cold War nuclear arms race may be a good analogue for an initial race to build AI,[56] though a better analogue would be the initial race to build nuclear weapons. An essential feature of the initial development of nuclear weapons is the extreme geopolitical tensions of that era. It appears to be a historical coincidence that the relevant scientific breakthroughs in nuclear physics occurred during the run-up to and fighting of WWII, since there is no clear link between the initial development of nuclear physics and increasing tensions in Europe. This geopolitical context may, however, explain the very rapid progression from the 1939 discovery of nuclear fission[57] to the establishment of nuclear weapons development projects in each of Germany, Japan, the Soviet Union, the UK and the US (1939 to 1942; exact project start dates are ambiguous), and finally to the first detonations of nuclear weapons

(1945). Indeed, reading this history today, it is remarkable how quickly the events unfolded and how extensive were the contacts between scientists and high-level government officials.[58] The fast pace was motivated by a desire to build nuclear weapons first and therefore achieve a major—perhaps decisive—advantage in WWII and its aftermath.[59]

An implication of this is that an AI race could be avoided or at least managed more carefully if major geopolitical tensions can also be avoided. This point applies not just to advanced AI but also to near-term AI and other technologies of military significance. The matter is well-documented by Scharre[60] in interviews with military officials and experts and accompanying analysis. Scharre documents that militaries have thus far largely abstained from deploying autonomous weapons or have at most proceeded rather cautiously, due to a variety of concerns, including cost, safety and ethics. (Autonomous weapons can be defined as weapons capable of selecting and firing on targets without human input.[61]) However, Scharre finds that militaries are much more likely to use autonomous weapons if a major war breaks out and countries find themselves compelled to do whatever it takes to win. One expert compares the situation to the US abstention from unrestricted submarine warfare prior to the bombing of Pearl Harbor on 7 December 1941. In regards to whether the US would deploy autonomous weapons, the expert asks, "Is it 6 December or 8 December?" It follows that if a race for advanced AI is to be avoided, it may be important, perhaps even crucial, to avoid major wars between the countries that could build advanced AI.

Another important lesson from the nuclear weapons race for a potential AI race concerns secrecy. The nuclear weapons projects were highly secretive, and espionage was sometimes but not always successful. Notably, the US and its allies did not know how little progress the German nuclear weapons programme was making until August 1944.[62] Because beating the German programme was a primary goal of the US programme, had the US known earlier, it is possible that it would have ended its own programme or at least pursued its programme more carefully. Similarly, if future AI programmes learn of rival programmes' struggles and cessations, then they may also stop or proceed more carefully. This possibility runs counter to the proposed idea that information about rival AI projects increases risks.[63]

If an AI race is won, such that there is only one group in possession of advanced AI, then the situation may resemble the period spanning from 1945 to 1949 in which only the US possessed nuclear weapons—the so-called nuclear monopoly period.[64] It is sometimes proposed that advanced AI may involve a strong first-mover advantage, sometimes referred to as "winner takes all."[65] While the extent to which the nuclear-weapon monopoly involved the same dynamic is unclear and may have been more limited, there were nonetheless serious proposals for using the power of nuclear weapons to maintain a monopoly.

One proposal sought to keep the nuclear monopoly under US control. The US would have threatened nuclear attack against any country that attempted to build nuclear weapons, or, if need be, executed such an attack.[66] One view held that this would be preferable to permitting catastrophic nuclear proliferation.[67] It also would have given the US a strong and potentially dominant position in global politics. US President Truman ultimately declined to follow this proposal, which may suggest that the first party to build advanced AI may likewise decline to use it to maintain a monopoly and a dominant global position.[68] However, there is no guarantee that other leaders would have made the same choice as Truman.

Another proposal—the Baruch Plan—called for an International Atomic Development Authority that would consolidate nuclear expertise and oversee the global use of nuclear power for both peaceful and military purposes. Such an arrangement could have maintained much of the geopolitical status quo; in particular, it would theoretically not have required US dominance. The Soviet Union nevertheless rejected the Baruch Plan; apparently out of concern that the US and its allies would in practice dominate the new international atomic authority.[69] Potentially, had the US threatened nuclear war if the Soviet Union refused to terminate its nuclear weapons programme, it might have been more inclined to accept the Baruch Plan, though it is unclear how the Soviets would have reacted in this circumstance.

The Baruch Plan is perhaps the best historical precedent for several proposals for global AI governance backed by the power of AI.[70] The essence of these proposals is to first build an AI capable of monitoring rogue AI development projects, and then to use this AI as the basis for enforcing global compliance with safety and ethics standards. In some variants, the AI itself could conduct the enforcement. Such a scheme could leave humans in charge, and could perhaps buy humans the time needed to carefully reflect on how best to build a more powerful AI, including an AI that humans could not or would not control. However, just as the Baruch Plan struggled to gain international consensus, so too could a comparable plan for AI. Indeed, consensus on AI may be more elusive due to important and potentially divisive questions about which types of AI to build.[71] (A milder variant of this scheme is for an international AI research centre that consolidates resources for AI development, modelled after CERN.[72] However, the CERN model aims for scientific breakthrough, not safe development of technology in the public interest, and it may likewise be more applicable to the initial development of AI than the subsequent monopoly.)

The US nuclear monopoly ended in 1949 following the Soviet development of nuclear weapons. Since then, the world has persisted with multiple nuclear powers. Similarly, some AI scenarios involve multiple advanced AIs. Such scenarios have been considered especially in the context of AIs based on the digitisation or emulation of human brains,[73] though they could also occur for other forms of AI.

A central feature of the ongoing era of multiple nuclear powers is the doctrine of nuclear deterrence, in which the threat of nuclear attack dissuades rival countries from waging major wars. The absence of a global war since WWII arguably affirms the effectiveness of nuclear deterrence,[74] though this is controversial: other factors may explain international stability after WWII, including a desire to avoid any major war, nuclear or non-nuclear, and the general satisfaction of the Soviet Union and the United States with their positions in global affairs.[75] Similarly, deterrence could potentially facilitate the nonviolent and reasonably peaceable coexistence of rival AI powers. Scholarship on and experience with nuclear deterrence suggests that an AI deterrence regime may be most successful if (1) no side has the ability to destroy rivals or disable their AI systems without suffering devastating retaliation, an ability sometimes referred to in the nuclear weapons literature as "primacy"[76] and in the AI literature as "decisive strategic advantage,"[77] (2) rival parties have incentives to avoid crises, or to deescalate crises if they occur, a condition sometimes referred to in the nuclear weapons literature as "crisis stability,"[78] and (3) miscalculations on the intentions and activities of rivals can be avoided. These and other aspects of nuclear deterrence could prove valuable for managing a world of multiple rival advanced AI powers.

5.5 GLOBAL WARMING

Out of all the global risks, global warming has probably been the subject of the most extensive interdisciplinary scholarly inquiry—indeed, it is probably the most extensive by a large margin. There are robust literatures on the psychology of global warming,[79] the economics,[80] the epistemic and policy implications of catastrophic risk,[81] military dimensions,[82] and much more. The voluminous scope of global warming research makes it a rich source of insight for many other global risks, including AI.

Existing AI studies have just begun to scratch the surface of insight from global warming literature. One study draws on the psychology of global warming to inform the design of both formal regulations and informal community-based measures to improve AI outcomes.[83] Another draws on the politics and psychology of scepticism and misinformation about global warming to explore how similar dynamics could play out with AI.[84] These are important topics, but there is a lot more lurking in the extensive global warming literature.

The global warming literature may be of particular relevance for scenarios in which AI is developed in the private sector. National AI development projects are plausible (and more closely related to the pursuit of nuclear weapons), but AI is currently developed primarily in the private sector. Indeed, AI is an important technology for some of the largest corporations in the world. It is therefore worth studying cases in which corporate activity poses a global risk. The case of global warming and the fossil fuel industry serves this purpose well. What follows is a very brief history to illustrate some major dynamics.

For many years, the fossil fuel industry has sought to downplay the importance of global warming and dispute the underlying science.[85] However, this was not always the case. Initially, some fossil fuel companies were active in the mainstream science of global warming. This early history is of particular relevance for the current state of affairs in AI and is worth exploring in some detail.

In 1979, Exxon installed on its Esso Atlantic supertanker custom scientific equipment for measuring air and ocean carbon dioxide concentrations. The project assessed the ocean's uptake of atmospheric carbon dioxide, which at the time was an important uncertainty in the science of global warming. The supertanker project was part of a broader engagement by Exxon in the mainstream scientific study of global warming during the decade 1977–1987, as was recently documented in an investigative journalism project by InsideClimate News.[86]

1988 marked the beginning of serious policy interest in addressing global warming, at least in the US. Prompted in part by a severe drought and heatwave, the US Senate Energy and Natural Resources Committee held a hearing in which NASA's James Hansen delivered a now-famous testimony expressing 99% certainty that global warming had begun. As reported in a *New York Times* article, which ran at the top of the front page, several Senators on the Committee concurred that global warming was a threat and that action should be taken to counteract it.[87]

At around the same time, Exxon began supporting efforts to amplify uncertainty about the science of global warming, apparently as a strategy to stymie policy restrictions on its fossil fuel business. This change in practice is seen, for example, in the Global Climate Coalition, an industry lobbyist group that Exxon co-founded in 1989. Exxon continued its scientific research on global warming, much of which continued to support the mainstream scientific consensus, but its public-facing communications tended to question the science and oppose policy action.[88]

The divergent content of its scientific research and public communications served different purposes. As reported by InsideClimate News, Exxon wanted its own sound science to guide its internal planning, confer it legitimacy to help it influence policy, and adhere to scientific standards.[89] In contrast, public communications were a business strategy aimed at avoiding costly regulations. This strategy has a long history, dating to 1950s tobacco industry efforts to question the science linking tobacco to cancer, and it remains in use across multiple industries, including fossil fuels.[90] Exxon's science/public divergence permits it to claim it accepts the reality of global warming while actively thwarting efforts to seriously address it.

The AI issue may now be where global warming was in the late 1970s to early 1980s: public recognition has begun, but policy regulations are not yet in serious consideration. This may explain why AI corporations are active in efforts on AI ethics: acknowledging that AI poses serious ethical issues is not yet a threat to their core business model. Indeed, the corporations may wish to demonstrate that they are responsible actors on AI and therefore do not need to be regulated. (They may even want to show that they are more responsible than their competitors, such that their competitors need to be regulated and they do not.)

The history of global warming shows that if corporations view the issue as a significant threat to their profits, then addressing the issue becomes quite a lot more difficult. The corporate ethics statements may continue insofar as it improves the corporations' public image without committing them to any costly restrictions on their business activities. Meanwhile, the companies may seek to publicly downplay the risks associated with their technology, and to lobby governments to prevent regulations. This is what the fossil fuel industry did, despite global warming posing a significant risk of global catastrophe that has long been backed by extensive mainstream science. The risk of global catastrophe from AI has a much more tenuous scientific basis and thus may be considerably easier for the industry to sow doubts about.[91] (Conversely, improving expert consensus on AI risk could help counteract industry obfuscation.[92])

An important difference between global warming and AI is that whereas all fossil fuels can increase global warming, not all AI technology poses a global risk. For example, contemporary AI systems designed to play games like chess and Go may be a significant cultural phenomenon, but they are not significant threats to human welfare. In order to avoid an AI catastrophe, only certain forms of AI may need to be restricted, specifically those that could cause a catastrophe. It thus follows that a key question for AI governance is whether the restrictions need to avoid catastrophe would cover forms of AI that are also profitable. In this context, Baum[93] coins the term "AGI profit–R&D synergy," defining it as "any circumstance in which long-term AGI R&D delivers short-term profits." If there is AGI profit–R&D synergy, then corporations may resist restrictions on the development of AGI, even though the technology could pose a global risk. The extent of AGI profit–R&D synergy could be an important—perhaps even crucial—factor in the safe governance of AI.

Some arguments against regulating fossil fuels may also apply to AI. First, it is sometimes argued that regulation stifles innovation and economic growth and restricts consumer lifestyles. This has been a common refrain in global warming debates[94] and is starting to be heard for AI.[95] Second, it is sometimes argued that regulations should be delayed until the risks are adequately understood. This has also been a common refrain in global warming debates, although the argument is sometimes, though not always, made disingenuously.[96] The same argument might also be made for AI, potentially, but not necessarily, disingenuously. Whether any particular regulation would bring net benefits (by reducing the risks from a technology more than it restricts the potential benefits) and when regulations should be introduced are important matters for policy analysis but are beyond the scope of this chapter.

It is important to note that the pathologies of global warming governance do not apply equally across the globe. The case of Exxon as discussed above applies in particular to the US. Overall, the US has been relatively susceptible to corporate influence on global warming due to a variety of political, economic and cultural factors. For example, Sheldon Whitehouse, a US Senator and strong advocate for environmental protection, attributes much of the problem to the 2010 US Supreme Court decision in the case of *Citizens United v. Federal Election Commission*, which permitted unlimited corporate spending on election-related communications.[97] Whitehouse reports that after this court case, many politicians abstained from supporting action on global warming out of concern that the fossil fuel industry would support their political opponents. In countries with more restrictive campaign finance rules, the fossil fuel industry may tend to have less influence on global warming policy. The same could hold for AI policy as well.

Finally, the history of global warming also provides a more general lesson regarding the role of scholarly expertise in public debates about science and technology issues. In public debates about global warming, corporate messaging has diminished the influence of the scientific consensus. Similarly, recent public debates about AI have given extensive attention to science and technology celebrities with limited AI expertise, such as Bill Gates, Elon Musk and the late Stephen Hawking.[98] The history of global warming shows that public debates can diverge from expert opinion for an extended period of time. Public debates have different dynamics and epistemic standards. Efforts to improve the quality of public debates about AI should proceed accordingly.

5.6 ASTEROID COLLISION

In several respects, asteroid collision and AI are very different types of issue. They differ in their origin (outer space vs technology), their empirical basis (which is much stronger for asteroid collision), and their degree of social consensus (AI is much more controversial). Indeed, asteroid collision is notable for being perhaps the most well-characterised global catastrophic risk in terms of the probabilities and severities of the risk.[99] Nonetheless, both asteroid collision and AI involve the prospect of extreme global catastrophe. Concern about the risk of global catastrophe has motivated high-level efforts to address asteroid collision by both the international scientific community and major national governments. These successes have only been partial—more work to address asteroid collision remains to be done—but they nonetheless suggest a pathway for high-level attention to AI risk even if AI catastrophe is perceived as unlikely.

Asteroid collision should be a quintessential case of what Jonathan Wiener[100] calls "the tragedy of the uncommons": a risk so rare that it is overlooked by the lay public and policymakers. Yet, the history of the risk shows that this has not been the case. (The history below draws heavily on Chapman.[101])

Scientific awareness of the asteroid collision threat began in the 1940s, but was largely dormant until the early 1980s, following the landmark

Alvarez et al.[102] study of the Cretaceous-Paleogene extinction and an important workshop in 1981. Public interest grew in the late 1980s via a trade press book[103] and the "near miss" of asteroid 1989FC (it was "near" in astronomical terms but not in terms of its danger to Earth). Policy interest was sparked by a position paper published by the American Institute of Aeronautics and Astronautics.[104] This outreach culminated in the 1990 US House NASA Authorization Report Language calling for NASA attention to the asteroid threat. The text of the Report Language is illuminating:

> The chances of the Earth being struck by a large asteroid are extremely small, but since the consequences of such a collision are extremely large, the Committee believes it is only prudent to assess the nature of the threat and prepare to deal with it. We have the technology to detect such asteroids and to prevent their collision with the Earth.[105]

This text shows the US House of Representatives reaching the conclusion that an extreme catastrophic risk should be taken seriously and addressed even if its probability is extremely low. The logic here mirrors the logic found throughout academic studies advocating attention to global catastrophic risks,[106] including the risk of runaway AI.[107] The asteroid threat therefore offers an important precedent, one that may be worth revisiting in policy debates about AI.

The 1990 US House NASA Authorization Report Language is no anomaly. The US government has remained engaged in the asteroid threat. Most recently, the US National Science and Technology Council, an Executive Branch advisory group, published the *National Near-Earth Object Preparedness Strategy and Action Plan*.[108] The US has also sponsored astronomy studies to detect asteroids, as have other countries. Scientists report the detection of over 90% of large asteroids, none of which are found to be on earthbound trajectories.[109] Ongoing detection programmes scan for smaller (and thus harder to detect) asteroids. The US and other countries are also developing techniques for deflecting away earthbound asteroids. The US has taken at least some formal steps toward operationalising those techniques: the US National Nuclear Security Administration is holding onto an important component of nuclear explosives for "potential use in planetary defence against earthbound asteroids."[110] While more could be done, it is nonetheless clear that the asteroid threat has significant high-level policy recognition and support for efforts to address it.

The nature of the asteroid threat may have made it easier for governments to recognise it than it would be for the AI threat. The Cretaceous-Paleogene extinction provides what appears to be a clear proof of principle, and the overall science of asteroids is relatively well understood. Scientists routinely publish figures graphing the frequency of collision as a function of asteroid size based on well-established empirical data.[111] This makes it easier for government officials to believe in the validity of the threat. Furthermore, the asteroid threat involves no human enemies whose livelihood may be put at risk by efforts to address the threat—the only thing put at risk is the asteroid itself. Likewise, there is likely to be less in the way of institutions lobbying against asteroid risk reduction.

However, the history of the asteroid threat shows that it did in fact struggle to gain serious recognition, and it did also have to overcome institutional opposition. Early media coverage included a significant "giggle factor" and portrayed concerned astronomers as "Chicken Littles" playing up concern to generate funding for their research.[112] Additionally, many scientists, including those in leadership at NASA, pushed back against efforts to address the asteroid threat. The scientists did not want the "giggle factor" tarnishing their reputations, and they did not want the applied mission of the asteroid threat to pull scarce funds away from pure (non-applied) scientific research.[113] Recognition of the AI threat faces very similar challenges. For the asteroid threat, these challenges have been overcome with at least some modest success. This fact should provide some encouragement to efforts to gain serious attention for the AI threat.

Furthermore, the human dimensions of asteroid risk are not as well understood as the physical and environmental dimensions. This holds in particular for potentially globally catastrophic human harm.[114] While asteroid risk is probably the most well-characterised global catastrophic risk, the exact risk estimates are nonetheless uncertain. This uncertainty has not precluded policy action; either the uncertainty has gone unnoticed by policymakers, or the policymakers opted to act anyway. The willingness of policymakers to act despite uncertainties in the risk is an encouraging precedent for AI, which is a considerably more uncertain risk.

5.7 LESSONS LEARNED

Several overarching lessons for the study of AI can be drawn from the four global risks surveyed in the preceding sections. First and foremost, the extreme severity of global risks does not on its own ensure they will be addressed successfully. The severity of global risks does sometimes move key actors to take action, such as US Congressional action on asteroid risk. Other actors have not been persuaded by the severity, such as academic biotechnologists reluctant to adopt RRI and the fossil fuel industry opposing global warming policy. There are compelling theoretical reasons to prioritise reducing global risks, but these reasons are not always persuasive in practice.

Second, perceptions of global risks can be strongly influenced by people's incentives and by their cultural and intellectual orientations, especially where the size of the risk is uncertain. Global risks are highly uncertain due to the complexity of global events and the rarity of (and thus lack of data on) global catastrophes. Even the risk of an asteroid collision, which derives from relatively simple and well-understood astronomical processes, has significant uncertainties with respect to human consequences. Communicating asteroid risk has also been challenging due to the risk's "giggle factor." Other risks are more contentious. Global warming risk is disputed, perhaps disingenuously, by a fossil fuel industry that has an incentive to avoid regulation. GOF-PPP risk is disputed by different populations of experts, with those conducting GOF-PPP experiments sometimes finding the risk to be lower than those who emphasise the security dimensions of biotechnology. The size of AI risk is also currently disputed within expert communities, could also come to be disputed by industry, and might be difficult to communicate due to its own distinct "giggle factor." Efforts to characterise and raise awareness about AI risk should be mindful of these dynamics to mitigate biases in analysis and public discourse.

Third, whether the response to global risks is successful may depend on buy-in, especially from those who stand to lose as a result of risk reduction measures. Out of all the cases studied in this paper, two stand out as relatively successful stories of risk reduction: recombinant DNA and asteroid collision. The former involved a moratorium that had broad buy-in from the relevant scientific community. The latter involves response measures that do not implicate or restrict anyone to any significant extent. Contrasting examples abound. Biotechnology RRI initiatives face resistance from academics concerned about intellectual freedom. Biological and nuclear weapons arms control initiatives face resistance from states concerned about losing strategic advantage. Initiatives to reduce greenhouse gas emissions face pushback from the fossil fuel industry. Obtaining buy-in for AI risk reduction may be especially challenging because many key actors, including academics, states, and industry, could stand to lose as a result of risk reduction initiatives. AI risk reduction initiatives may need an unusually large and multifaceted effort to achieve buy-in in order to succeed.

Finally, risks and risk reduction initiatives can be heavily shaped by broader socio-political conditions. GMO regulation has been stricter in Europe than in the US due to Europe's less business-friendly political culture and its recent experience with mad cow disease. Fossil fuel regulation has also been relatively lax in the US, perhaps due to its relatively permissive campaign finance laws (which are closely tied to the business-friendly US political culture). Nuclear weapons technology was developed extremely quickly because certain breakthroughs in nuclear physics happened to coincide with the extreme international competition of the 1930s and 1940s. Likewise, AI risk reduction initiatives will not take place in a vacuum. To succeed, the initiatives should account for the particular socio-political conditions and the (possibly unforeseen) circumstances in which they will take place.

5.8 CONCLUSION

History is not doomed to repeat itself. Past failures to manage global risks do not necessarily portend future failures—especially if important lessons are learned. At the same time, past successes do not necessarily portend future successes. While AI is relatively new as a social, risk, and policy issue, it has much to learn from other global risks.

This chapter proposes that it is possible to accelerate the study of AI as a social, risk, and policy issue by leveraging the existing scholarship on and experience with other global risks. To demonstrate this possibility, the paper presents examples from four other classes of global risk: biotechnology, nuclear weapons, global warming, and asteroid collision. Although it would be valuable to expand the study of these four cases to broader international contexts, they shine considerable light on how to understand the prospects for AI catastrophe, how such an outcome could be avoided and how AI outcomes can be improved more generally.

In addition, these sorts of historical case studies may hold some rhetorical value for efforts to improve AI outcomes. History may help some people take certain AI scenarios more seriously, especially scenarios involving long-term, high-stakes AI. Many people in academia, government, and other sectors may be dismissive of such scenarios,[115] instead preferring to focus their attention on more near-term and empirically robust issues. The history of other global risks can provide at least an indirect empirical basis for some important aspects of long-term AI, and can likewise demonstrate that similar issues have often gotten substantial high-level attention. The history may be of particular value for relating long-term AI to people with a background in other global risks because it can help to make long-term AI seem more familiar.

At the heart of this chapter is a claim that transferring lessons from other global risks can be an efficient and productive means of advancing progress on AI. In putting forward this claim, we do not mean to imply that lessons from other global risks are sufficient for studying issues in AI. On the contrary, AI will inevitably pose some novel challenges that require dedicated original analysis. Furthermore, we do not mean to claim that transferring lessons from other risks will be the most efficient and productive research strategy for all groups working on issues in AI. This approach will tend to work best for research groups, such as our own, that already have a background in other risks. The merits of this approach for research groups that are more narrowly specialised in AI is an important question and is beyond the scope of this paper. Instead, this paper serves to demonstrate the intellectual and practical benefits that can be gained from transferring lessons from other global risks to the study of AI.

ACKNOWLEDGEMENTS

Maurizio Tinnirello and two anonymous reviewers provided helpful comments on an earlier version of this chapter. Jake Stone assisted in formatting the manuscript. Any remaining errors are the authors' alone.

NOTES

1. S. J. Pan and Q. Yang, "A Survey on Transfer Learning," *IEEE Transactions on Knowledge and Data Engineering* 22, no. 10 (2010): 1345–1359.
2. A. R. Zamir et al., "Taskonomy: Disentangling Task Transfer Learning," *Proceedings of the IEEE Conference on Computer Vision and Pattern Recognition* (2018): 3712–3722.
3. D. N. Perkins and G. Salomon, "Transfer of Learning," in *International Encyclopedia of Education*, 6452–6457. (Oxford: Pergamon Press, 1992); Perkins and Salomon, "Knowledge to Go: A Motivational and Dispositional View of Transfer," *Educational Psychologist* 47, no. 3 (2012): 248–258.
4. D. Crevier, *AI: The Tumultuous History of the Search for Artificial Intelligence* (New York: Basic Books, 1993); J. Markoff, *Machines of Loving Grace: The Quest for Common Ground between Humans and Robots* (New York: HarperCollins, 2016); P. McCorduck, *Machines Who Think: 25th Anniversary Edition* (Natick: AK Peters, 2004).

5. N. Wiener, "Some Moral and Technical Consequences of Automation," *Science* 131, no. 3410 (1960): 1355–1358; I. J. Good, "Speculations Concerning the First Ultraintelligent Machine," *Advances in Computers* 6 (1965): 31–88.
6. S. Butler, "Darwin among the Machines," *The Press*, 13 June 1863.
7. N. Bostrom, *Superintelligence: Paths, Dangers, Strategies* (Oxford: Oxford University Press, 2014); Callaghan et al., *Technological Singularity* (Berlin: Springer, 2017); Eden et al., *Singularity Hypotheses* (Berlin: Springer, 2015); K. Sotala and R. V. Yampolskiy, "Responses to Catastrophic AGI Risk: A Survey," *Physica Scripta* 90, no. 1 (2015): 018001. https://doi.org/10.1088 /0031-8949/90/1/018001.
8. Some notable examples include K. Grace, *The Asilomar Conference: A Case Study in Risk Mitigation* (MIRI Technical Report 2015-9, 2015); K. Grace, *Leó Szilárd and the Danger of Nuclear Weapons: A Case Study in Risk Mitigation* (MIRI Technical Report 2015-10, 2015); J. Altmann and F. Sauer, "Autonomous Weapon Systems and Strategic Stability," *Survival* 59, no. 5 (2017): 117–142; S. D. Baum, "On the Promotion of Safe and Socially Beneficial Artificial Intelligence," *AI & Society* 32, no. 4 (2017): 543–551; S. D. Baum, "Countering Superintelligence Misinformation," *Information* 9, no. 244 (2018); A. Grotto, "Genetically Modified Organisms: A Precautionary Tale for AI," *AI Pulse*, 24 January 2019. https://aipulse.org/genetically-mod-ified-organisms-a-precautionary-tale-for-ai-governance-2; M. Maas, "How Viable is International Arms Control for Military Artificial Intelligence? Three Lessons from Nuclear Weapons," *Contemporary Security Policy* 40, no. 3 (2019): 285–311.
9. G. Allen and T. Chan, *Artificial Intelligence and National Security* (Belfer Center for International Affairs, Harvard Kennedy School, July 2017).
10. As is argued, for example, by Bostrom, *Superintelligence*. For a counterargument, see S. Pueyo, "Growth, Degrowth, and the Challenge of Artificial Superintelligence," *Journal of Cleaner Production* 197, no. 2 (2018): 1731–1736.
11. S. Legg and M. Hutter, "Universal Intelligence: A Definition of Machine Intelligence," *Minds & Machines* 17 no. 4 (2007): 391–444.
12. B. Goertzel, "Superintelligence: Fears, Promises and Potentials," *Journal of Evolution and Technology* 25, no. 2 (2015): 55–87.
13. McCorduck, *Machines Who Think*.
14. Bostrom, *Superintelligence*; A. H. Eden, J. H. Moor, J. H. Søraker, and E Steinhart (eds), *Singularity Hypotheses* (Berlin: Springer, 2012); Sotala and Yampolskiy, "Catastrophic AGI Risk,"; Callaghan, *Technological Singularity*.
15. R. Brooks, "I, Rodney Brooks, am a Robot," *IEEE Spectrum*, 1 June 2008, https://spectrum.ieee.org/computing/hardware/i-rodney-brooks-am -a-robot; J. J. Bryson and P. P. Kime, "Just an Artifact: Why Machines Are Perceived as Moral Agents," in *Proceedings of the Twenty-Second International Joint Conference on Artificial Intelligence*, 1641–1646, edited by Toby Walsh (Vol. 2. Barcelona, July 2011); for an overview, see Baum, "Countering Superintelligence Misinformation."

16. S. Kaplan and J. Garrick, "On the Quantitative Definition of Risk," *Risk Analysis* 1, no. 1 (1981): 11–27.
17. A. Atkinson, *Impact Earth: Asteroids, Comets and Meteors—The Growing Threat* (London: Virgin, 1999).
18. S. D. Baum and I. C. Handoh, "Integrating the Planetary Boundaries and Global Catastrophic Risk Paradigms," *Ecological Economics* 107 (2014): 13–21.
19. e.g. D. Parfit. *Reasons and Persons* (Oxford: Oxford University Press, 1984); J. G. Matheny, "Reducing the Risk of Human Extinction," *Risk Analysis* 27, no. 5 (2007): 1335–1344.
20. N. Bostrom, "Existential Risks: Analyzing Human Extinction Scenarios and Related Hazards," *Journal of Evolution and Technology* 9, no. 1 (2002); S. D. Baum et al., "Long-Term Trajectories of Human Civilization," *Foresight* 21, no. 1 (2019): 53–83.
21. A. Wyckoff, *OECD Directorate for Science, Technology and Industry Committee for Scientific and Technological Policy Report*, DSTI/EAS/STP/NEST1/RD(2001)30, 2001, as discussed in A. S. Dahms, "Biotechnology: What it Is, What it Is Not, and the Challenges in Reaching a National or Global Consensus," *Biochemistry and Molecular Biology Education* 32, no. 4 (2006): 271–278.
22. P. R. Dormitzer, "Rapid Production of Synthetic Influenza Vaccines," *Current Topics in Microbiology and Immunology* 386 (2015): 237–273.
23. National Academies of Sciences, Engineering, and Medicine, *Gene Drives on the Horizon: Advancing Science, Navigating Uncertainty, and Aligning Research with Public Values* (Washington: The National Academies Press, 2016).
24. Gryphon Scientific, *Risk and Benefit Analysis of Gain of Function Research* (Washington: Gryphon Scientific LLC, 2015).
25. Biological and Toxin Weapons Convention 2011, *Scientific and Technological Developments that May Be Relevant to the Convention.*
26. P. Arntz et al., "When Artificial Intelligence Goes Awry: Separating Science Fiction from Fact," (Malwarebytes, 2019), https://resources.malwarebytes.com/resource/artificial-intelligence-goes-awry-separating-science-fiction-fact.
27. Grace, *The Asilomar Conference.*
28. Grace, *The Asilomar Conference.*
29. Grace, *The Asilomar Conference*, 20.
30. Baum, "Socially Beneficial Artificial Intelligence."
31. R. A. Posner, *Catastrophe: Risk and Response* (Oxford: Oxford University Press, 2004); G. Wilson, "Minimizing Global Catastrophic and Existential Risks from Emerging Technologies through International Law," *Virginia Environmental Law Journal* 31 (2013): 307–364.
32. Bostrom, *Superintelligence.*
33. R. Yampolskiy and J. Fox, "Safety Engineering for Artificial General Intelligence," *Topoi* 32, no. 2 (2013): 217–226.
34. B. Joy, "Why the Future Doesn't Need Us," *Wired*, 1 April 2000.

35. J. J. Hughes, "Global Technology Regulation and Potentially Apocalyptic Technological Threats," in *Nanoethics: The Ethical and Social Implications of Nanotechnology*, edited by F. Allhoff et al., 201–214 (Hoboken: John Wiley, 2007); J. O. McGinnis, "Accelerating AI," *Northwestern University Law Review* 104, no. 366 (2010): 366–381.
36. D. Dewey, "Long-Term Strategies for Ending Existential Risk from Fast Takeoff," in *Risks of Artificial Intelligence*, edited by V. C. Müller, 243–266 (Boca Raton: CRC, 2015); McGinnis, "Accelerating AI,"; Tomasik, *International Cooperation vs. AI Arms Race* (Foundational Research Institute, 2016), https://foundational-research.org/files/international-cooperation-ai-arms-race.pdf.
37. For example, R. A. M. Fouchier, "Studies on Influenza Virus Transmission between Ferrets: The Public Health Risks Revisited," *mBio* 6, no. 1 (2015): e02560–14, https://doi.org/10.1128/mBio.02560-14.
38. For example, M. Lipsitch and T. V. Inglesby, "Moratorium on Research Intended to Create Novel Potential Pandemic Pathogens," *mBio* 5, no. 6 (2014): e02366–14, https://doi.org/10.1128/mBio.02366-14; M. Lipsitch and T. V. Inglesby, "Reply to 'Studies on Influenza Virus Transmission between Ferrets: The Public Health Risks Revisited,'" *mBio* 6, no. 1 (2015): e00041–15, https://doi.org/10.1128/mBio.00041-15.
39. Fouchier et al., "Pause on Avian Flu Transmission Research," *Science* 335, no. 6067 (2012): 400–401.
40. Gryphon Scientific, *Risk and Benefit Analysis*.
41. M. J. Imperiale and A. Casadevall, "Zika Virus Focuses the Gain-of-Function Debate," *mSphere* 1, no. 2 (2016): e00069–16, https://doi.org/10.1128/mSphere.00069-16.
42. D. Reardon, "Ban on Pathogen Studies Lifted," *Nature* 553 (2018): 11.
43. J. Kuzma and P. Roberts, "Cataloguing the Barriers Facing RRI in Innovation Pathways: A Response to the Dilemma of Societal Alignment," *Journal of Responsible Innovation* 5, no 3 (2018): 338–346.
44. B. Ribeiro et al., "Introducing the Dilemma of Societal Alignment for Inclusive and Responsible Research and Innovation," *Journal of Responsible Innovation* 5, no. 3 (2018): 316–331.
45. Kuzma and Roberts, "Cataloguing the Barriers."
46. S. D. Baum, *A Survey of Artificial General Intelligence Projects for Ethics, Risk, and Policy* (Working Paper Global Catastrophic Risk Institute 17-1, 2017).
47. Kuzma, "Cataloguing the Barriers."
48. Grotto, "Genetically Modified Organisms."
49. For example, S. Armstrong et al., "Racing to the Precipice: A Model of Artificial Intelligence Development," *AI & Society* 31, no. 2 (2016): 201–206; C. Shulman, "Arms Control and Intelligence Explosions," (Paper presented at the 7th European Conference on Computing and Philosophy, Bellaterra, Spain, 2–4 July 2009).
50. E. Schlosser, *Command and Control: Nuclear Weapons, the Damascus Accident, and the Illusion of Safety* (New York: Penguin, 2013).

51. For example, Shulman, "Intelligence Explosions"; Armstrong, "Racing to the Precipice."
52. Baum, "A Survey of Artificial Intelligence."
53. N. Thompson and I. Bremmer, "The AI Cold War that Threatens Us All," *Wired*, 23 October 2018, https://www.wired.com/story/ai-cold-war-china-could-doom-us-all.
54. D. Welch and E. Behrmann, "Who's Winning the Self-Driving Car Race?" *Bloomberg*, 7 May 2018, https://www.bloomberg.com/news/features/2018-05-07/who-s-winning-the-self-driving-car-race.
55. Shulman, "Intelligence Explosions"; S. Cave and S. S. Ó hÉigeartaigh, "An AI Race for Strategic Advantage: Rhetoric and Risks," in *Proceedings of the 2018 AAAI/ACM Conference on AI, Ethics, and Society—AIES '18*, 36–40 (New Orleans: ACM Press, 2018); W. Naudé and N. Dimitri, "The Race for an Artificial General Intelligence: Implications for Public Policy," *AI & Society* (2019), https://doi.org/10.1007/s00146-019-00887-x.
56. A. Ramamoorthy and R. Yampolskiy, "Beyond MAD?: The Race for Artificial General Intelligence," *ICT Discoveries* no. 1 (2 February 2018); Shulman, "Intelligence Explosions"; Tomasik, "*International Cooperation.*"
57. O. R. Frisch, "Physical Evidence for the Division of Heavy Nuclei under Neutron Bombardment," *Nature* 143, no. 3616 (1939): 276; L. Meitner and O. R. Frisch, "Disintegration of Uranium by Neutrons: A New Type of Nuclear Reaction," *Nature* 143, no. 3615 (1939): 239.
58. R. W. Clark, *The Birth of the Bomb* (New York: Horizon Press, 1961); M. Gowing, *Britain and Atomic Energy 1939–1945* (London: Macmillan, 1964); K. Macrakis, *Surviving the Swastika: Scientific Research in Nazi Germany* (New York: Oxford University Press, 1993).
59. H. L. Stimson, "The Decision to Use the Atomic Bomb," *Harper's Magazine*, February 1947, 98–101.
60. P. Scharre, *Army of None: Autonomous Weapons and the Future of War* (New York: Norton, 2018).
61. Scharre and Horowitz, "An Introduction to Autonomy in Weapon Systems," (Working paper, Center for a New American Security, 13 February 2015), https://www.cnas.org/publications/reports/an-introduction-to-autonomy-in-weapon-systems.
62. S. A. Goudsmit, *Alsos* (New York: Henry Schulman, 1947).
63. Armstrong et al., "Racing to the Precipice."
64. G. H. Quester, *Nuclear Monopoly* (New Brunswick: Transaction Publishers, 2000).
65. Shulman, "Intelligence Explosions"; Cave, "An AI Race"; Naudé, "Artifical General Intelligence."
66. Quester, *Nuclear Monopoly*.
67. B. Russell, "The Bomb and Civilization," *Forward* 39, no. 33 (18 August 1945).
68. Dewey, "Ending Existential Risk."
69. Dewey, "Ending Existential Risk."

70. Dewey, "Ending Existential Risk"; Shulman, "Intelligence Explosion"; Goertzel, "Superintelligence."
71. Dewey, "Ending Existential Risk."
72. G. Marcus, "Artificial Intelligence is Stuck. Here's How to Move it Forward," *New York Times*, 29 July 2017, https:// nytimes.com/2017/07/29/opinion/sunday/artificial-intelligence-is-stuck-heres-how-to-move-it-forward.html.
73. R. Hanson, *The Age of Em: Work, Love, and Life When Robots Rule the Earth* (Oxford: Oxford University Press, 2016); R. A. Koene, "Embracing Competitive Balance: The Case for Substrate-Independent Minds and Whole Brain Emulation," in *Singularity Hypotheses: A Scientific and Philosophical Assessment*, edited by A. H. Eden et al., 241–267 (Berlin: Springer, 2012).
74. K. Waltz, "The Spread of Nuclear Weapons: More May Better," *Adelphi Papers* 21, no. 171 (1981); R. Rauchhaus, "Evaluating the Nuclear Peace Hypothesis: A Quantitative Approach," *Journal of Conflict Resolution* 53, no. 2 (2009): 258–277.
75. J. Mueller, "The Essential Irrelevance of Nuclear Weapons: Stability in the Postwar World," *International Security* 13, no. 2 (1988): 55–79; W. Wilson, *Five Myths about Nuclear Weapons* (Boston: Houghton Mifflin Harcourt, 2013).
76. For example, K. A. Lieber and D. G. Press, "The End of MAD? The Nuclear Dimension of US Primacy," *International Security* 30, no 4 (2006): 7–44.
77. For example, Bostrom, *Superintelligence*.
78. For example, Altmann, "Autonomous Weapon Systems."
79. For example, Centre for Research on Environmental Decisions, *The Psychology of Climate Change Communication: A Guide for Scientists, Journalists, Educators, Political Aides, and the Interested Public* (New York: Columbia University Center for Research on Environmental Decisions, 2009).
80. For example, N. Stern, *The Economics of Climate Change: The Stern Review* (Cambridge: Cambridge University Press, 2007).
81. For example, M. L. Weitzman, "On Modeling and Interpreting the Economics of Catastrophic Climate Change," *Review of Economics and Statistics* 91, no. 1 (2009): 1–19.
82. For example, CNA Military Advisory Board 2014.
83. Baum, "Socially Beneficial Artificial Intelligence."
84. S. D. Baum, "Superintelligence Skepticism as a Political Tool," *Information* 9, no. 209 (2018); Baum, "Countering Superintelligence Misinformation."
85. N. Oreskes and E. M. Conway, *Merchants of Doubt: How a Handful of Scientists Obscured the Truth on Issues from Tobacco Smoke to Global Warming* (New York. Bloomsbury, 2010).
86. N. Banerjee, L. Song, and D. Hasemyer, "Exxon: The Road Not Taken," *Inside Climate News*, 16 September 2015, https://insideclimatenews.org/content/Exxon-The-Road-Not-Taken.
87. P. Shabecoff, "Global Warming Has Begun, Expert Tells Senate," *New York Times*, 24 June 1988.

88. G. Supran and N. Oreskes, "Assessing ExxonMobil's Climate Change Communications (1977–2014)," *Environmental Research Letters* 12, no. 8 (2017): 084019, https://doi.org/10.1088/1748-9326/aa815f.
89. Inside Climate News, "The Road Not Taken."
90. Oreskes, *Merchants of Doubt*.
91. Baum, "Superintelligence Skepticism."
92. Baum, "Countering Superintelligence Misinformation."
93. Baum, "A Survey of Artificial Intelligence," 19.
94. J. D. Collomb, "The Ideology of Climate Change Denial in the United States," *European Journal of American Studies* 9, no. 1 (2014), https://doi.org /10.4000/ejas.10305.
95. e.g. Gurkaynak et al., "Stifling Artificial Intelligence: Human Perils," *Computer Law and Security Review: The International Journal of Technology Law and Practice* 32, no. 5 (2016): 749–758, https://doi.org/10.1016/j.clsr .2016.05.003 2016; D. Castro, "The U.S. May Lose the AI Race Because of an Unchecked Techno-Panic," *Center for Data Innovation*, 5 March 2019, https://www.datainnovation.org/2019/03/the-u-s-may-lose-the-ai-race -because-of-an-unchecked-techno-panic.
96. Oreskes, *Merchants of Doubt*.
97. S. Whitehouse, *Captured: The Corporate Infiltration of American Democracy* (New York: New Press, 2017).
98. V. Galanos, "Exploring Expanding Expertise: Artificial Intelligence as an Existential Threat and the Role of Prestigious Commentators, 2014–2018," *Technology Analysis & Strategic Management* 31, no. 4 (2019): 421–432.
99. S. D. Baum, "Uncertain Human Consequences in Asteroid Risk Analysis and the Global Catastrophe Threshold," *Natural Hazards* 94, no. 2 (2018): 759–775.
100. J. Wiener, "The Tragedy of the Uncommons: On the Politics of Apocalypse," *Global Policy* 7, no. 1 (2016): 67–80.
101. C. R. Chapman, "History of the Asteroid/Comet Impact Hazard," *Southwest Research Institute*, https://www.boulder.swri.edu/clark/ncarhist.html.
102. L. W. Alvarez et al., "Extraterrestrial Cause for the Cretaceous-Tertiary Extinction," *Science* 208, no. 4448 (1980): 1095–1108.
103. C. R. Chapman and D. Morrison, *Cosmic Catastrophes* (New York: Plenum, 1989).
104. American Institute of Aeronautics and Astronautics, *Dealing with the Threat of an Asteroid Striking the Earth* (Reston, VA, 1990).
105. US House, *Report Language to H.R.5649, National Aeronautics and Space Administration Multiyear Authorization Act of 1990* (Washington: United States House of Representatives, 1990). Quote at p. 30.
106. e.g. Posner, *Catastrophe*; Wiener, "Tragedy of the Uncommons."
107. Sotala, "Catastrophic AGI Risk."
108. National Science and Technology Council, *National Near-Earth Object Preparedness Strategy and Action Plan* (Washington: US National Science and Technology Council, 2018).

109. A. Mainzer et al., "The Population of Tiny Near-Earth Objects Observed by NEOWISE," *Astrophysical Journal* 784, no. 2 (2014):110, https://doi.org/10.1088/0004-637X/784/2/110.
110. Government Accountability Office, *Nuclear Weapons: Actions Needed by NNSA to Clarify Dismantlement Performance Goal* (Washington: Government Accountability Office, 2014).
111. For example, A. W. Harris et al., "Asteroid Impacts and Modern Civilization: Can We Prevent a Catastrophe?," in *Asteroids IV*, edited by P. Michel et al. (Tucson: University of Arizona Press, 2015).
112. Chapman, "History of the Asteroid."
113. Chapman, "History of the Asteroid."
114. Baum, "Uncertain Human Consequences."
115. For example, Brooks, "I, Rodney Brooks"; Bryson, "Just an Artifact."

CHAPTER 6

Vulnerability, AI, and Power in a Global Context

From Being-at-Risk to Biopolitics in the COVID-19 Pandemic

Mark Coeckelbergh

CONTENTS

6.1 INTRODUCTION

The COVID-19 or coronavirus pandemic raises personal-existential and political questions concerning vulnerability and power in a global context. At a personal level, it has created fear and anxiety, and on a global scale it has impacted different people and societies in different ways, often depending on how governments have handled the risks. Moreover, artificial intelligence (AI), in particular machine learning and data science methods, have been used to tackle the pandemic. Consider the use of big data, next to tracking apps, to monitor the spread of the virus in the population, or the analysis of people's behaviour in public spaces in order to monitor compliance with social distancing rules. At first sight, such

DOI: 10.1201/9780429446726-6

measures seem a good idea: together with medical interventions, these technologies can help to save human lives. But the collection, analysis, and use of these digital technologies and data has also sparked controversy and ethical and political concerns, for example, about privacy and freedom. Seen in a global context, there are also stark differences with regard to the use of AI in the pandemic: governments that are more authoritarian (for example, China and Russia) have used it in different ways than Western liberal democracies. What does this mean, for example, for issues concerning justice and equality?

Drawing on Heidegger and Foucault, this chapter maps and analyses some of these problems regarding existence and power by focusing on the relation between COVID-19 and the use of technology and data science, in particular AI. First, it is argued that AI and data science shape the experience of risk and vulnerability in the pandemic, creating a particular kind of knowledge of risk that stands in tension with other subjective, personal, and cultural experiences of risk. Further developing previous work, the concept of being-at-risk[1] is used to argue for a non-dualist view of pandemic risk and vulnerability that goes beyond the objective/subjective binary. In addition, and inspired by McLuhan, I show that this being-at-risk and the related fear and anxiety also have a global dimension. I also argue that our use of technologies to tackle the pandemic creates new risks and vulnerabilities, thus transforming our being-at-risk. This leads me to the second part of the chapter, which outlines some political questions raised by AI and data science that are used to respond to the pandemic: technology is used for what Foucault calls biopolitics. Different techniques are used, including separation, disciplining, and statistical analysis. These were already used in historical times, but now digital technologies, including AI, transform them. This creates not only threats to privacy but also to freedom, justice, and equality—also in a global context. I conclude with a summary of the chapter and a plea for global governance of both the pandemic and AI and for thinking beyond the human/non-human dichotomy. Foucault had already started to bring together issues concerning life and political questions; it is time to do the same for thinking about technology and thinking about politics. I end with a note on our obsession with control in the context of the Anthropocene.

6.2 EXISTENTIAL-EPISTEMOLOGICAL ISSUES

The pandemic reminds us that we are vulnerable and mortal beings: a small virus is enough to make us sick or kill us, and on top of that entire societies and economies have been heavily disrupted, which creates further vulnerabilities at the individual level; COVID-19 is and has been a global disaster. Yet typically humans tend to not accept such natural occurrences and struggle against their vulnerability and (in the case of transhumanism) even against their mortality. Technology and science are used for this purpose: they are anti-vulnerability strategies. They are used to make us less vulnerable—or at least that is the aim. Medical science seeks to protect us as much as possible from disease and death. Moreover, transhumanists such as Bostrom and Kurzweil embrace the possibility of using technologies to "enhance" humans above normal levels, making them more intelligent and more resilient against disease. But the border between this "human enhancement"[2] and therapy is not so clear. For example, medical science has already resulted in an increased lifespan. In the case of the pandemic, vaccination is used to protect people against deadly consequences of COVID-19 infection, and data science is used by governments to monitor COVID-19 in the population in order to take measures against the further spreading of the virus and to protect people: the aim is to render persons, bodies, and populations less vulnerable. Such interventions are therapeutic, but overall, since the 20th century, vaccination has "enhanced" us in the sense that we are now protected against a range of diseases that people would previously die from.

Yet new technologies do not only intervene in vulnerability and risk as mere means and instruments to reach a particular goal; they also change our knowledge and experience of risk and vulnerability and create new risks.[3] With the help of AI and data science, "objective" knowledge is created regarding COVID-19 risk. The statistics are communicated to the public, and government measures are justified by referring to data and their analysis. This shapes our experience of COVID-19 risk: what COVID-19 is and what risks it presents are mediated by the technologically and scientifically produced knowledge about it. COVID-19 comes in the form of numbers: how many people are infected, how much distance needs to be observed, how many people are allowed in a particular space, and so on. This gives us an idea of the risk we are exposed to.

At the same time, however, there is also the very personal and existential experience of *my* vulnerability in the pandemic. This experience cannot be reduced to numbers but involves feelings and concerns: fear, uncertainty, anxiety, despair. We may feel fearful when we see the numbers, but also when something happens that is less distant from us, for example, a friend who tested positive. We may fear for the health of others (for example, family members) but also fear our own death. COVID-19 becomes then less a matter of statistics than of existential *angst*. Suddenly the pandemic is not something that happens "in the world" but something that is also about *me*.

In philosophy, phenomenology and existentialism have something to say about this. In *Being and Time*, Heidegger proposed the two concepts of being-towards-death and authenticity. It is certain that we are going to die, although we do not know when it is going to happen. We can consider death because we are always ahead of ourselves. We are concerned about the future. But when it comes to our own death, we try to ignore or forget it, or society discourages thinking too much about it. In everyday life, we do not want to confront our own finitude. According to Heidegger, this is inauthentic: we should confront it and see our lives against the horizon of our death.

This analysis of inauthenticity connects back to the question of what kind of knowledge and experience is produced in the pandemic. Usually, I think of the death of others: I know, by means of statistics about COVID-19, for example, that "one" dies. Others die. But I do not really face that *I* can and will die. Death is then always the death of others. Heidegger writes:

> The publicness of everyday being-with-one-another "knows" death as a constantly occurring event, as a "case of death." Someone or another "dies," be it a neighbour or a stranger. People unknown to us "die" daily and hourly. "Death" is encountered as a familiar event occurring within the world … One also dies at the end, but for now one is not involved.[4]

Science and technology such as AI and data science seem to encourage such a distant and inauthentic epistemological relation to death and vulnerability. The numbers show that "one" can get infected, that "one" can end up in an intensive care unit of a hospital, and so on. But it is quite another thing to fully face the personal, existential fact that *I* will die—in the pandemic or at some time in the future. Authentic living, by contrast, means that we become aware of that ultimate possibility. Once we realise it, we get existential angst. We look into the abyss of our own mortality. This is very confronting, but it is at least authentic. Heidegger writes: "In Angst, Da-sein finds itself faced with the nothingness of the possible impossibility of its existence."[5]

COVID-19 thus gives us a chance to achieve such Heideggerian authenticity. But the way knowledge about the virus and the risk is produced seems to create barriers for such an existential transformation. Through science and technology, we generally only get the knowledge that "one" may die and that "one" should be careful. This avoids angst, but also removes the possibility of authentically confronting the possibility of our own death—caused by COVID or not.

Angst is thus different from mere fear, although the latter of course also plays a role in the pandemic. Here we can use Heidegger's phenomenology of fear. For Heidegger, fear is part of our being-in-the-world: "Da-sein as being-in-the-world is fearful."[6] Heidegger writes that when I fear, there is a threat: something can get me. Maybe it will get me, maybe not. This enhances fear.[7] When it comes near, it becomes alarming and creates terror. This phenomenology of fearful being-in-the-world can also be applied to fear in the pandemic: when I fear the threat of the COVID-19 virus, I fear that the virus will get me. It is a threat. But I do not know if that will happen. The virus may "pass me by." But when it gets me or others nearby, I am alarmed. There is terror, for example, when the virus appears in the family, the school, the group of friends.

Since, however, the "objective" knowledge about COVID-19 risk and the pandemic cannot be completely disentangled from our experience of it (fear, for example), I have proposed the quasi-Heideggerian concept "being-at-risk"[8] to capture that there is no strict separation between science and lifeworld, between technology and feelings, between risk and existence. We are-at-risk in the sense that we are always directed towards some threat or object of risk, but at the same time there is no risk-in-itself but always an experience of, interpretation of, and emotional response to that risk. Even if data science gives me the numbers, I never experience *mere* numbers; the numbers already mix with my fear. Pandemic risk, then, is a form of this being-at-risk. It is a risk that is measured, quantified, analysed, and "produced" by medicine, science, and technology, but it is never a risk-in-itself: it is always already experienced, interpreted, and so on.

Moreover, risk and vulnerability are not just a passive experience, something that happens to us or might happen to us. We actively *render* ourselves vulnerable and put ourselves at risk. For example, if I go to a place where there are a lot of people, I put myself at risk and I know that. I might even feel some fear. Nevertheless, I have taken the decision to go there. Risk, then, is never completely objective but also subjective and related to my capacity for action and agency. I can do things or not. I can make decisions. Being-towards-death and being-at-risk also open up possibilities for freedom. Furthermore, part of what I do takes the form of concern (Heidegger: *Sorge*): I am concerned about the risk, but I also care about and for others. This may be translated into action (or not). For example, one could go to the supermarket for an elderly person who is scared of getting infected by the virus. But being concerned about others (and about myself) also creates extra risk and vulnerability: once I care, I render myself vulnerable. Just as the fear of the virus itself creates an extra vulnerability, concern also renders me vulnerable. This vulnerability is rooted in my capacity to be concerned as an individual human being, but also in the basic sociality that I have. We are social beings, and hence we care about and for others. The least vulnerable amongst us (in this sense, at least) are those *who do not care*. But these are also the least social amongst us.

In addition to this care related to others, the pandemic has also created or at least increased opportunities for practices of self-care, for what Foucault calls "technologies of the self": techniques that permit individuals to affect by their own means or with the help of others a certain number of operations on their own bodies and souls, thoughts, conduct, and way of being, so as to transform themselves in order to attain a certain state of happiness, purity, wisdom, perfection, or immortality.[9]

In his histories of sexuality, Foucault analyses how ancient Greek and Roman philosophers, but also Christian church fathers, proposed various techniques and practices of the self, self-care, and self-disciplining in order to gain self-knowledge and transform themselves. Similarly, today in the pandemic, people try to increase their resilience and engage in all kinds of exercises to maintain or increase their physical and mental health. This can also be seen as a strategy of risk mitigation and vulnerability coping. Some people even see the pandemic as an opportunity for self-improvement and self-transformation. It is to be expected that technologies such as AI will play an increasingly important role in such self-care and self-improvement practices.[10]

However, while the result of our technological and scientific interventions is that one risk diminishes and one vulnerability is reduced, often other vulnerabilities and risks are created. For example, vaccination is a medical, technoscientific method that reduces our vulnerability to COVID-19, but at the same time creates its own risks (some known, some unknown). For example, the AstraZeneca vaccine became infamous for producing a thrombosis risk: the formation of a blood clot, which is itself a way in which the body protects itself against bleeding, but which might lead to unconsciousness and death. Moreover, even if the statistics show that, overall, a particular medical intervention works, there are no *guarantees* that anti-vulnerability technologies work in an individual case. Medical science cannot completely guarantee that there will be no deaths, no severe side effects, etc. Thus, while it could be that my overall vulnerability is reduced by vaccination, it would be an illusion to think that I am now completely safe or shielded against death. I remain vulnerable.

Now so far this analysis assumes that the world in which we live and act is a local one, or at most a national one. But due to the role of digital media and technologies (among other factors), our world has expanded and has acquired a global scope. McLuhan has described the psychological and existential consequence of this: anxiety. In his introduction to *Understanding Media*, he says that our nervous system is extended by new media, and that this makes us feel we are responsible.[11] Our consciousness has been expanded, but the price is that we now know what happens everywhere on the planet and become aware of the consequences of our actions. This makes us anxious. In *The Medium is the Massage*, he writes:

> The media work us over completely. They are so pervasive in their personal, political, economic, aesthetic, psychological, moral, ethical, and social consequences that they leave no part of us untouched, unaffected, unaltered.[12]

With regard to the pandemic, we also experience this anxiety, which is enhanced by media reports about the virus that cover the whole globe. We now experience the risk and the numbers not only locally, but also come to know what happens in other countries and the world as a whole. We do not only have knowledge about COVID-19 but about a *pandemic*: a worldwide phenomenon and risk. This makes us concerned about people that are distant from us and can in principle also lead to care in the sense of "care for." But it is not always clear what we can do on a global scale. We feel powerless. This contrasts with our enhanced global awareness: through the mediation of the internet, social media, and so on, I am now anxious and concerned about the whole world. I now know not only that "one" dies in my city or country, but also that "one" dies from COVID-19 everywhere in the world. AI and data science can also play a role here in producing global knowledge about "the pandemic." We get global statistics. This extension of our awareness also *globalises* our being-at-risk: we experience the risks and vulnerabilities associated with the pandemic in a way that relates us to the whole world. This increases anxiety.

6.3 POLITICAL-EPISTEMOLOGICAL ISSUES

However, AI and data science do not only inform and create knowledge and shape experience; they are also used to influence and steer human behaviour. More generally, they have effects on power. This takes us to the politics of AI and the pandemic. This topic can be discussed in terms of governmental policy regarding these issues, but use of these technologies also has more fine-grained consequences for the fabric of power as it pervades our lifeworld. Foucault's theory of power can help here, especially what we could call his *political epistemology*.

Foucault offers a number of concepts that can be used to theorise the role of AI and data science in the pandemic. The first concept is *biopolitics*. In his lectures for the Collège de France, he defines this concept as follows:

> The set of mechanisms through which the basic biological features of the human species became the object of a political strategy, of a general strategy of power, or, in other words, how, starting from the 18th century, modern Western societies took on board the fundamental biological fact that human beings are a species. This is what I have called biopower.[13]

Interestingly given the topic of this chapter, Foucault describes biopolitics in more detail by focusing on how society dealt with infectious diseases in the past. As Sarasin puts it,[14] Foucault identifies different "models" of how governments dealt with people under various biopolitical regimes: leprosy, plague, and smallpox. In his *History of Madness*, he describes how leprosy infirmaries were used to exclude the poor, vagabonds, the sick, and the mad from society; in *Discipline and Punish*, he describes how in the 17th century disciplining and the surveillance measures were used in response to the plague, and in his lectures for the Collège de France he describes smallpox and the use of statistical analysis: smallpox becomes a problem of epidemics and statistical effects.

The latter is of course very relevant to the topic of AI and data science in the pandemic. In the current pandemic, governments have used all of these methods, but this time propelled by AI and data science. Quarantine, disciplining, and statistical analysis are still used, but now time AI helps to monitor if people observe quarantine and distance, surveillance by AI can lead to disciplinary measures, and statistical analysis and data collection are the basis of machine learning AI, which is used for instance in the form of analysis of big data about the pandemic at a national and global level. Artificial intelligence and data science thus enable new forms of population control and management, new biopolitics.

Consider, for example, how in the pandemic people were (are?) put under surveillance by means of drones and AI: Sylvia mentions the use of drones with loudspeakers in China, analysis of biometrical data and social distance in the US, and the use of AI and cameras to monitor if people observe quarantine in Russia.[15] New technologies thus enable old forms of biopolitics which, as Foucault shows, were already used in response to earlier epidemiological problems. But with AI these forms of separation, discipline, and analysis are much more efficient and enhance the possibilities of control: control of the population, control of bodies, and control of individuals. This raises concerns about authoritarianism and even totalitarianism: AI seems to enable "total" control and manipulation of people.

Using concepts from political philosophy, one can discuss the political problems with regard to AI in the pandemic by focusing on well-known political principles such as freedom, justice, and equality.

With regard to freedom, there are not only potential privacy violations (consider, for example, tracking apps), but also potential violations to the bodily autonomy of people and restrictions to freedom such as curfews that might become the new normal. There is always a risk of normalisation; governments extending a "state of exception."[16] The risk is not only or not so much that regulations will persist, but also that cultural ways of doing will continue.[17] Think about social distancing, for instance: will this continue after the pandemic? Will people continue to self-discipline? Moreover, often there are no direct and open restrictions to what Berlin calls "negative freedom"[18]—interference with one's actions and decisions—but rather various forms of covert manipulation and surveillance that also have a disciplinary effect.

To analyse this, Foucault's work is useful again. In Discipline and Punish, Foucault points to a form of discipline that is based on Bentham's design of the panopticon. The concept was initially applied to prisoners: the guards could see the prisoners, but the prisoners could not see the guards. In other words, they did not know if they were being watched, but they could be being watched. This had a disciplining effect on the prisoners. Foucault writes: "the inmate must never know whether he is being looked at any one moment; but he must be sure that he may always be so."[19] This "automates" power.[20] Similarly, in the pandemic, the presence of police surveillance combined with digital methods, including the use of

AI, have been used as methods of "panoptic" and automated surveillance: one keeps to the COVID rules from the government not so much because the police *actually* intervene a lot with the liberty of people, but because they *could* do so, *might* do so. Or in the case of AI: the cameras present in the public space *could* be linked to facial recognition software and biometric measuring *might* be in operation. Like speed camera boxes, of which one never knows if they are actually "occupied" by a speed camera, this has a disciplining effect on people, without the need for much actual police intervention. It's a form of discipline that encourages self-disciplining. It is not necessary to use force;[21] people discipline themselves.

Other issues raised by the pandemic concern justice. The pandemic has impacted some people—the most vulnerable, those with small businesses, those in some parts of the world (e.g. Latin America), etc.—more than others. This can be seen as an issue of justice: it is unfair, and this unfairness should be undone by taking measures that restore some for more distributive justice. Consider, for example, the unequal effects on the labour market,[22] but also racist biopolitics[23] and pandemic othering and blaming,[24] such as for example violence towards Chinese people in the US. In the context of the pandemic, often these matters of justice are also a matter of life and death: some people are given preferential treatment over others, which may result in the survival of the former and the death of the latter. Furthermore, there are intergenerational justice issues: who should take priority, young or old? There are diverging views on that across the globe.

Some of these issues can also be framed as issues concerning equality rather than justice. As António Guterres, Secretary-General of the United Nations, has put it:

> The virus is shining a spotlight on inequalities of all kinds. It poses the highest risk to the health of the most vulnerable, and its social and economic impact is concentrated on those who are least able to cope. Unless we act now, 100 million more people could be pushed into extreme poverty and we could see famines of historic proportions.[25]

Vulnerability is not only a useful term to talk about existential problems, but also a key concept that enables us to raise *political* questions—here injustices and inequalities.

If combined with the use of technologies such as AI, the worry is that these problems of injustice and inequality, including bias and exclusion, are exacerbated. It is well-known that AI and algorithms can be biased and, for example, reinforce racism.[26] Given that some people and groups are *already* disproportionately vulnerable to health risks and discrimination, including increased risk for exposure to COVID-19, the use of AI may make things worse: some groups might not be properly represented in training datasets, AI tools for decision making in clinical settings may be more harmful to members of these groups, and the AI tools themselves might have discriminatory effects.[27] In this way, AI threatens to further increase the vulnerability of people belonging to groups and communities that are already vulnerable. In a global context, the use of AI in the pandemic can have "colonial" aspects, at least in so far as it risks to further support the maintenance of the health of those that are already advantaged because they live in affluent societies. If and in so far it has these effects, it thus leads to the continuation of forms of injustice and inequality.

Problems concerning freedom, justice, and equality in a global context are also linked to problems with democracy: people who live in democracies might have fewer problems when AI is used to tackle the pandemic than people living in authoritarian states: through the use of AI, the latter are likely to be even *more* vulnerable to threats to their freedom than they already are, and this continues the unequal and arguably unjust distribution of vulnerability at a global level.

6.4 CONCLUSION

The pandemic reveals many existential and political vulnerabilities, including problems at the intersection of pandemics and the use of AI and data science. Influenced by Foucault and Heidegger, I have conceptualised some of the existential and political challenges raised by the pandemic and efforts to deal with it. This has led to reflections on our experience and knowledge of technological risk and existential vulnerability, also in a global context, but also to a brief overview of some political issues regarding the use of (biopolitical) power, restrictions to freedom, and threats to justice and equality—which again has global dimensions. Here, too, we could make a link to knowledge issues. For example, the panopticon produces a particular kind of knowledge and experience, which leads to self-discipline, and bias in a training dataset will likely lead to more bias and discrimination when AI is used in particular contexts, for example, in a medical context. The result is a map of existential and political issues and some useful starting points for the analysis of these problems.

One could ask, however, what *solutions* can be offered for these problems. Next to the protection of vulnerable people and the promotion of the mentioned political principles in the development of the technology (for example, design of AI that is less biased, avoidance of totalitarian tendencies in the use of AI), I recommend more work on the global dimension of the problems and the solutions. I already mentioned McLuhan in the context of thinking about fear and anxiety in "the global village" and I pointed out that there may be justice and equality issues regarding the global distributions of the consequences of the pandemic and the use of AI. But more philosophical discussion and research is needed on the psychological-existential and political aspects of the pandemic and AI in a global context, and on global ways of dealing with these issues.

For example, in an opinion article,[28] I have argued that global problems such as the pandemic and AI require global solutions. International cooperation is needed, but also a more supranational form of governance to effectively deal with a problem—COVID-19—that does not recognise national borders. One could also question the anthropocentric thinking in both the current analyses of the pandemic and thinking about the role of technologies such as AI in society. With his concept of biopolitics, Foucault brought life into politics but did not sufficiently criticise his anthropocentrism and failed to sufficiently conceptualise the role of technology in knowledge production; it is also necessary to bring *technology* into politics and vice versa. Resources from sociology and anthropology such as Latour's work (especially *We Have Never Been Modern*),[29] environmental philosophy, and posthumanist theory could be used to develop a less anthropocentric and perhaps less modern approach to thinking about the pandemic and AI, and more generally about politics, nature, and technology.

Furthermore, the pandemic also provides an excellent opportunity to critically question the idea that we should control the pandemic and control nature. Could it be that too much control is problematic? Asking this question is especially important in the so-called Anthropocene,[30] when humanity has become a geological force: we are faced with the problem that the hyper-agency of humanity has caused a lot of environmental problems, including a significant contribution to climate change. Is the pandemic also an *environmental* problem, perhaps one that is not completely natural but always already social and political? Is it an example of how our relation to nature has become so problematic that it is now turning against us? Is our modern way of dealing with nature *part* of the problem? Heidegger provides some starting points for such a reflection in his work on *Gelassenheit* (Heidegger 1999).[31] He argued that instead of more control, we should let go and adopt an attitude of releasement. It is not clear what this means and where such an investigation might lead us. But as human vulnerability is being transformed by new viruses, new technologies, and experimental medical interventions—also in a global context—we better reflect a little harder on this problem of control, on our attitude to nature, and indeed on the very concepts of "politics," "life," and "nature" themselves.

To conclude, the pandemic reminds us about our existential vulnerability (even if "one" is relatively "safe," *I* realise that *I* will die, sooner or later), makes us concerned and care (about ourselves and others), and creates biopolitical opportunities that should be critically evaluated by means of political epistemology and political principles such as freedom, justice, and equality. In this chapter, I have mapped the problems and shown how Heidegger's and Foucault's work can be mobilised to conceptualise them. More work is needed at this intersection of interesting topics, on their global dimension, and in the end also on philosophical questions regarding the nature of politics, its relation to technology, and the role and place of human beings on this planet. Like AI, the pandemic invites us to re-think what it means to live and exist here and now in a global and planetary environment pervaded by digital technologies, to question the kinds of knowledge and experience produced by science and technology, and to revisit the political challenges that keep infecting our societies and continue shaping the vulnerability and daily lives of concrete, living humans.

NOTES

1. Mark Coeckelbergh, *Human Being @ Risk: Enhancement, Technology, and the Evaluation of Vulnerability Transformations* (Dordrecht: Springer, 2013).
2. Julian Savulescu and Nick Bostrom, eds., *Human Enhancement* (Oxford: Oxford University Press, 2011).
3. Coeckelbergh, *Human Being @ Risk*.
4. Martin Heidegger, *Being and Time* (Albany: State University of New York Press, 1996), 234.
5. Heidegger, *Being and Time*, 245.
6. Heidegger, *Being and Time*, 133–134.
7. Heidegger, *Being and Time*, 132.
8. Coeckelbergh, *Human Being @ Risk*.
9. Michel Foucault, *Technologies of the Self: A Seminar with Michel Foucault*, edited by Luther H. Martin, Huck Gutman, and Patrick H. Hutton (Amherst: University of Massachusetts Press, 1988), 18.

10. Mark Coeckelbergh, *Self-Improvement* (New York: Columbia University Press, 2022).
11. Marshall McLuhan, *Understanding Media: The Extensions of Man* (New York: Mentor, 1964), 26.
12. Marshall McLuhan, *The Medium is the Massage: An Inventory of Effects* (Harmondsworth: Penguin, 1967).
13. Michel Foucault, *Security, Territory, Population: Lectures at the Collège de France 1977–78*, edited by Michael Senellart, translated by Graham Burchell (London: Palgrave Macmillan, 2007), 16.
14. Philipp Sarasin, "Understanding the Coronavirus Pandemic with Foucault?" *Foucaultblog*, 31 March 2020. https://doi.org/10.13095/uzh.fsw .fb.254.
15. J.J. Sylvia, "The Biopolitics of Social Distancing." *Social Media + Society* 6, no. 3 (2020). https://doi.org/10.1177/2056305120947661.
16. Giorgio Agamben, *State of Exception* (Chicago: University of Chicago Press, 2005).
17. Danielle L.Couch, Priscilla Robinson, and Paul A. Komersaroff, "COVID-19—Extending Surveillance and the Panopticon." *Journal of Bioethical Inquiry* 17 (2020): 809–814.
18. Isaiah Berlin, "Two Concepts of Liberty." In *The Proper Study of Mankind*, edited by Henry Hardy and Roger Hausheer, 191–242 (London: Chatto & Windus, 1997).
19. Michel Foucault, *Discipline and Punish: The Birth of the Prison* (New York: Vintage Books, 1995).
20. Foucault, *Discipline and Punish*, 202.
21. Foucault, *Discipline and Punish*, 202.
22. International Labour Organization (ILO), "World Employment and Social Outlook: Trends 2021." https://www.ilo.org/global/research/global-reports /weso/2021/WCMS_795453/lang--en/index.htm.
23. Sylvia, "The Biopolitics."
24. Kim Yi Dionne and Fulya Felicity Turkmen, "The Politics of Pandemic Othering: Putting COVID-19 in Globan and Historical Context." *International Organization* 74, no. S1 (2020): E213–230. https://doi.org/10 .1017/S0020818320000405.
25. António Guterres, "Tackling the Inequality Pandemic: A New Social Contract for a New Era." 18th Nelson Mandela Annual Lecture, 18 July 2020. https://www.unodc.org/ropan/en/message-of-the-secretary-general -in-the-nelson-mandela-day_-tackling-the-inequality-pandemic_-a-new -social-contract-for-a-new-era.html.
26. Safiya Noble, *Algorithms of Oppression: How Search Engines Reinforce Racism* (New York: NYU Press, 2018).
27. David Leslie, Anjali Mazumder, Aidan Peppin, Maria K. Wolters, and Alexa Hagerty, "Does 'AI' Stand for Augmenting Inequality in the Era of COVID-19 Healthcare?" *BMJ* 372 (2021). https://doi.org/10.1136/bmj.n304.

28. Mark Coeckelbergh, "Coronavirus and the Need for Global Governance." *E-International Relations* (April 2020). https://www.e-ir.info/2020/04/06/opinion-coronavirus-and-the-need-for-global-governance/.
29. Bruno Latour, *We Have Never Been Modern* (Cambridge: Harvard University Press, 1993).
30. Paul Crutzen, "The 'Anthropocene.'" In *Earth System Science in the Anthropocene*, edited by Eckart Ehlers and Thomas Krafft, 13–18 (Berlin: Springer, 2006).
31. Martin Heidegger, *Gelassenheit* (Stuttgart: Neske, 1999).

CHAPTER 7

Using Decision Theory and Value Alignment to Integrate Analogue and Digital AI

Mahendra Prasad

CONTENTS

DOI: 10.1201/9780429446726-7

7.1 INTRODUCTION

> For by Art is created that great LEVIATHAN and called a COMMON-WEALTH, or STATE, (in latine CIVITAS) which is but an Artificiall Man.[1]

We might interpret Thomas Hobbes as describing the state as an artificial man (or what we might call today an "artificial intelligence" (AI)), where the laws are algorithms by which this AI leviathan operates. This understanding could potentially be extended to any corporate entity, where the corporate entity acts as an "analogue AI" agent on behalf of human principals. This Hobbesian analogy is quite useful for understanding the relation between digital AI and politics. All known digital AI was created by humans (or by digital AI that was ultimately created by humans). The rules, procedures, and algorithms that regulate a digital AI were ultimately created by humans who were regulated by rules, procedures, and laws. These institutions are framed and developed by politics and group decision-making processes, and in democracies, by elections. In other words, roughly speaking, the laws, procedures, and institutions of government may be understood as analogue AI that regulates much of the development and usage of digital AI. For example, the analogue group decision-making procedures that decide the American presidency, Chinese paramount leadership, EU unity, Russian presidency, and UK prime ministership have huge downstream effects on the development and usage of digital AI, especially in an international race towards artificial general intelligence (AGI) (i.e. AI that has the general intelligence of a human).

For example, as we will later discuss in more detail, of all the 2016 Republican US presidential candidates, Donald Trump had the lowest approval rating among Republican voters during nomination process contests, but because of the particular group decision processes by which Republicans chose their nominee, Trump was able to win the Republican nomination. Additionally, despite not receiving the most popular votes, Trump still won the presidency, again because of the particular decision procedures used to elect the president. The fact that Trump was elected has had huge impacts on US policy with regards to COVID-19, which has killed over 100,000 Americans, and the George Floyd protests, which led to changes in policing policy (such as Amazon and Microsoft stopping sales of its surveillance technology to police) (Levy 2020). Thus, regardless of whether the downstream policy space is international security, nuclear proliferation, biosecurity, climate change, or AI safety, we know the rules, procedures, and laws (or algorithms) of analogue AI leviathans matter.

Additionally, group decision-making algorithms have an important impact on how digital AI behaves. For example, suppose a couple co-owns an autonomous vehicle, and one person wants to go to the movies and the other to dinner. How does the car decide where to go? At some level, it will have to take information from the human principals and aggregate it into a group decision binding on both passengers. Consider another example, the standard practice for an app is that the developer has a long contract specifying the terms of usage written up, and app users just click "agree." Today, many people have AI personal assistants, whether it be Google or Alexa or whatever. Barring catastrophe, is it unreasonable in 10 or 20 years for us to expect that our personal assistants will be reading the terms and conditions of an app, and highlighting any clauses which might concern us? In the coming decades should we expect that the AI personal assistant of an app developer and the many AI personal assistants of the app users and potential users negotiate the terms of usage of the app? What about countries using AIs to negotiate and enforce treaties and agreements between each other? Whatever exactly happens, we should reasonably expect that in the coming years, much group decision-making will be the interaction of multiple AIs, whether it be for appointment scheduling or traffic control of autonomous vehicles or treaty negotiations.

Roughly speaking, social choice theory is the science of group decision-making processes. Historically, since the 1950s, social choice has been a province of politics, economics, and philosophy, but interest has slowly declined since the 1970s such that by 2000, social choice research was primarily relegated to subfield journals in those disciplines. But since the late 1980s, interest in social choice has grown in computer science, such that by the 2000s, it might be reasonable to claim that "sovereignty" of the social choice province was transferred to computer science. For example, at the annual conference of the Association for the Advancement of Artificial

Intelligence (AAAI), there is an entire subtopic keyword dedicated to social choice submissions (e.g. "Game Theory and Economic Paradigms: Social Choice/Voting").[2] Because modern social choice started out in the economics and politics literatures, the terminology of the field was based on voting and elections examples. When social choice became a part of computer science, computer science inherited much of this voting and elections language. One thing that should become eminently clear by the end of this chapter is how thoroughly intertwined politics and multiagent AI systems languages have become at the junction of group decision-making. But it is important to note that social choice is more general than just voting in political elections. While the language used carries the artefacts of elections and voting, it can basically be used to understand any group decision-making process where individual entities submit information to a system, where the system then uses this information to decide which action the group should take.

Typically, digital AI and analogue AI are studied separately; this can lead to large oversights on the big problems of the world where these two kinds of AI interact. In case studies I examine, I hope to show that decision theory (including but not limited to expected utility theory, empirical decision theory, algorithmic game theory, mechanism design, and social choice) and value alignment can offer a unifying framework to deal with big real-world problems that involve digital and analogue AI overlapping.

We proceed in the following manner. First, we provide background on value alignment and social choice, which forms a general framework for dealing with them. Second, as a simple case, we will non-technically discuss how using social choice to treat an analogue AI as a multiagent system allows us to use the same language for digital AI and analogue AI decision-making. After the first case, we will discuss two other mini-cases (2a on AI safety and 2b on Critch's theorem) that could also benefit from a holistic approach. My hope is that by the end of this chapter, researchers will shift from a paradigm that treats digital and analogue AI as distinct domains to be examined separately, towards one where these two kinds of AI are understood holistically (using value alignment and decision theory).

7.2 VALUE ALIGNMENT: WHEN ONE AI AGENT REPRESENTS MULTIPLE HUMAN PRINCIPALS

AI value alignment is the problem of aligning the behaviour of AI agents with the values of their respective human principals. Because human principals, represented by the same agent, may disagree about fundamental values and about what the agent should do, the agent can be confronted with the difficult problem of aggregating information from its principals to form a coherent decision on how to act. This is exactly the problem of social choice, which has made the social choice literature especially relevant to the AI value alignment problem. Mahendra Prasad provides a technical overview of social choice and value alignment, but unfortunately there is no reasonably comprehensive non-technical overview of social choice with respect to the value alignment problem.[3] Here we hope to provide a brief non-technical overview.

7.2.1 Baum's Taxonomy

Seth Baum argued that there are three kinds of questions that must be asked when using social choice to align AI: standing, measurement, and aggregation.[4] Standing refers to the identification of entities that have input in the group decision-making process. For example, this might be shareholders within a corporation or city residents in a municipal election. In an autonomous vehicle, it might be the passengers in the vehicle. Measurement refers to what information should be gathered from those with standing to make the group decision. For example, with plurality voting (i.e. first-past-the-post), each voter is asked to submit their top preference candidate, but with a single transferable vote (also known as Hare's method, instant runoff voting, and ranked-choice voting), each voter is asked to submit a rank ordering of candidates. When MIT's moral machine tried to construct the ethics of an autonomous vehicle, they asked over a million humans to make multiple binary decisions in hypothetical driving situations.[5] Finally, aggregation refers to how the system aggregates the information from those with standing, and outputs a group decision. For example, plurality voting chooses the candidate that is the top preference of the greatest number of voters.

It is important to emphasise how Baum's taxonomy intimately intertwines social choice with multiagent AI systems (MASs), an important subfield of AI. A MAS is a system of AIs that share information with the system, information which the system then uses to decide for the group of AIs. Standing specifies which AIs are voters. Measurement identifies what kind of information (i.e. ballots) AIs are allowed to submit. Aggregation determines how the system will aggregate the ballots into a group decision for the MAS.

7.2.2 Paradox of the Democratic Imposition Problem

We assume that a necessary (but not sufficient) condition of a democracy is that its decisions have procedural legitimacy, in the sense that decisions have procedural legitimacy if the procedures which output them are legitimate. In the context of democratic group decision-making, there is the democratic imposition problem. Specifically, suppose a group of individuals want to make a group decision democratically. Given that different voting systems can lead to different decisions (even if voters' underlying preferences and opinions remain unchanged), if the group wants to ensure a democratic decision, they have to democratically decide which voting system is legitimate (i.e. democratically decide how to decide). This can become an infinite regress unless there is unanimity, or a decision procedure imposed. Thus, in all likelihood, for large groups, democracy's procedures are paradoxically imposed. What the democratic imposition problem highlights is that social choice, while perhaps necessary, is not sufficient to democratically resolve group ethics and decision-making. Other things must also be taken into consideration to break the regress.

7.2.3 Four-Stage Sequence Heuristic

To address this regress, John Rawls borrowed Kenneth Arrow's four-stage sequence heuristic.[6] Prasad adapts these four stages (bureaucratic, legislative, constitutional, and principal) for AI. The bureaucratic stage refers to decisions an AI makes with almost no direct input from principals, but decisions at this stage are bounded by regulations created in the other three stages. At the legislative stage, the AI makes decisions with input from some or all of the principals, but these decisions are bounded by regulations created at the principal and constitutional stages. The constitutional stage represents the form, structure, and design of the AI. It regulates and specifies the legislative and bureaucratic stages, and is regulated by the principal stage. The constitutional stage can also specify a process for amending itself. The principal stage is the stage where the constitution is created and specified; it bounds and regulates the lower three stages.[7]

7.2.4 Procedural Legitimacy

Procedural legitimacy refers to the idea that if a procedure is legitimate, then the output of such a procedure is legitimate. While some take the strong stance that procedural legitimacy is sufficient for the democratic legitimacy of a corporation, government, or AI, a more commonly held view is that procedural legitimacy is a necessary condition of democratic legitimacy. This is because, for any large group of individuals, it is highly unlikely any unanimity will occur in group decision-making; thus, principals must at some level agree that while they may not be unanimous on a particular group decision, the group's decision is legitimate because it is procedurally legitimate. All of this suggests that to help ensure democratic legitimacy of corporations, governments, and AIs (that are acting as agents on behalf of groups of humans), procedural legitimacy of bureaucratic, legislative, and constitutional decisions flows from the principal stage, which is likely imposed to break the regress.

7.2.5 Risk Aversion Principle

Another principle that plays an important role is the risk aversion principle. Roughly speaking, it asserts that as we proceed along the four-stage sequence from bureaucratic to principal stages, we should become more risk-averse in our decision-making. This is because, as we proceed through the stages in this manner, the decisions become more important and more widely affecting. Under such important and wide affecting circumstances, we will want to give greater weight to choosing good enough with high probability, rather than risk system-wide catastrophe for the best.[8]

7.2.6 Mechanism Design

An important distinction to make is that between social choice and mechanism design. Most often, social choice is used to refer to the study of group decision-making processes; however, an (admittedly confusing) distinction is sometimes made in the literature between social choice, in a narrow sense, and mechanism design. Roughly speaking, in this narrow sense, social choice assumes voters honestly express their beliefs in ballots, while mechanism design assumes voters may misrepresent their beliefs to create a favourable outcome. For example, suppose that in the 2016 US presidential election, a voter honestly prefers Jill Stein over Hillary Clinton over Trump, and the voting system used is plurality voting. If the voter is honest, then they would submit a ballot for Stein. But suppose the voter believes Stein has no chance of winning, but Clinton does. To create a favourable outcome, this voter may misrepresent their beliefs and vote for Clinton instead.

We might seek to avoid using group decision rules that incentivise such misrepresentations of beliefs. Unfortunately, the Gibbard-Satterthwaite theorem and related results have, for virtually all practical purposes, demonstrated that no group decision rule can disincentivise all possible misrepresentations.[9] As a result, both the (narrow) social choice and mechanism design literatures have blossomed. Roughly speaking, social choice in this narrow sense will ask, "given voters are honest, what properties ought our group decision rule have, and what group decision rules have these desirable properties?" In other words, this narrow social choice focuses extensively on what the objective function of our group decision procedure should be. On the other hand, mechanism design tends to focus on the question, "given that voters may misrepresent their beliefs, what should be our group decision-making mechanism to best replicate the objective function assuming honest voters?"

7.2.7 Non-Deterministic Voting and Voting as a Game

There are two additional points to make that are especially important with respect to the two highest stages of the sequence (i.e. principal and constitutional). One is that the higher the stage, the more hesitant we should be about using non-deterministic decision-making rules. First, due to the risk aversion principle, we seek less risk in decision-making at higher stages, and non-deterministic decision rules tend to be riskier. Second, non-deterministic voting systems, which tend to be more robust to misrepresentation, also tend not to take advantage of the law of large numbers, which make them less likely to make competent decisions. Third, as the stakes of decision become larger, it greatly incentivises some players to corrupt the non-deterministic process used to make the decision, because it is more difficult to prove corruption of non-deterministic processes than deterministic ones. For example, there have been lottery games with million-dollar prizes that were corrupted by the lottery administrators to ensure their friends won the lotteries and shared the prizes.[10]

Second, some have argued that given the endemic nature of misrepresentation in voting, rather than treating voting systems as attempts to identify a corporate entity's will, we should treat voting as a game where voters are understood to misrepresent their opinions to win the game of the election. If everyone understands this is the nature of the election, and the optimal strategy is intractable to determine, then it can be a fair game if everyone has some possibility of not losing. What this treatment fails to consider is that this interpretation is highly advantageous for those with extensive computational resources. For example, take a relatively simple game like chess or Go. We might say it is fair if Magnus Carlsen, the current world chess champion, is the world champion because no unaided human can currently defeat him in a chess match. But let us say I were to team with DeepMind to compete against an unaided Carlsen. I would crush him. That may sound trivial, but this could easily extend to international relations. For example, a treaty or agreement may decide that when some conflict arises, the conflict is resolved with some intractable negotiation game. Such a mechanism would be hugely biased to those who have resources, because like chess, while no one may be able to currently optimally solve it, those with computational resource advantages could potentially easily crush others.

7.2.8 Condorcet, Social Choice, and Institutional Design

Arguably, the first theorem in the study of MASs was Condorcet's jury theorem, which is also considered one of the first theorems in social choice. Discovered by the 18th-century French mathematician, philosopher, and revolutionary, Nicolas de Condorcet, approximately speaking the theorem can be stated as follows: suppose a true-or-false proposition is presented before a group of voters. With respect to the proposition, each voter either votes true or votes false. Condorcet's theorem roughly states that if voters are sufficiently honest, knowledgeable, independent thinking, and numerous, then the probability that a majority of voters are correct in their judgement of the statement asymptotically approaches one.

To ensure democracy tended to track correct judgements, Condorcet contended that society needs background institutions that promote honesty, knowledge, independent thinking, and numerousness among voters. For example, Condorcet argued that education should be universally free for all persons to promote knowledge, and that suffrage should be universal regardless of race, sex, or sexuality to increase the numerousness of voters.[11]

Condorcet understood different sets of background conditions could suggest different decision procedures to aggregate votes to lead to better decisions. For example, in the case where a group of low knowledge and low independent thinking 3-year-old preschoolers and a high knowledge adult preschool teacher are deciding when the class should cross the road, it is easy to model the situation and show that if we want to maximise the probability of the class crossing the road safely, we should effectively allow the adult teacher to be a dictator when it comes to deciding when to cross the road.[12] Unfortunately, for Condorcet, he did not have access to computers that would allow him to approximate good enough decision methods when background conditions were not simple corner case examples, like the ones he could easily calculate. Fortunately for us, we have access to computational resources and MASs, which allow us to get approximate answers to two questions: (1) given a particular set of background conditions, what are best or good enough voting methods by which to aggregate individual judgements into an aggregate group judgement? And (2) given the goal to use a particular group decision-making process, how do we need to change background conditions so that the particular group decision-making process produces good judgements? For example, with respect to the preschool class case, teacher dictatorship is the best decision rule given the background conditions, but let us suppose our goal is for each student to eventually learn how to cross the road using their own judgement. Given such a goal, it is clear that we must increase the knowledge and independence levels of the preschoolers, perhaps through institutions that teach kids how to cross roads. Again, this is just a corner case, but more complicated cases can be dealt with using MASs and algorithmic game theory.[13]

7.2.9 Sociopathy and Sen's Paradox

One thing Condorcet seemed to believe was that as a person becomes more enlightened (roughly speaking, more knowledgeable and rational), then the more likely that person will be altruistic. However, many today would argue that this is not necessarily the case; for example, they might note the classic prisoners' dilemma as disproving this assertion. Roughly, we might describe someone as having a sociopathic utility function if (a) that person's utility increasing is dependent on other people's utilities decreasing (i.e. others suffering) or if (b) that person requires their utility to be greater than that of other people (i.e. envy), even if this means lowering everyone's individual utilities.[14] For example, there exists several excellent group decision-making processes and properties (e.g. Pareto efficiency, Vickrey auctions, Brams-Taylor procedure) that have normatively desirable characteristics when people behave in a manner that can be modelled with non-sociopathic utility functions, but can lose those desirable characteristics when people have sociopathic utilities.

For example, Pareto efficiency requires that when all voters prefer x over y, then the group decision process should socially rank x above y. This has intuitive normative appeal. But Sen's paradox shows how when people experience envy, Pareto efficiency can cause unexpected and arguably undesirable results. To see this, consider Louie and TOM, who are respectively the mascots of archrivals, the University of Louisville (L) and the University of Memphis (M). Louisville plays at the KFC Yum! Center, while Memphis plays at the FedEx Forum. The colours of Louisville are red and black (RB), and the colours for Memphis are blue and grey (BG). Suppose that the colours of the home courts are decided by Louie and TOM voting. There are only two colour schemes under consideration in each court: L's home court painted RB (LRB), L painted BG (LBG), MRB, and MBG. Because each court can only be painted in accordance with one scheme, there are four possible alternatives under consideration by Louie and TOM: (1) painting both courts in Memphis' colours, (2) painting both courts in their rival's colours (3) painting both courts in their respective home team colours, and (4) painting both courts in Louisville's colours. Obviously, both Louie and TOM would most prefer that both courts be painted in their respective school colours (e.g. Louie would prefer both courts be painted RB, while TOM wants BG for both courts), while both mascots would least prefer that both courts be painted in their rival's colours (e.g. Louie would least prefer both courts painted BG, and TOM least prefers RB for both courts). However, assume both mascots have sociopathic utilities where they would prefer they both suffer than they both being happy (e.g. Both Louie and TOM prefer painting both courts in their respective rival's colours, rather than painting courts in concordance with their home's colours). In other words, for example, Louie would prefer (to suffer and see TOM suffer) than (to be happy and see TOM happy). Thus, any Pareto efficient decision procedure would choose painting both team courts in the rival's teams' colours over painting both team courts in their respective home colours. If, on the other hand, the mascots only had restricted domains of influence (e.g. Louie chooses Yum! Center colours and TOM chooses FedEx Forum colours), then these restrictions would produce a Pareto non-efficient outcome.

Sen's paradox highlights the important relationships between social choice, interdependent utilities, and domains of influence (e.g. property rights).[15] Better understanding these relationships can help us create and structure analogue and digital AI that minimise sociopathy.

7.3 THE 2016 REPUBLICAN PRESIDENTIAL NOMINATION PROCESS: CASE STUDY 1

Historically In US politics, party elites have shaped party nomination processes, whether through political wrangling of political bosses in "smoke-filled rooms" or invisible primaries.[16] Because elites framed nomination processes, they could narrow down the number of candidates and proposals available in popular primaries, caucuses, and referenda to a very small number. Since there were so few candidates, the fact that many primaries and caucuses used plurality voting could be virtually inconsequential.

Today, things are different. First, the rise of the internet has allowed candidates and interest groups to find funding, publicity, and organisation outside of traditional political elites.[17] For example, it is much easier now with the internet for a candidate to raise millions of dollars by receiving many small (less than a thousand dollars) donations. The 2016 Republican nomination of Trump in the US and Brexit passage in the UK are evidence of this global trend of support and bases arising from outside of traditional elites.

Second, in the US context, the *Citizens United* ruling has effectively allowed candidates to run indefinitely long campaigns if they can find a few donors that are willing and able to bankroll an entire campaign. There is a strong incentive for a donor to donate in such a manner because even if the candidate has a small chance of winning, if they win, the winning candidate is deeply beholden to the few donors. In the past, because of campaign contribution limits, US candidates had to find several donors who could contribute medium amounts (thousands of dollars) to sustain a campaign. Under such circumstances, the donor did not feel the candidate was beholden to the donor, and it became much harder for a candidate to raise enough money to sustain a campaign. They would drop out.

With these reduced constraints, the number of candidates in nomination processes has ballooned. In the 2016 Republican presidential nomination race, there were 17 major candidates; in April 2019, there were 19 major Democratic candidates for president.[18]

The fact that the internet has given candidates the ability to develop bases outside of traditional elites can be interpreted as being more democratic. The problem is that election mechanisms have not evolved to handle this technological change.

The current election mechanism in almost all primaries and caucuses in the US is *plurality voting*. Under plurality voting, each voter chooses one candidate, and the candidate with the greatest number of voters wins. The problem with plurality voting is that as the number of candidates increases, its susceptibility to the spoiler effect increases quickly. Because under plurality voting, each additional candidate reduces the number of votes necessary to win, each additional candidate acts as a potential spoiler allowing some candidates with a low amount of support to win the election.

7.3.1 What's the Matter with Plurality Voting?

When there are two candidates in a plurality voting race, a candidate needs at least 50% of the voters to have a mathematical chance of winning. If there are three candidates, at least 33.3%; four, 25%; five, 20%.[19] With 17 candidates (as there were in the 2016 Republican presidential nomination race), the winner needs at least 5.9% of the vote. With 19 candidates (as there were in the 2020 Democratic presidential nomination race in April 2019), the winner needs at least 5.3%.

This means that a candidate with a really small voter base can potentially win the election because of all the vote splitting. We can see this in the 2016 Republican presidential nomination race. During the 2016 US presidential race, Hart Research Associates/Public Opinion Strategies conducted occasional NBC News/Wall Street Journal surveys of nationally representative Republican primary/caucus voters.[20] The "Date" column in Table 7.1 specifies approximately when such polls were conducted, starting in March 2015 and ending with April 2016 (Trump, de facto, secured the Republican nomination at the beginning of May 2016). Almost all polls listed in Table 7.1 contained two questions.

First, there was a *support question* which was roughly stated as "I'm going to mention a number of people running for president in 2016. For each one, please tell me, yes or no, whether you could see yourself supporting that person for president in 2016."[21] The poll lists the percentage

TABLE 7.1 Trump's Rankings among 2016 Republican Presidential Candidates as Ranked by Republican Voters

Date	Trump Support	Trump Plurality	# of Candidates
Mar-15	12th	NA	14
Jun-15	12th	11th, 12th, 13th	16
Jul-15	7th	1st	17
Sep-15	6th	1st	15
Mid Oct-15	3rd	1st	13
Late Oct-15	2nd	2nd	13
Jan-16	3rd	1st	11
Feb-16	4th	2nd	6
Mar-16	4th	1st	4
Apr-16	2nd & 3rd	1st	3

Hart Research Associates/Public Opinion Strategies, "NBC News/Wall Street Journal Survey." I want to thank Rohit Shetty for finding this data set: Shetty, Rohit. 2016. "Trump, Product of a Flawed Balloting System." *HuffPost*. April 25. https://www.huffpost.com/entry/trump-product-of-a-flawed_b_9773370.

of Republican voters that express support for each Republican candidate. This measurement is akin to approval ratings. Using this information, we can rank order Republican candidates based on the percentage of support they received from Republican voters. The column, "Trump Support" in Table 7.1, expresses Trump's rank among Republican candidates based upon Republican voter support.

Second, there was a *plurality question* which was roughly stated as "And, if the Republican primary for president were being held today, which one of the following candidates would you favor."[22] This is akin to a plurality voting election. Using this information, we can rank order the Republican candidates based on the number of plurality votes they would receive. The "Trump Plurality" column in Table 7.1 expresses Trump's rank among Republican candidates based upon Republican voter plurality votes. With this, we can now look at Table 7.1.

Let's go over a few rows of Table 7.1 to clarify how it is read. For the poll conducted in March 2015, Trump ranked 12th out of 14 Republican candidates with respect to Republican voter support. (The plurality question was not asked in the March 2015 poll.) In April 2016, when there were only three candidates left, Trump was tied for second and last place in terms of Republican support; however, he had the most Republican voters that ranked him as their top choice.

What Table 7.1 makes eminently clear is that among Republican presidential candidates, Trump never seems to have had the most support from Republican voters. Even at the end, when there were only three candidates left, Trump tied for last place. However, in the last eight polls, he always had the largest plurality, except on two occasions, when he came in second. Because Republican primaries and caucuses use plurality voting, and Republican Party delegates are roughly apportioned on the winner-take-all principle, Trump would consistently win delegates even when he had plurality voting victories based on a very small base within the Republican Party.

I want to emphasise the fact that plurality voting can lead to the election of candidates with very few supporters is a non-partisan phenomenon. For example, it could be argued that conservative Ross Perot served as a plurality voting spoiler to 1992 Republican presidential candidate George H.W. Bush, who would lose to the Democratic nominee, Bill Clinton. In other words, the plurality voting spoiler effect hurts both left- and right-wing candidates.

Approval voting could have avoided the spoiler effect. Under approval voting, each voter marks each candidate she supports.[23]

Whichever candidate is supported by the greatest number of voters wins. The NBC News/Wall Street Journal surveys show that the plurality voting winner would have been different from the approval voting winner (i.e. candidate with the most support) in the 2016 Republican presidential race. That is an empirical argument. What I hope to show in the next sections are normative arguments for approval voting in party nomination races.

7.3.2 Condorcet's Paradox

There are several normative arguments for majority rule on two alternatives. The big caveat here is two alternatives, because these arguments can collapse when we generalise majority rule to multiple alternatives with majority preference. To see how, consider Condorcet's paradox, displayed below in Table 7.2.

Note that in Table 7.2, there are three voters and three candidates (x, y, and z). Voter 1 prefers x over y over z. And so on. Now let us suppose that between every pair of candidates, there is a majority preference race. The results of those majority preference races (based on preferences in Table 7.2) are in Table 7.3.

Table 7.3 is straightforward to read. For example, consider a race between x and y. A majority of two voters (i.e. voters 1 and 3 from Table 7.2) prefers x over y, while only one voter (i.e. voter 2) prefers y over x. With a victory margin of 2 to 1, x is the majority preference winner.

Notice, a majority prefers x over y, and a majority prefers y over z. If majority preference were transitive, then this should imply that a majority prefers x over z. This is in fact not the case. A majority prefers z over x.

TABLE 7.2   Condorcet's Paradox Example: Ballots

	1st Preference	2nd Preference	3rd Preference
Voter 1	x	y	z
Voter 2	y	z	x
Voter 3	z	x	y

TABLE 7.3   Condorcet's Paradox Example: Majority Preference Pairwise Winners

Race	Majority Preference Winner	Victory Margin
x vs. y	x	2 to 1
y vs. z	y	2 to 1
z vs. x	z	2 to 1

In other words, a majority prefers x over y over z over x. This is akin to saying "3 > 2 > 1 > 3." Just as that intransitivity of numbers makes the notion of three as the largest of the listed numbers meaningless, the intransitivity of majority preference makes the notion of the best candidate meaningless. The preference of the majority can be meaningless.

7.3.3 The Paradox of Unanimous Consent and Majority Preference

Suppose three broke graduate students are out late at night and are hungry. Suppose only one place is open at this time, which is a pizzeria, which only sells three kinds of whole pizza pies: (b)eef pepperoni, (c)heese, and (p)ork sausage. Each student only has one dollar to spend, each pie costs $3, and the pizzeria does not sell slices. The three students decide to vote on which pie to buy. Each of the three students submits the following information, as expressed in Table 7.4.

Note in Table 7.4, pizzas that a voter would consent to purchasing are bolded. From Table 7.4, we know that voter *1* prefers pork over beef over cheese, but would consent to purchasing any of them. Voter *2* prefers pork over cheese over beef, but consents only to pork and cheese. Voter *3* prefers cheese over beef over pork, but consents only to cheese. Notice pork is preferred by a majority over cheese, and also preferred by a majority over beef. So pork is the majority preference winner. On the other hand, beef is consented to by one voter, pork by two voters, and cheese by three voters. Cheese maximises the number of voters who consent to the winning pie, so the cheese is the consent of the majority winner. There are two things to notice about Table 7.4.

(1) The majority preference winner is distinct from the consent of the majority winner.

(2) Majority preference does not necessarily choose a candidate with unanimous consent, though one exists.

While consent of the majority always chooses a candidate with unanimous consent when one exists, the consent of the majority winner does not have

TABLE 7.4   Paradox of Unanimous Consent and
Majority Preference: Example

	1st Preference	2nd Preference	3rd Preference
Voter 1	p	b	c
Voter 2	p	c	b
Voter 3	c	b	p

to have unanimous consent, because unanimous consent does not always exist. What is interesting is that majority preference fails to choose a candidate with unanimous consent, *even when one exists*. This should be troubling for social contract theorists. For both John Locke and Jean-Jacques Rousseau, the social contract must have consent, in some form, from each citizen, to be legitimately binding on all citizens of a state. Given unanimous consent is near impossible in large societies, some might concede that majority preference is enough because it is the closest we can get to unanimous consent. However, this is erroneous because even when there is a candidate with unanimous consent, it can fail to be chosen by majority preference.

7.3.4 Approval Voting

These are all nice normative points about the consent of the majority, but the question arises, how is this implemented when there are multiple candidates? This is through approval voting. Each voter marks each candidate she is willing to consent to, and whichever candidate is consented to by the greatest number of voters is selected the winner.

For example, if each candidate is conceived of as a potential contract, and each voter marks each contract she is willing to consent to, then the contract that the greatest number of voters consents to is implemented by approval voting. Because approval voting can maximise the number of consenting voters, it maximises the number of voters who are self-determined. If a candidate that did not maximise the number of consents is elected (i.e. an approval voting winner is not elected), then the number of voters subjected to a winning candidate that they did not consent to is increased. Very importantly, approval voting is transitive when there are multiple candidates, so the intransitivity problems which arise, when majority preference is generalised to multiple candidates, do not occur.

7.4 TWO GLOBAL POLITICS MINI-CASES IN NEED OF FUTURE WORK

We will examine two mini-cases here: AI safety and Critch's theorem.

7.4.1 AI Safety: Case Study 2a

> Artificial intelligence is the future, not only for Russia but for all humankind. It comes with colossal opportunities, but also threats that are difficult to predict. Whoever becomes the leader in this sphere will become the ruler of the world.[24]
>
> Vladimir Putin

There is a widespread belief in the AI global politics community that whichever country dominates AI will dominate the world.[25] A growing fear in the AI safety community is that with countries like the US, China, Russia, and others rushing to dominate AI, they will place safety concerns on the backburner. With safety only given secondary considerations, the concern is that an AI catastrophe is just waiting to happen. The hope of the AI safety community is that AI researchers will cooperate in their efforts to develop AI; hopefully, this cooperation will help build trust that allows for safety to be taken seriously. But the process of developing trust includes the ability to come to agreements and keeping them. This is one facet in which approval voting can be useful.

Typically, we want safety agreements that are strong but not so strict that no major player is willing to accept the terms of the agreements. At the same time, we want a broad consensus that major players will abide by, but we don't want to require a consensus that is so dispersed, a minor player has veto power over important safety features. Approval voting provides a mechanism (or at least the starting point for the design of a mechanism) for the construction of AI safety agreements that have the largest possible number of major players consenting.

Another aspect of such international AI safety agreements is the issue of who is negotiating the agreements. Presumably, the negotiators (at least from democracies) will be elected officials or persons ultimately appointed by elected officials. Ensuring that elected officials represent the broad consensuses of their respective countries, as opposed to narrow interests, is important to ensure that those countries actually implement international agreements in the long run. The use of approval voting in single-winner elections, especially within party nomination processes, can significantly stabilise democratic decision-making.

7.4.2 Critch's Theorem: Case Study 2b

In the immediate future, there is a very low probability that states will use digitally implemented algorithms to do the bulk of negotiating international agreements and treaties. However, we know that today in securities markets, such as stock markets, algorithms make the overwhelming majority of trading decisions. In the coming decades, while there is no guarantee, there is a reasonable possibility that international political/governmental interactions will become so complex and fast, it will become the case that governments, corporations, and NGOs will use algorithms to make, negotiate, and implement agreements and decisions.

This leads us to an important mathematical result that affects that possibility. Andrew Critch generalised Löb's theorem to proof systems with bounded computational resources.[26] With this result, Critch was able to demonstrate that if the algorithm players in classic non-cooperative games (e.g. prisoners' dilemma) are able to read each other's source codes, then such expected utility-maximising players can achieve mutual cooperation. For example, in the two-player prisoners' dilemma, when expected utility-maximising players know each other's source codes, players will both cooperate or both defect, but never be in a situation where one cooperates and one defects. This is a superior equilibrium for both players compared to the classic Nash equilibrium, where both players defect.

This has huge implications on treaties, agreements, and contract negotiations. Conceivably, Critch's scheme could be used by states, NGOs, or any other parties involved in a dispute to negotiate solutions to collective action problems, like armed conflict, climate change, trade wars, and epidemic response. While each party could delegate their negotiation responsibilities to a digital AI algorithm, there is still a huge analogue AI component in play, in terms of (1) determining the source code of their AI negotiator, (2) ensuring its source code's transparency, and (3) ensuring other players are being transparent with their source code. The usefulness of Critch's scheme cannot be fully developed without serious examination of this analogue AI.

7.5 CONCLUSION

Traditionally, political problems and digital AI problems are considered in separate problem spaces. But as more problems overlap both spaces, the need to examine these problems holistically across both spaces arises. In this chapter, we hope we have demonstrated that by interpreting the rules and procedures of states and other corporate entities as the algorithms of analogue AI, we are better able to integrate these two spaces with decision theory and value alignment in order to better solve our problems. The body of our argument consisted of three sections.

Analogue AI typically takes the form of group entities, such as governments and corporations. The science of group decision-making is social choice. In our first section, we summarised important aspects of social choice. One, Baum's taxonomy broke group decision-making into three parts: (1) which individuals have standing, (2) what information is taken from individuals with standing, and (3) how is that information aggregated to form a group decision? Two, the four-stage sequence specifies a hierarchy of group decision-making levels, which in reverse order are: (4) bureaucratic group decision-making which is done with little or no consultation with the principals and is bound by the higher three levels, (3) legislative group decision-making, which is ordinary group decision-making that is done with consultation of some or all of the principals and is bound by the higher two levels, (2) constitutional group decision-making specifies the form, structure, and design of legislative and bureaucratic decision-making, and (1) principals group decision-making, where the principals decide how they want their constitutional level structured. Three, the risk aversion principle asserts that because the higher levels of group decision-making are what make AI sustainable in the long run, typically as we ascend higher in the four-stage hierarchy, we want AI to be more risk-averse in its decision-making. This suggests that, heuristically speaking, as we ascend the hierarchy, decision-making should become less non-deterministic. Four, institutions which promote honesty, independent thinking, knowledge, universal suffrage, and disincentivise sociopathy among individuals in a group can be systematically important in improving group decision-making.

In the second section, we non-technically covered a case where the group decision-making procedures of an analogue AI could be understood as a multiagent system. Specifically, despite Republican voters giving Trump the lowest approval rating among Republican presidential candidates, and despite Trump not receiving the most popular votes, the decision-making institutions of the US elected Trump as president in 2016. This of course had huge implications on American policy towards Afghanistan, China, Iran, North Korea, Russia, space militarisation, COVID-19, and the George Floyd protests.

In the third section, we covered two mini-cases, where the integration of analogue and digital AI needs more examination. In the first mini-case, we discussed how AI safety is heavily dependent on getting states to cooperate towards non-belligerent and cautious development of AI. In the second mini-case, we discussed how Critch's theorem, a recent result in logic, could significantly improve cooperation and agreement between states involved in collective action problems. However, for this theoretical result to be put to practical use, we must better understand how to integrate the analogue AI state's behaviour with that of digital AI acting on behalf of the state.

The COVID-19 pandemic is an instructional analogy regarding the importance of studying analogue and digital AI, both at their interfaces and holistically. That horrible pandemic had both dire health and economic consequences. Healthcare professionals are taught to focus on minimising the spread of disease. Economists are taught to avoid recessions. During April 2020, healthcare professionals argued for sheltering in place, and the elimination of non-essential economic activities that could not be done in the shelter, to reduce the number of pandemic deaths. Some economists have argued that shutting down such economic activity will cause layoffs, debts, and bankruptcies leading to a recession severe enough to lead to a number of indirect deaths dwarfing those that would be caused by the pandemic; this is partially why Sweden (in April 2020) was rejecting near-universal calls to order sheltering in place. During the middle of this crisis (during which this is being written), it is virtually impossible to say what is the proper tradeoff between the epidemic and recession, given that both can cause a large number of deaths, because relatively few resources have been dedicated to understanding these tradeoffs.

What I have tried to demonstrate in this chapter is similar to the pandemic situation. Specifically, I want to emphasise that analogue AI has a huge impact on digital AI, and vice versa; hueing our research focus to fit academic specialisations rather than real-world problems can lead to catastrophes. As I hoped to have demonstrated in my examples, decision theory and value alignment offers a means of a more holistic approach that better bridges the interfaces of the different kinds of AI.

ACKNOWLEDGEMENTS

This chapter has been improved by comments from Maurizio Tinnirello, two anonymous reviewers, and a copyeditor. All remaining errors are those of the author alone.

NOTES

1. Hobbes, Thomas. 1651. *Leviathan*. http://www.gutenberg.org/files/3207/3207-h/3207-h.htm. The many grammatical errors (by 21st-century English standards) in this Thomas Hobbes quote from the *Introduction* of Hobbes' *Leviathan* have been left uncorrected.
2. AAAI. 2020. "AAAI-19 Keywords." *Association for the Advancement of Artificial Intelligence*. 2 March. https://aaai.org/Conferences/AAAI-19/aaai19keywords/.
3. Prasad, Mahendra. 2018. "Social Choice and the Value Alignment Problem." In *Artificial Intelligence Safety and Security*, edited by Roman V. Yampolskiy, 291–314. Boca Raton: CRC Press.

4. Baum, Seth. 2017. "Social Choice Ethics in Artificial Intelligence." *AI & Society*: 35, 1–12.
5. Noothigattu, R., S. N. S. Gaikwad, E. Awad, S. Dsouza, I. Rahwan, P. Ravikumar, and A. D. Procaccia. 2017. "A Voting-Based System for Ethical Decision Making." *ArXiv.org.* https://arxiv.org/pdf/1709.06692.pdf.
6. Arrow, Kenneth J. 1963. *Social Choice and Individual Values.* New York: John Wiley and Sons; Rawls, John. 1999. *A Theory of Justice.* Revised. Harvard University Press, Cambridge, Massachusetts.
7. Prasad, "Social Choice and the Value Alignment Problem": 297.
8. Prasad, "Social Choice and the Value Alignment Problem": 297–298.
9. Taylor, Alan D. 2005. *Social Choice and the Mathematics of Manipulation.* Cambridge: Cambridge University Press.
10. Prasad, "Social Choice and the Value Alignment Problem": 299–300.
11. Prasad, Mahendra. 2019. "Nicolas de Condorcet and the First Intelligence Explosion Hypothesis." *AI Magazine*: 40, 29–32.
12. Prasad, Mahendra. 2019. "Rational Group Decision-Making." *YouTube.* Centre for Effective Altruism. 18 December. https://www.youtube.com/watch?v=6KqjT21fbT8.
13. Prasad, "Rational Group Decision-Making."
14. Prasad, "Social Choice and the Value Alignment Problem": 308–311.
15. Sen, Amartya. 1970. "The Impossibility of the Paretian Liberal." *Journal of Political Economy*: 78, 152–157.
16. Cohen, Marty, David Karol, Hans Noel, and John Zaller. 2008. *The Party Decides.* Chicago: University of Chicago Press.
17. By "traditional elites" or "elites of a party" in the US context, I am primarily referring to elected government officials, party leadership and high level bureaucracy, major donors and fundraisers, and large-membership organisations that align with the respective party at the federal, state, or local levels.
18. By "major candidate," I mean a candidate who at some point was a CEO, congressperson, senator, governor, or secretary of a federal department. I have also added Pete Buttigieg due to his popularity in April 2019. It should be added that plurality voting with a large number of candidates does not guarantee that a candidate with low support will win; rather, increasing the number of candidates increases the probability that such a low support candidate will win. This is why it is possible for Joe Biden, who had large support within his party, to be the presumptive 2020 Democratic nominee (as of June 2020).
19. If there are n candidates, a candidate needs at least $1/n$ of the votes to have a shot at winning.
20. Hart Research Associates/Public Opinion Strategies. 2015, 2016. "NBC News/Wall Street Journal Survey."
21. Hart Research Associates/Public Opinion Strategies. March 2016. "NBC News/Wall Street Journal Survey": 9.
22. Hart Research Associates/Public Opinion Strategies. March 2016. "NBC News/Wall Street Journal Survey": 12.

23. Alternatively, each voter could be asked to mark each candidate she "approves." Or each candidate she "consents to."
24. RT. 2017. "'Whoever Leads in AI Will Rule the World': Putin to Russian Children on Knowledge Day." *RT*, 1 September. https://www.rt.com/news /401731-ai-rule-world-putin/.
25. Scharre, Paul. 2019. "The Real Dangers of an AI Arms Race." *Foreign Affairs*. https://www.foreignaffairs.com/articles/2019-04-16/killer-apps.
26. Critch, Andrew. 2019. "A Parametric, Resource-Bounded Generalization of Löb's Theorem, and a Robust Cooperation Criterion for Open-Source Game Theory." *Journal of Symbolic Logic*: 84, 1368–1381.

CHAPTER 8

Nomadic Artificial Intelligence and Royal Research Councils

Curiosity-Driven Research Against Imperatives Implying Imperialism

Vassilis Galanos

CONTENTS

DOI: 10.1201/9780429446726-8

8.1 INTRODUCTORY REMARKS ON SCOPE, METHOD, AND THEORY: WHY AN EXAMINATION OF ARTIFICIAL INTELLIGENCE RESEARCH AS AN ARENA OF NOMADS AGAINST THE ROYALS

[T]he policy, practice, or advocacy of extending the power and dominion of a nation especially by direct territorial acquisitions or by gaining indirect control over the political or economic life of other areas. Broadly: the extension or imposition of power, authority, or influence.

(Second definition of "imperialism" in
Merriam-Webster)

[D]esire to know.

(First definition of "curiosity" in
Merriam-Webster)

What are we to make of terms such as "imperial" or "royal" applied in artificial intelligence (AI) research and discourse? While the phrase "global politics of AI" may pinpoint to political impacts AI technologies have at a global level, in order to avoid a technologically deterministic and speculative point of view (as suggested in Science and Technology Studies (STS) literature[1]), it may be far more productive to look at what kind of politics are already imbued in the social history and construction of AI. For reasons of economy and scope, in this chapter, I examine research practices mostly in the UK (occasionally compared to US- and EU-related practices) using the conceptual metaphor of royal and nomadic science.[2] Further explained below in this introduction and throughout the chapter, this theoretical template (not a sharp framework) suggests that radical science progresses in a nomadic, mobile manner, allowing researchers-nomads to make the most out of available resources in order to develop what might be recognised as innovative science. Opposed to them are State regimes, exploiting or withholding resources, aiming to absorb the nomadic knowledge to their advantage, keeping nomadic researchers in controlled stasis. I recommend that due to lessons from the history of AI (further analysed below), the metaphor of a nomadic AI can be a particularly useful tool to map the political processes of global movement in AI research.

8.1.1 A Note on Method: Theoretical and Empirical Tools

8.1.1.1 First Lessons from Interviews with AI Specialists in the UK

While writing this chapter, I am conducting long-term interview-based research on AI specialists[3] with research questions very different to the ones posed here. At the time writing, I have collected 23 interviews lasting between one and two hours of people who work in areas related to AI, such as machine learning, algorithmic training, bioinformatics, computer vision, autonomous vehicles, intelligent robotics, and several areas in-between or around these disciplines. The selection of candidate interviewees involved systematic research within academic institutional websites, according to the usage of such terms on academics' personal biographic notes. Of the 23 interviews, only few 11 of them were transcribed by the time writing; hence, direct quotes reflect only but part of the research; however, the remaining 12 interviews do not deviate largely from what this chapter reports on, and the present chapter is only a stepping stone towards more concise empirical research on the complexities of a sociology of AI. The interviews are anonymised, hence allowing the informants to express themselves as honestly as possible. My interviewees are invited to share the reasons they chose to work in their current institution(s) and describe their working routines and funding sources. The general view I have obtained so far has to do with the serendipity involved in the process, as none of the interviewees so far have claimed that they had a specific goal to work in their respective (and respected within the AI community) institutions; they usually accepted an offer they have been made. Their everyday routine appears to be essentially fund-oriented. None of them so far have spoken of their personal inspirations and aspirations unless asked; they have not spoken of an institutional agenda either. Instead, the available government-based Research Council projects shape the expectations of what is to be produced by their laboratories.

8.1.1.2 Nomadic and Royal Science: From Cybernetics to AI
The theoretical framework to analyse the above observation stems from philosopher Gilles Deleuze and psychoanalyst/philosopher Félix Guattari's book *A Thousand Plateaus: Capitalism and Schizophrenia*, and in particular in their brief, yet rich, analysis of what they designate as a framework of royal (or State) and nomadic types of science.[4] The chapter applies this framework by dividing it into two main directions— roughly speaking: hypotheses—and relating these to AI research and regulation dynamics: first, I examine whether there is reason enough to consider the royal/nomadic metaphor within AI domains and if this is the case, to what extent, if any, AI researchers manage to take advantage of the State, and/or whether the State manages to appropriate and regulate AI research. I quote the few sentences that Deleuze and Guattari use to develop their concept in the case of networks and hierarchies of AI-related institutions, in order to show the complex dynamics AI practitioners face amidst the wave of a recent AI hype, which involves speculation disseminated by non-practitioners, and a race towards governmental monetary support, strangely benefitting each other, according to my reading of recent relevant policy documents, the aforementioned interviews and other related material from historical and social studies of AI. At this point, I should state that the present work would greatly benefit from a concise history of AI. To my knowledge, the only existing reference works on the topic are (1) Crevier's 1993 work (that I heavily draw upon throughout the chapter), which is as much invaluable due to its uniqueness as it is also outdated and relatively partial (for example, UK and Japan histories of AI are referred to only scarcely as means of comparison to American developments); and (2) Nilsson's 2010 detailed tome on the development and history of AI, which is very rich in explicitly conceptualising the differences between the schools of AI (and related approaches) thought, but again, and maybe unavoidably, partial since it reflects on a single US-based person's—nonetheless impressive— memory and understandings. A similar case for UK developments can be found in the surprisingly uncited 1982 work by Fleck (1982), which is still in need of updates from the last three decades. Thankfully, due to conference visits, I am now aware of work being conducted on the history of AI, as well as great sociological work on comparing AI policymaking attempts; however, such work remains unpublished to date (Plasek's 2016 paper *On the Cruelty of Really Writing a History of Machine Learning* explains some of the cruelties, although, only a fraction of

them; unpublished work by Jon Agar and Jacob Ward will make a great contribution to the AI history jigsaw puzzle). If such work is eventually produced, the hype might have served its purpose.

I do not claim any radical originality in applying Deleuze and Guattari's scheme of nomadic/royal sciences on the field of AI, as this chapter can be seen as a continuation of STS theorist Andrew Pickering's usage of this theoretical framework as an explanatory device of the social history of cybernetics.[5] Given that AI can be seen as one of the key intellectual successors of cybernetics, I suggest that applying Deleuze and Guattari's thinking on AI research and development is contributing to Pickering's existing analyses and has a double benefit: first, Deleuze and Guattari's (and Pickering's) framework is proven to be relevant in a field more contemporary than the 1950s–1970s timeframe of early cybernetics examined in Pickering's work; second, but most importantly, AI, which happens to be hyped for the third time in its history will benefit from an early analysis of the politics involved in its development (see Grudin's 2009 work for an early suggestion of the third hype cycle; Sluckin's 1960 Pelican popular science book *Minds and Machines* is a particularly good resource showing the transition from cybernetics to AI and it also stands as evidence that AI was hyped in the late 1950s).

To understand the conceptual metaphor of nomadic science without overly analysing the vast Deleuzian (or Deleuzoguattarian) oeuvre, it suffices to mention the context of *The Thousand Plateaus*, which is a broader philosophical metaphor rejecting traditional convenient geometrical metaphors and accepting that reality can better be described in geological terms, or in terms of land movement; for example, and punning after philosopher Friedrich Nietzsche's book *The Genealogy of Morals*, they prefer to examine *The Geology of Morals*.[6] Within that broader geological metaphor employed in their *Thousand Plateaus*, Deleuze and Guattari place emphasis on the importance of science and technology progress and decide to view scientists as nomads who travel and harness the vast geological terrains (to analyse more of their theory would go far beyond the scope of this chapter). What suffices to say, and while Deleuze and Guattari do not explicitly mention it, while it becomes obvious while reading their text, is that they draw a distinction between (a) settled States who try to expand their grounded authority in territories beyond their settlements, and (b) nomadic scientists whose curiosity leads them to explore science and who travel in order to find the best conditions (climatically or financially) in order to do so. As it will be shown below, this distinction becomes fluid depending on the circumstances. This is how Pickering introduces the concept in question:

> The royal sciences are the modern sciences, which function as part of a stable social and political order—which prop up the State. The nomad sciences, on Deleuze and Guattari's reading, are a different kind of science, one which wanders in from the steppes to undermine stability.[7]

My personal choice for the employment of this metaphor (that I first explored several years ago but never applied to any research output) was inspired first by some interview statements (quoted below) of surprising coherence with the theory, and second by its previous usage in Pickering's work. Pickering suggests then that early cybernetics was a nomadic scientific movement that was born precisely as an outcome of the radical, anti-establishment, counterculture, even psychedelic tendencies of the mid-20th century.[8] In his reading, the royal sciences are "aligned with the established order" and "aspire to grasp the inner workings of the world through knowledge and thus to dominate it and put it entirely at our disposal";[9] thus, they make use of nomadic knowledge production in order to control and dominate. This brings us to the important two-faced meaning of the word control: on the one hand, early cybernetics[10] had to do with the advancement of a science of control and communication, that is, a strategy for humans to navigate between the chaotic structures of the universe and create controllable "intelligent" machines to produce desired outcomes; on the other, the establishment's control and maintenance of social order as a means of domination. The *royal* sciences, as shown below, are acting in ways that absorb the nomadic sciences' advancement of control strategies to their own merit. Pickering speaks of a "protean" quality in cybernetics, using as examples the career paths (both intellectual and physical) of early pioneering cyberneticists such as Ross W. Ashby and Gray Walter, whose "nomadic wandering" allowed them to develop their cybernetic thinking and adjust the nature of their jobs (and use their resources) to develop cybernetics further. That much for the nomadic mobility of cybernetics. Pickering further comments on the radical nature of this scientific nomadism that sometimes threatens the commonly accepted order:

> Bateson was intensely critical of orthodox psychiatry, and his analysis [...] implied a drastic departure from orthodox modes of

therapy [...] Here we approach Deleuze and Guattari's sense of the nomad as a threat to the State and the established social order.[11]

If AI is treated as a product of early cybernetics,[12] and since cybernetic thinking drew largely from mathematical reasoning,[13] it is particularly interesting to note that Deleuze and Guattari place emphasis on the history of mathematics to substantiate their argument on royal and nomadic science:

> Democritus, Menaechmus, Archimedes, Vauban, Desargues, Bernoulli, Monge, Carnot, Poncelet, Perronet, etc.: in each case, a monograph would be necessary to take into account the special situation of these savants whom State science used only after restraining or disciplining them, after repressing their social or political conceptions.[14]

Given such a lineage of the struggle between the radical mathematicians who evolved, partly, into cyberneticists, it may be reasonable to claim that something similar is happening with AI researchers. However, this further highlights a mild weakness of the metaphor when it comes to AI. Opposed to abstract mathematics in the age of antiquity and/or the Renaissance, AI, in most cases, requires much more expensive equipment. This appears to render the theory incompatible with AI; however, I suggest that it acts like a precise point of departure to speak about ways in which the clear boundary does not actually work—which is this chapter's main assertion.

At this point, it seems that the position I hold presently is at odds with Pickering's interpretation of the movement from cybernetics to AI. Pickering makes an argument on the marginality of cyberneticists becoming even more intense, precisely because the "military bought it" and "[a]lmost all the funding for AI research was provided by the US military," leading cybernetics to lose "much of its social basis in the universities from the mid-1950s onward; the cyberneticians became even more marginal there than they had been before."[15] My objection, which I think complements Pickering's observations on the nomadic nature of such sciences, is that no matter the label, AI or cybernetics, the same division between royal or nomadic sciences has been preserved, and a closer look at the inner workings of both Deleuze and Guattari's nomadic war machines (next section) and the oscillation of AI workers between royal and nomadic statuses will exemplify the precise nomadic nature of the field.

This chapter's scope does not offer any suggestions on whether AI is or is not possible, or how research should be shaped in order to achieve "true" AI, as several other works have covered this area.[16] Instead, it is recommended that the critical recognition of AI research as overly driven by competitive national strategies should give rise to more free-moving, curiosity-based research. Finally, it should be stated that the present metaphor of royal/nomadic sciences is not, by all means, the only way to speak about the relationship between networks of "core" scientists, governments, media, consumers (and so on)—in the case of AI, for example, I have shown elsewhere, by applying Collins and Evans' third wave of expertise scheme,[17] how prestigious influencers with little or no expertise in AI influence media portrayals of AI as well as policy negotiations.[18]

8.2 NOMADS SURVIVING AI WINTERS: DARPA AND THE WAR MACHINES

It would seem that a whole nomad science develops eccentrically, one that is very different from the royal or imperial sciences. Furthermore, this nomad science is continually "barred." Inhibited, or banned by the demands and conditions of State science.[19]

8.2.1 How to Become a Nomad by Applying for State Grants

Developing AI is expensive. It requires the collaboration and coordination of several different tribes of nomads: computer scientists, mathematicians, electrical engineers, neurologists, linguists, psychologists, just to name a few of the main disciplines that AI relates to.[20] It further requires the coordination of groups of people with very different backgrounds and methodologies; such requirements are very difficult and expensive tasks in academia. Moreover, the material side of AI, the hardware, machinery, storage, and so on, requires additional financial support. In order to secure grants for developing such projects, AI founders gave to potential funders grandiose promises until they eventually crystallised an AI niche amidst the competition of different scientific fields in the early 1950s.[21] These stakeholders included the institutions which had an interest in appropriating the knowledge of such technical advancements: the military was a good candidate to ask for grants. Crevier[22] offers a very detailed account of the mobility of early AI developers such as Marvin Minsky and John McCarthy until, eventually, after a series of conferences and working space dislocation, Minsky and McCarthy were settled at the Massachusetts Institute of Technology (MIT) by 1962.

> On 27 June 1963, MIT received a $2,220,000 grant from a newly created Defense Department agency: the Advanced Research Projects Agency (ARPA) was created after Sputnik to ensure that America would never again be caught with its technological pants down [...] Minsky [...] was to be the principal beneficiary of the part of the grant that went to the AI group, a full third of the total amount.[23]

Hubert Dreyfus, known for his early critiques against AI imaginary promises,[24] spoke more recently of "first-step fallacies" (cf. Turing's 1950 well-cited future views and the most famous 1958 predictions by Simon and Newell[25]). The unrealisability of such early promises, after a big expenditure of government money, has led twice to the phenomenon of AI winters, that is, "[...] pessimism in the AI community, followed by pessimism in the press, followed by a severe cutback in funding, followed by the end of serious research."[26] Two such AI winters have been observed so far: the first is considered to be the period between 1974–1980 and the second from 1987 to 1993, while some specialists have expressed concerns for a third AI winter.[27] The first winter was marked by the document *Artificial Intelligence: A General Survey*, authored by Sir James Lighthill,[28] ordered by the then Science Research Council in the UK, and offered a particularly pessimistic view on the promises given by AI researchers until that time. Crevier points out that the report resulted in severe funding cuts not only in the UK but also in the US. Moreover, it led to a nomadic movement of certain AI researchers from the UK to the US:

> As a result, his 1973 report called for a virtual halt to all AI research in Britain. This recommendation led to the quasi-dismantling of top-flight research groups, such as that at the University of Edinburgh, and to the emigration of eminent British AI workers to the United States.[29]

That much for the first AI winter, resulting from an initial settlement of AI nomads in institutions that were military-funded, eventually dismantled since the State disproved their ability to help with their agenda. The second AI winter followed a similar cyclical pattern of grandiose expectations followed by disillusionment. The first step is succinctly synopsised by Grudin:

> In 1981 as in 1958, a foreign threat reinvigorated AI funding. Japan, brimming with success in manufacturing, launched the "Fifth-Generation" AI effort, built upon the logic-based Prolog language. Reaction was swift. The US Congress amended antitrust laws to permit the founding of the AI-based consortium MCC in 1982. In 1983, US government funding for speech understanding and other AI technologies ramped up sharply, with DARPA again leading the charge. Annual funding for its Strategic Computing Initiative (SCI) rose over time, reaching $400 million (in today's US dollars) in 1988. The European ESPRIT and UK Alvey programs began in 1984 with annual AI expenditures of over $200 million [...] As the 1980s ended, DARPA was unhappy. It had spent $2 billion (in today's dollars), and there were no autonomous land vehicles. There were no pilot's associates or battlefield management systems. Natural language-understanding products foundered in the marketplace. Funding was cut, and a long winter set in.[30]

This rise-and-fall pattern observed in AI funding and cuts, hype and disillusionment, has also been described as AI's phoenix-like cycle of rebirth.[31] An interesting characteristic of this rebirth is the protean transformation of AI names to mask the relevant content from grant application evaluators who may be aware of the previous branding: AI then transformed into various "new" technologies such as expert systems, multiagent systems, fifth-generation computers, machine-aided cognition, neural networks, and so on. Something similar can be said to have happened in post-2010 AI hype with buzzwords such as machine learning or deep learning, occasionally misplacing references to AI (although one may argue that all these technologies are sub-disciplines of the broader field of AI). One may think of an explanatory principle based on the comparison between short- and long-term effects of AI winters: in the short-term, AI winters cause stagnation of funds, something which might happen in the case of any disillusioned technological novelty presented as innovative (as shown by Rayner's conceptualisation of the "novelty trap"[32]); in the long-term, I suggest that the discontinuities of research in AI combined with the allusive AI imaginary expressed in science fiction, as opposed to other sciences, results into the constant reinvention of hype. Whatever is the case, scientific AI nomadism advances thus in two ways: AI researchers mobilised themselves aiming at taking advantage of military operations to advance their technologies; and AI *per se* changed its appearance to fit within application schemes. This leads to a twofold question given the last decade's concern with the impact of AI/robotics research on autonomous weapons and other military operations:[33] does AI research and development become a tool of the State's image, and what is to be expected of AI scientists' responsibility when signing up for military grants? The next subsection is an initial attempt at elucidating this double—and admittedly complex—question.

8.2.2 Using War to Make AI, Not War

War does not necessarily have the battle as its object, and more importantly, the war machine does not necessarily have war as its object, although war and the battle may be its necessary result (under certain conditions).[34]

Maybe academic scientists have no time to think of war in times of academic competition and maybe their everyday routines in terms of securing grants are obscuring some of the unintended outcomes of their technologies' development. When asked about the difference or overlap between an individual and an institutional agenda, one of my interviewees explained the funding procedures which enabled his multidisciplinary large-scale collaborative project to continue and perform as the members (and him as the leader) wish it to do so. His constant references to a tribalism of academics was actually one of the main reasons which inspired the present reflections on Deleuzian nomadism:

But in fact, what happens is the money comes in, and because [this is] the way the funding works in the UK, there's no checkpoints after that, the money is given as a block grant, it's not sort of doled out on a three-monthly basis or on a six-monthly basis; so there's no incentive really for people to collaborate What there really is, [is] an *incentive* for people to say that they'll collaborate. That's a very scathing view of it, but it's actually true, when you work on very large multi-scale projects with lots [of] different partners, it's really the way that it works out: once the money comes in, people revert back to their sort of tribal nature, and they try and push their agenda towards their own sort of career promotion and making their name in this specific field as opposed to working objectively on projects without any regard to sort of hierarchy and interdependence of people's positions on one another.

(INTERVIEW 6; AI-ROBOTICS RESEARCHER
WELL-KNOWN FOR SEVERAL SUCCESSFUL
INTERDISCIPLINARY PROJECTS)

This captures particularly well the way in which AI researchers need to act nomadically in order to push forward their own academic agendas, taking advantage of the available grants provided for reason A and using them opportunistically for reason B (or a modified reason A). Another researcher, however, expresses a rather confrontational relationship between nomadic and State sciences by referring to the lack of curiosity-driven research, similar to the early mathematical foundations of cybernetics and AI described in the introduction:

> [G]overnment organisations always have to be doing something different to justify their existence, I guess. So, you'll find you have a special programme, and let's say electric cars, and then they'll say "right, that's been done, let's move on to the next one." And the problem may not always be solved. So you are limited by what the Research Council is funding. Allied to that [is] the balance between Research Council or indeed industry-driven research and the abstract maths I was talking about. You know, what would you call curiosity-driven research, nobody's interested [in] and has definitely changed; a lot. So it's harder now to have PhD students that are completely free in their topic.

(INTERVIEW 4, AUTONOMOUS VEHICLES AND
COMPUTER VISION SENIOR SPECIALIST)

In this sense, we see the emergence of a double form of nomadic existence. On the one hand, the marginalised nomad, limited and confined by the State's programmes (military operations, (D)ARPA, Research Councils, national strategies)—very similar to the marginalised nomads-mathematicians described by Deleuze and Guattari above, and their cyberneticist successors as described by Pickering. On the other hand, the nomadic war machine, the opportunity-seeker and tribal leader (or member) who transforms the State grants into a nomadic craft, something which has not really been advanced by Pickering's reading of Deleuze and Guattari. It might be worth questioning whether, by acting so, AI specialists become, in a sense, traitors of their anti-establishment pack. When asked about the possibility of threats in research, a senior researcher working on the intersection between AI, robotics, human–computer interaction, systems engineering, and virtual environments with a long "migratory" career from specialism to specialism and institution to institution, responded "I think if there's a threat, I'll, I'll just move. You know, I'll go where the money is. Yeah [laughs]." Later, in the same interview I asked him to relate this possibility of moving with his interdisciplinary institution's long-term visions and unity politics. His response exemplifies exactly the way academic opportunism in AI (and related fields) is built through a dialectic of survivability of the institution if there is sufficient connectivity between disciplines and survivability of the individual should the institution collapse:

> If you find yourself more to the computing side, you probably live there, you'll be very comfortable in your own space, but it'll be very difficult for you when you go to another dimension, you know, another space, because it's outside your comfort zone. And this is exactly what the [name of institution] has: many uncomfortable zones where people don't actually interact. Yeah? I mean, you can see from my research here I do lots of stuff, because I come from a systems point of view. Yeah? I do coding; I do AI, do neuro, I do neuroscience, I do social science, I do physiology. Yeah? So, for me, communication isn't an issue because it's the research that I do; I cross many, many sectors. And I don't care whether I apply my technology to robotics or not. This is to me, it's just another sector. I have tools that can bridge any one of them, so I'm not worrying where I go. That's why I say I can leave at any time. It doesn't bother me.
>
> (INTERVIEW 11)

The question can be viewed in light of this two-way stretch between the poles of tribal opportunism and marginalisation; however, a possibly pragmatic response may be that the phenomenon is rather messy and liminal, on the borderline between responsibility and survival;[35] AI scientists are aware of the potential unintended outcomes of their research, but have no other option when sources are limited. As Deleuze and Guattari ascertain: "Most significant are perhaps borderline phenomena in which nomad science exerts pressure on State science, and, conversely, State science appropriates and transforms the elements of nomad science[36]" or as further explained later:

What we have [...] are two formally different conceptions of science, and, ontologically, a single field of interaction in which royal science continually appropriates the contents of vague or nomad science while nomad science continually cuts the contents of royal science loose. At the limit, all that counts is the constantly shifting borderline.[37]

To put it more simply, convenient divisions between "good" AI scientists versus "evil" governments (or conversely, "mad" AI scientists and "heroic" regulatory bodies) are not realistic, as the two "formally different" groups of scientific progress *in tandem* and of course at many different levels (a national strategy for science and technology appears different to pure military operations, but what certifies that the two categories are not benefitting from each other?).

This borderline shift is captured in the statements of two interviewees (one of them being quoted again above) when they elaborate on their views on autonomous weapons development and the general relationship between AI and the military. The first quote further illustrates the continuation of the nomadic nature of AI funding past the second AI winter, as this recently retired researcher describes events happening in the early 1980s:

And then I got money from the Defence Technology Centre, and that was where we did the autonomous vehicle work. Then again, that was quite open-ended; I am not a pacifist, I'm not a militarist; I don't like weapons. I think there's no point in having armed forces that are not the best in the world instead of having second best-armed forces in the world, but I despise and loathe the arms trade and the selling of arms to third parties, but it gave, doing autonomous vehicles research, gave us space to do the research we wanted to do. So we had, yeah, 4–5 years funding from there, but almost entirely it's been government funding with a little bit of industrial support, but largely the industrial support has been peripheral because they've been interested in exploiting the possible outcomes rather than actually being engaged with research right from the start

(INTERVIEW 1, COMPUTER VISION, AUTONOMOUS VEHICLES SPECIALIST, WITH PARTICULAR "HOBBYIST" INTEREST IN THE HISTORY OF AI).

The same interviewee who reflected earlier on the more abstract problem of the lack of research about abstract mathematics in AI, in agreement with the previous informant, encapsulates the paradoxical condition where, while having weapons and warfare is questionable in the first place, given that there are weapons, more accurate ones are desired:

So are you saying, I mean, is a guided missile ethically worse than an unguided missile? [pause] You could argue [...] I mean, look, you could argue that a guided missile is actually better because there's less collateral damage. Certainly, it's a debate you should have. I mean, I realise it's a debate about whether you should fire a missile at all. But, I mean, if you think of the Second World War carpet bombing, they just, you know, it just hammered Dresden. How many were killed in Dresden? I don't know, but surely guided missiles are better than that. So they just bombed indiscriminately because they couldn't target accurately.

(INTERVIEW 4)

So far, this section has explored in more detail one of the two movements in the reciprocal nomad–State science relationship of appropriation, namely, how AI researchers managed to establish their field and survive AI winters by the early circulation of promises and the strategic (or opportunistic) use of funding schemes. The next section will explore the strategies developed (intentionally, unintentionally, or semi-intentionally) by the State to appropriate, regulate, and limit AI research.

8.3 2013–2016: RESEARCH COUNCILS IMPERATIVES AS ROYAL SCIENCE IMPERIALISM

The fact is that the two kinds of science have different modes of formalisation, and State science continually imposes its form of sovereignty on the inventions of nomad science.[38]

With the exception of the introduction and conclusion, Deleuze and Guattari's *A Thousand Plateaus* consists of 13 chapters whose headlines are year numbers; significant events that happened during a certain period act as points of departure for their philosophical analyses. This section will focus on a short period instead of a year, in order to capture a specific moment in the dynamic between royal and nomadic sciences to support the argument in question: 2013–2016. The reason is that in 2016 several proposals and attempts at AI regulation and policymaking were made,[39] and the preceding three years, as I intend to show, played an important role in the preparation of this. In other STS contexts, Sørensen[40] has spoken of "learning by regulation," that is, the process in which studying the ways different relevant players involved in the production, dissemination, and adoption of a technology may try to regulate each other in order to effectuate their plans; usually, studying this *dynamic* (and not the "winners" or "losers") can be revealing with regard to what the technology actually is or does. Therefore, I suggest that examining how and in what context the State aimed to *appropriate, regulate*, and further *portray* AI (the three are interwoven and form a single mechanism, as I argue below), can be revealing in several ways when it comes to a sociology of AI. The regulations examined are not yet in practice, at least by the time of writing. But being able to historicise the *attempts* at regulating should be an interesting way to understand how the State's "apparatus of capture" works (to use another term from Deleuze and Guattari).

As happened in the early 1970s and the late 1980s (the two aforementioned AI winters), this royal apparatus of capture is a mix of factors such as parliamentary discussions, academic debates about AI-as-an-existential-threat, and the generalised journalistic hype which started around 2014 (more on this, below). This section's discussion will first take a look at a specific policy document from 2013, which can be understood as the beginning of a novel hype cycle, at least in the UK.

8.3.1 The Imperialism of Eight Great Technologies: Upon Examining How Royal Science Integrates Nomads and How Nomads Are Willing to Partake in the Game

As Summer's 2014 work shows in exceptional historical detail, computer-related rhetoric played a significant role in post-war Britain. His article begins by citing the influential 1978 BBC2 documentary *Now the Chips are Down*, in which the narrator states: "Programming is a particularly British skill. In fact, we invented it." Summer demonstrates how technology in Britain was used as a means to promote a nationwide technocratic vision of competence, in which the commercial hype of the 1950s about "electronic brains" was no exception. As Summer puts it succinctly in one of his article's subheadings: "Making British computers, and making computers British."[41] The same temperament was kept throughout the first wave of AI in the 1960s–1970s to the Thatcher era in which the Alvey programme emerged as a response to the Japanese Fifth-Generation Computers programme. Keeping this in mind as a line of historical context, let us examine the post-2010 hype-and-policy conundrum in AI and robotics. David Willetts, then a Member of Parliament, Minister for Universities and Science in the UK, published a policy report entitled *Eight Great Technologies* through the UK's largest think tank, Policy Exchange, in which he recommended that the "[g]overnment should be promoting with further capital investment and technology support"[42] with the aim to "make Britain the best place in the world to do science."[43] The use of such wording ("best place in the world") to promote a country's technological development seems like *imperative implying imperialism*; or, at least, given the vast complexity of the term "imperialism," a form of cryptoimperialism, masquerading as healthy international competition. Keeping in mind the distinction between nomadic and royal sciences, it is quite tantalising—for the sake of an empirical pun—to notice that this "report was published alongside the Chancellor's important speech to the Royal Society."[44] The Royal Society, literally coinciding with royal science, is in the UK context mainly responsible for the allocation of government funds for research, and was eventually convinced to support Willetts' eight great technologies (among which were robotics and autonomous systems) with a "£1.5bn of extra science capital investment."[45] In the same passage, he asserts that the technologies were selected according to three main criteria: their importance in terms of scientific advance, Britain's distinction in each respective area, and the identifiability of commercial advantages for each of these areas' technological output.

After comparing robotics advancements in Japan and Germany, Willetts set a clear national agenda of competition between the UK and the US: "In the US as well as Government setting a regulatory environment[46] DARPA has been promoting these technologies through sponsoring grand challenges and funding them. We are not leaving the development of these technologies to others."[47] In the same style of national strategy rhetoric, the technological concepts of "algorithms," "autonomous systems," "data flows," or "clinical medicine" are used as assets of UK's "comparative advantage" to other countries; and to those "world-class" assets, the national superiority of the British humanities are added:

Through the strength of the Humanities in our universities we also have a strong position in the ethical issues that arise—programming a scavenging robot and defining how it acts and in what circumstances should not be done in an ethical vacuum.[48]

A final point needs to be made about Willetts' 2013 report through the following quote, to situate the entire text more clearly within the royal-nomadic understanding of scientific advancement:

Research Councils provide grants for future research and training. Some of this funding pursues specific goals; much of it is driven entirely by the curiosity of researchers. Quite rightly, this adds up to a substantial level of freedom for academics to pursue curiosity-driven research while also making space for the pursuit of specific challenges.[49]

In a sense, the State created an obligatory distinction between Royal Society funding schemes (royal science) and curiosity-driven research (nomadic science) precisely by means of *linking* the two through an initial formal demonstration (a Policy Exchange report written by a MP): by being inviting towards nomad scientists in a rhetorical passive-aggressive manner, the State manages to regulate what their research agenda will be. Two interviewees have spoken to me about their relationship to Research Councils with regard to their work; I will use a few quotes to illustrate the argument set forth on the research constraints set by the rush of the State which relates, as shown by Willetts' report to the national competition:

I think research councils are under pressure, as I say, to get results. And perhaps they make promises that you know, "if we put an extra hundred thousand into electrical vehicles we will reduce pollution levels by ..." and the question is are they quoting academic studies? I guess the problem is the verifiability of those academic studies. So, [pause] when you're writing research proposals you have to write an impact study [...] So the question is when I'm writing a research proposal I guess I have to be kind of bullish about what doing this research may achieve [...] The

Research Council's expecting me to produce results [...] So if you can say this has generated a spinoff company, employed 40 people and that's enabled us to go to Mars, that's good, you know so, so, it's got to generate income, it's gotta generate income, and pay our salaries, it's gotta generate results to justify the government expenditure.

(INTERVIEW 4)

This particular interviewee stated earlier in the same interview that he had no particular involvement with advising Research Councils. This quote, then, expresses the opinion of a senior researcher with a long-time experience moving from grant application to grant application, funding body to funding body with no particular say in the process of what is eventually being funded. The next quote comes from a person being quite successful, albeit not as senior as the previous interviewee, with a certain degree of greater experience in being involved in scientific advisory panels:

So, if I'm a person of particular esteem in my community, then I'd be advised, I would advise the Research Councils [...] I've been on some of these things, consultation is what's up and coming in robotics that we should be looking into, you know, what are the sorts of future horizon-scanning things that we should be looking into that will help deliver on our Research Council's strategic goals, right? [...] so really, it all ties back to the top level of government and what they're looking for from the Strategic Advisory Panel is topics that fit within a scientific agenda that advance the things that come down from the top-level strategic priorities from the government. So at the moment, an example, a top, you know, example of this is in the Industrial Strategy Challenge Fund, right? So the Industrial Strategy Challenge Fund is not something that scientists are doing because they want to advance the economy in the UK. It's something which comes from a very, very, very top-level strategic position from the government, comes down through the base to Research Council UK, RCUK consults with members of esteem in the community, those members of esteem say these are the sorts of things which I or we collectively as a sort of council think we should be doing. They put out the call, the call comes down and then people, you know, effectively tend against that call; they put in their bid against that call. The problem with the system is that obviously the people [who] are best placed to take the money are the people that advised the research councils in the first place. So if I advise the Research Council that we should definitely be working on [area where the interviewee is specialised], for example, because it will help to underpin that UK strategic priorities in industrial innovation, they put out a call for robotics, for [this area] in particular using wording that I developed in my scientific advisory panel, I then apply against it, and I get the money, you know. The world is not a meritocracy.

(INTERVIEW 6)

The opposition between nomadic AI/robotics scientists and State science is not a clear-cut binary. As shown earlier through the war machine metaphor (DARPA funds appropriated by early cyberneticists and AI researchers), nomadic scientists compete to find niches to build their habitats. Nomads of different tribes are not members of a universal nomadic "proletariat"; they push forward their own agendas to get funds and survive in the next years. At this point, let us recall what the previous interviewee questioned about the quality of academic research being pushed forward and promoted via the Research Council imperative (or the royal science imperialism) and further question the relationship between pure curiosity-driven research and State-appropriated research. Could this be a reciprocal process of making science? If yes, is this form of appropriation an appropriate way? If not, are there winners and losers? A return to theory is relevant here: "State science retains of nomad science only what it can appropriate; it turns the rest into a set of strictly limited formulas without any real scientific status, or else simply represses and bans it."[50] That this science is of questionable quality—to the extent that, at least seemingly, curiosity-driven, pure abstract mathematics do not require the same amount of expensive equipment as compared to grant-driven, impact-based practical AI—is the concern of the next subsection.

8.3.2 Extending Royal Science to a Constellation of Mainstream Media and State Academics

If we wish to focus on the State's impact on science and technology research, it is useful to treat the abstract concept of "State" as something which extends beyond Research Councils and crystallises through media portrayals or supportive academic publications from different nomadic tribes who aim to establish their own habitats. Past Willetts' policy document, a novel wave of AI-related hype seems to have occurred. While a thorough analysis and presentation of this would exceed the present chapter's scope, in previous work[51] I have traced the impact of public statements made by prominent influential researchers such as Stephen Hawking, Elon Musk, and others, whose expertise in fields such as cosmology or entrepreneurship is undeniable, although their knowledge of AI matters is rather contestable. This latter phenomenon of "expert opinion" media coverage is denoted as "expanding expertise," that is, the concentration of prestige on one individual enabling a process of "gurufication" in the eyes of the press and the consumers of the press.[52] Simply put, people associated with prestigious institutions like Hawking and Musk have been quoted in the media of mass consumption on their views of AI being one of the most important and yet one of the most existentially threatening inventions of humanity and in three years' time generated a popular dystopian future view of AI. Such views are linked historically to older imaginaries of machines exceeding human intelligence capacities and have occasionally been denoted as "ultraintelligence" by Irwin J. Good in 1965, "singularity" by Victor Vinge in 1991, and "superintelligence" by Nick Bostrom in 2014.[53] There is a resurgence of such singularity hypotheses in the post-2013 media hype, and some of my interviewees have spoken about the questionable credibility of such statements and expanding experts:

> It's rubbish. I mean these people don't know what they're talking about. Really it's rubbish. And again, it's the entitlement and the hubris of people who are experts in one area, assuming they can be experts in all areas. Hawking doesn't have a clue, and he should know better, really. It's nonsense, really—fuels, it fuels public fears.
>
> (INTERVIEW 1)

While this quote questions such public figures' expertise and reflects upon the hubris committed, the next one furthers the argument through a comparison with actual current capabilities:

> I think we are still an awfully long way away from the kind of thing they're envisaging. I don't know whether Stephen Hawking gets any ideas or has any area of expertise in this at all. I really

don't have a good handle on how up to speed with this kind of thing Elon Musk is really, he might have a good engineering background, but his engineering background is not particularly in the world of AI.

(INTERVIEW 5, SENIOR PROFESSOR WITH EXPERTISE
IN AI, WITH SEVERAL PERSONAL CONNECTIONS
TO PEOPLE INVOLVED IN THE FORMATION AND
IMPACTED BY AI WINTERS).

And the same criticism against the narrative of AI-as-an-existential-threat is supported by the previously quoted expert in interdisciplinary applications of robotics and AI:

So people talk about the singularity, right? [...] For people who work on the inside of artificial intelligence and robotics, then we know that robotics is an extremely long way away from having any sort of credible threat to people's work, to people's jobs, to anything like this. And lots of the stuff that's published is, you know, scaremongering and sort of 40 years out because the state of the art in robotics really hasn't moved on that much in the last 50 years. It's moved on a bit, but hasn't moved on as much as we would have people believe by showing them science fiction films and this sort of stuff.

(INTERVIEW 6)

From this quote, it becomes obvious that (at least some) AI nomads are aware of the impact of previous bold promises and that they should be cautious about projecting future visions (positive or negative) of their fields. A final quote from a specialist's opinion on the feasibility of such arguments is revealing when it comes to the additional pressure such nomadic specialists receive as they find themselves caught in a web of Research Council applications having to remain up to date and scientifically excellent and media portrayals promoting warnings against the inherent "dangers" of being "overly" up to date:

[...] and the press loves this. So [sounds of excitement], you know "Oh yes, put him on. Yeah, he's the expert." And this is complete rubbish [...] Especially the singularity is complete rubbish. But people love it, and the press, so everyone reads the stuff, and they go "yes, you know, yes, we should worry about this," but it is complete rubbish. And most of us researchers will say so when we get an opportunity, but we are researchers. We can't spend our lives trying to correct everything in the flaming press all the time, particularly when the press doesn't want to hear it.

(INTERVIEW 2, HEAD OF PROMINENT MATHEMATICS
AND COMPUTER SCIENCE DEPARTMENT SPECIALISED
IN AI-ROBOTICS OVERLAPS)

Nonetheless, such criticisms of AI researchers against proponents of AI-as-an-existential-threat narratives express a probable financial incentive on their behalf—however, a counterargument to this counterargument could be that the first quote comes from a retired interviewee and everyone's recommendation is much more credible, given at least their direct involvement with the production of such technologies. In any event, let us look now at ways the State uses popularised academic discourse to assist regulatory frameworks. To add some historical context, Hawking's first public warning was published in *The Independent*, on 1 May 2014. Two months later, Nick Bostrom's book *Superintelligence: Paths, Dangers, Strategies* was published on July 2014 by the major academic publishing house Oxford University Press, and became a best-seller according to the *New York Times* (23 February 2015), offering an analytical speculative account on how AI may achieve human-like and suprahuman (and maybe anti-human) intelligence and what strategies should be developed in order to avoid such a threatening scenario. Tracing the history of the empirical evidence Bostrom is basing his book upon (although he acknowledges it should be taken lightly) is an interesting way to show how the State science, in order to justify its own agenda's funding scheme, "turns the rest [of the non-appropriated scientific content] into a set of strictly limited formulas without any real scientific status."[54] Bostrom's work claims to be supported by expert opinions[55] and produces with an analytical table of five different polls bringing together 170 respondents being asked about when machines are expected to reach human-like intelligence, suggesting a 10% likelihood that this will be reached by 2022, a 50% by 2040, and a 90% by 2075. The particularly interesting, in my opinion, part of this table is that it refers to a footnote at the end of the book, decreasing the possibilities that an average best-seller reader will read its content. The footnote reads as such:

> The table shows the results of four different polls as well as the combined results. The first two were polls taken at academic conferences: *PT-AI*, participants of the conference *Philosophy and Theory of AI* in Thessaloniki 2011 (respondents were asked in November 2012), with a response rate of 43 out of 88; and *AGI*, participants of the conference *Artificial General Intelligence* and *Impacts and Risks of Artificial General Intelligence*, both in Oxford, December 2012 (response rate: 72/111). The *EETN* poll sampled the members of the Greek Association for Artificial Intelligence, a professional organisation of published researchers in the field, in April 2013 (response rate: 26/250). The *TOP100* poll elicited the opinions among the 100 top authors in artificial intelligence as measured by a citation index in May 2013 (response rate: 29/100).[56]

Once again, Bostrom acknowledges the relative bias of the results[57] (without need to mention the question concerning people who did not respond deliberately); however, given the magnitude of the book, perhaps acknowledgement is not enough, especially since Bostrom has been associated with (and initiated one of the) three well-known institutes for research about potential implications of AI: the Future of Humanity Institute (FHI, of which he is the founder and director), the Future of Life Institute (FLI, in which he is member of the Scientific Advisory Board), the Leverhulme Centre for the Future of Intelligence (CFI, in which he is a member; it should be noted that in the opening ceremony of which Stephen Hawking gave a public warning about AI's catastrophic future), as well as the Centre for the Study of Existential Risk (CSER, member of the Scientific Advisory Board), according to the websites of all these institutes.[58] (The very emergence of these institutes and centres is sociologically very telling of "future" becoming a new academic currency.) A final note on the story of Bostrom's empirical foundation of superintelligence is the fact that the aforementioned survey study came originally from a paper[59] which, during the time Bostrom's book was published, was still in press, and of which Vincent Müller is the first author and Bostrom is the co-author; it was eventually published two years after Bostrom's book (the paper was published in 2016, although a preprint was available in 2014). Out of this survey, used as the sole empirical ground, which, as said, and as Bostrom admits, has great limitations, the entire book unfolds and becomes a best-seller. By 2019, the time of writing, the actual research article has 221 citations according to Google Scholar, as opposed to 1,720 works citing Bostrom's best-selling book—in which the questionable empirical evidence is expelled in the back of the book (prior to blind review of the present paper the numbers were 187 and 1,447, respectively—the surprising increase in a span of only three months is also very telling). This shows an interesting case of how the popularity of an academic subject and strategic presentation of data can play into the establishment of an academic niche, further attached to a broader trope of anti-AI hype. While Bostrom himself has been careful enough to write in his 328-page book that such arguments should be taken lightly and that it is mainly credence that one should give towards *the possibility and not the certainty* of superintelligence, what really took off in this case was not machine intelligence, but the popularity of the book.

Hence, during 2015, a co-construction of AI-as-an-existential-threat took place through the continuation of similar statements (as well as tweets) by prestigious public figures, together with a general journalistic hype exaggerating any small piece of news that had to do with AI/robotics (robots killing workers, stepping over toddlers, disliking people of colour, passing self-awareness tests, and so on[60]). At the same time, members of the European Parliament started negotiations for a motion to regulate AI and autonomous robots, which eventually led the following year to a study "to evaluate and analyse, from a legal and ethical perspective, a number of future European civil law rules in robotics."[61] Surprisingly, the arguments justifying the motion's initiation were based mostly on hype and not expertise:

> In 2014 and 2015, Bill Gates, Stephen Hawking and Elon Musk warned of the dangers posed by artificial intelligence, which could potentially turn against humanity. As stated in paragraph I of the motion for a resolution, humanity may be at risk of "AI [surpassing] human intellectual capacity."[62]

Out of Hawking and Musk, it is probably only business magnate and Microsoft founder Bill Gates who can be said to have some authority in AI due to his computer science background. However, as shown elsewhere,[63] Gates has publicly declared completely opposing views on AI in 2015 and 2018 (without mentioning a reason for a change of mind, hence, one would assume, in order to promote different agendas at different times; hence justifying the label of what is now fashionably called an "influencer"—where the influence has more importance than the content). In 2016, similar justifications of concern were forwarded by another policy report, this time from the UK House of Commons, three years after Willetts' report, which appears contradictory to this rather alarming document (It is useful to note here that since Willetts was Minister of State for Universities and Science from 2010 to 2014, he probably did not have a say during the negotiations from 2015–2016):

> There is continuing debate about when such general artificial intelligence might be achieved, as well as whether it is even possible. According to Professor Stephen Hawking and others, while it might be "tempting to dismiss the notion of highly intelligent machines as mere science fiction [...] this would be a mistake, and potentially our worst mistake ever."[64]

The last State science policy document to be published in 2016 about AI and robotics came from the US, under the presidency of Barack Obama. This document refers to Müller and Bostrom's article[65] on the likelihood of possibilities that AI has to achieve and/or exceed human-level intelligence:

> Although it is very unlikely that machines will exhibit broadly-applicable intelligence comparable to or exceeding that of humans in the next 20 years, it is to be expected that machines will reach and exceed human performance on more and more tasks.[66]

The same report recommends "[o]ne way to elicit frequent judgements is to run 'forecasting tournaments' such as prediction markets, in which participants have financial incentives to make accurate predictions"[67]—thus, bringing us back to the strategies advanced by the State in order to incentivise scientific progress in a regulated manner. Such attempts at regulatory frameworks of AI suffered from a very vague understanding of what constitutes AI—in a sense, they were more speculation-based than evidence-based. AI can be seen as an umbrella term containing many component technologies and many output technologies which might call for regulation or are already being regulated (e.g. autonomous weapons in terms of future regulation and/or the General Data Protection Regulation framework of current regulation).

One may argue: since such regulation proposals are not in practice, then why be concerned? A response could come from lessons learned from previous AI winters, as regulations have an impact and are impacted by funding decisions. The State that funds AI nomads has nearly absolute power over their well-being as researchers; the building-up of a policy *condition* that is ready to accept a possible cut in funds through *possibilities* of regulation may be a good strategy to effectuate the cut if this is found to be needed; if the Research Council decided to fund a different type of project, arguments about the inherent (deterministic) dangers of AI can be used to stop funding without providing further explanations (and producing reports similar to Lighthill's in more contemporary, expanding experts contexts). Crevier quotes his communication with Hans Moravec and then Berthold Horn, showing how during the first AI winter government was able to regulate instantly even without preparatory work:

> So there were funding cutbacks in 1974. I think it was literally phrased at DARPA that "some of these people were going to be taught a lesson, were going to have their two-million-dollar-a-year contracts cut to almost nothing!" And, of course, they meant Stanford, MIT, and Carnegie Mellon! "There was almost no funding for a while," Berthold Horn confirmed to me at MIT.[68]

In this way, and if we treat policymaking and media coverage as two sides of the same State, the latter effectuates a double bind[69] which constrains the development of AI in State-approved desired levels: on the one hand, the UK has to develop AI and compete with other countries; on the other, this development shall be carefully regulated because it is dangerous according to prestigious commentators. The system is complex, and its complexity renders it partly invisible, as it is not so easy to see that people quoted in the press have politically important positions in institutions that affect AI funding, influencing them directly or indirectly. While, so far, this section has examined the role of institutions at large in the regulation and constrain of nomadic science, the next, and final, subsection will focus mostly on the role of individuals in this process.

8.3.3 Lucasian Men of the State: Airy, Lighthill, Hawking

[W]e find a very accurate appreciation of the irreducibility of nomad science, but simultaneously the concern of a man of the State, or one who sides with the State, to maintain a legislative and constituent primacy for royal science. Whenever this primacy is taken for granted, nomad science is portrayed as prescientific or parascientific or sub-scientific agency.[70]

When I began researching the social dynamics shaping the environment of AI research, I was mostly sensitised by group dynamics: I was looking for names of institutions, universities, policy offices, countries, networks, and so on. The passage from Deleuze and Guattari quoted above made lit-tle sense with respect to the argument I was seeking to explore, despite the fact that names such as Bostrom, Hawking, or Lighthill appeared increas-ingly more often in the documents I have been examining. However, I refused to believe (and I still do not wish to believe) that there is an intentional conspiracy against AI research. I was also unsure of whether I should attribute group dynamics to individuals' influence or individu-als' positions to group tendencies, until I read the following—hauntingly part-prophetic—passage from Crevier, which, very succinctly, synopsises the historicity of regulatory tensions between royal and nomadic sciences (one should keep in mind that Crevier wrote this in 1993, 21 years before Hawking's AI-related statements):

> A scathing report to their government on the state of AI research in England devastated their British colleagues. Its author, Sir James Lighthill, had distinguished himself in fluid dynamics and had occupied Cambridge University's Lucasian Chair of Applied Mathematics, presently held by Stephen Hawking. The British government traditionally requests scien-tific advice from past holders of the Lucasian Chair. Ironically, another ex-Lucasian, Sir George Biddel Airy, had been the one to advise Queen Victoria against continuing support for Charles Babbage's difference engine. Sir Lighthill pointed out to the Science Research Council of the UK that AI's 'grandiose objectives' remained largely unmet.[71]

To affirm both the nomadic nature of AI, as AI becomes a driver for research migration, I will quote an interviewee who engaged deeply with AI from the mid-1980s until the late 1990s, who, in one short passage, exemplified this, but also how the aforementioned issues of tribal oppor-tunism and the impact of the AI winter in the conceptualisation and masking of AI:

I've never seen so much research funding in my life again. It was kind of curious. So that meant I moved into the AI Department, I moved into this project, and this project was essentially about trying to use AI techniques, knowledge-based system techniques to support designers. We call this an intelligent knowledge base design support system. Because back in those days in the Alvey programme, we weren't allowed to call it AI because this was still post AI winter stuff and then the, what was the report of, I've forgotten the name of the guy ...

(INTERVIEW 7)

The "guy" obviously being Lighthill, this quote shows how the new guises of AI hype through deep neural networks, machine learning, and so on can be foretellers of a new AI winter. It might also be the case then that instead of asking for a formal new instalment of a "Lighthill report," recent governments implicitly "regulate" (in a less legal understanding of the term) AI through mass media commentary. "Scaremongering" and the fuelling of "public fears" can be seen as a method that State constellations of media and governments use to justify the regulation of AI research that its own Royal Society has been promoting, wearing the mask of openness towards curiosity-driven research. But how liberal can a State be if "experts" warn of AI dangers? With the final confirmation of this section's examination of royal/State strategies to regulate nomadic AI researchers (as well as mathematicians), we may be led to a few concluding remarks.

8.4 CONCLUSION: STATIONARY VOYAGES AND A MODEST PROPOSAL TO MAKE ROOM FOR CURIOSITY-DRIVEN RESEARCH

They are nomads by dint of not moving, not migrating, of holding a smooth space that they refuse to leave, that they leave only in order to conquer and die. Voyage in place.[72]

Pickering concludes in his study of cybernetics:

What we found throughout are the marks of continual social marginality of cybernetics: its hobbyist origins outside any institutional frame, its early flourishing in tenuous and ad hoc organisations like dining clubs and conference series, its continual welling-up outside established institutions and its lack of dependable support from them.

This is deeply reflected in career paths involving "part-time positions in universities" and lodging "in the world of business and industry."[73] This does not differ much from what the present study of AI researchers suggested, maybe with few differences of scale: certain lessons have been learned from previous AI winters, there is a greater population of AI specialists and tribes to seek nomadic niches, and the processes of grant applications have been entrenched enough to appear less risky. Also, due to the price of equipment, it may be more difficult to find AI hobbyists working from home. The present chapter started with a question concerning imperialistic dynamics as opposed to curiosity-based research in AI. It is curious to observe that terms containing the word "intelligence" (think intelligence agencies, intelligentsias, and of course AI) have been so deeply associated with imperialistic strategies instead of pure curiosity. Once again, the two poles do not express a binary. If a tentative answer is given, it is: imperialistic hierarchies in AI are quite messy; there is no simple division between ethical scientists-nomads and unethical governors-tyrants or unethical mad scientists-barbarians and ethical authorities-saviours. The nomad's metaphor implies a flexibility in terms of circumstances (geological, technological, social, or individual). As shown, AI and cybernetic nomads will not hesitate to take advantage of military or national strategy funds in order to occupy a territory, and likewise they will not hesitate to appropriate the money and negotiate its purpose, according to programmes they are finding more valuable. Similarly, the State claims to be in support of curiosity-driven research despite the fact that, at least when it comes to AI, it generates and sustains an ensemble of regulatory possibilities. Perhaps, what Pickering, or even Deleuze and Guattari, did not see in their treatises is that the royal and the nomadic sciences exist in a parasitical relationship.

It becomes clearer now that the game of contemporary AI environments is a thoroughly and complexly political one. Royal science wishes to encourage AI research, but only as long as it constrains its public image, so the citizens (i.e. taxpayers, funding the government) feel secure as long as the government regulates the fears its own media/best-selling system generates and perpetuates. This, as it seems from the present observations, works at three stages or levels: first, the State "locks-in" a policy which invites research; second, it spreads abstract expectations with little or very poor evidence that appear rigorous with the use of popularised evaluations about the potential harms of the same technologies; and third, based on the previous two, transferring the poorly assessed concerns into regulatory policy which in turn affects actual research in the name of safety.

Nonetheless, the present chapter has the following four limitations (and is open to further feedback): (1) it focuses mainly on the UK scene, and the evidence provided is partial: very few interviews, sudden jumps from the UK to the US and/or the EU. This happens, mainly because to speak of the politics of AI one needs to have references to the social history of AI, and with the exception of the few references provided, such research is lacking. What were the politics of AI in the 1950s? In the 1980s? In the 2000s? Why do we know so little about this? A thorough comparative history of the socio-political relationships between AI in America, Britain, Europe, and Japan (and elsewhere) would be of undeniable value for contemporary research, policymaking, and ethics of AI. A good starting point of comparison would be the recent thorough comparative examination of technological national pride rhetoric in Japan between the 1970s and currently as conducted in Robertson's 2018 book on the topic.[74] (2) There are further dimensions of the AI conundrum missing from this chapter: AI is not the sole product of academic scientists/technologists, militaries, and governments. It involves numerous players who contribute in different ways to innovation in a process that can be described as innofusion (innovation through social diffusion[75]) or social learning,[76] starting with taxpayers funding governments who in turn fund academic and military research, the industry and its existing or non-existing ties to academia or governments (of which the UK Industrial Challenge Fund is a good case to examine), the media representations of science and technology, science fiction, and more. (3) Moreover, such regulatory and funding schemes are not unique to AI at all; many similar cases can be found in different fields, and the present research would greatly benefit from comparisons of hypes areas such as synthetic biology, nanotechnologies, networked computer applications, and so on (Willets' text can be a great point of departure for such a comparison). (4) Finally, the content of my interviews ends in early 2019, and my readings mostly refer up to 2017; AI's allure is a producer of constant updates and reformulations so that a constant revisit of empirical data is needed at a time of grandiose rhetoric. All these may spark future research on the topic.

It is not only AI scientists (and cyberneticists and mathematicians) who are or have been nomadic, as it has been exemplified. The very concept of

AI is at the same time specific enough to become a pole of attraction and equally abstract to become nomadic itself. In this way, it becomes temporarily (and parasitically) attached to various individuals' works and institutions and generates hype as the impending invasion of a nomadic tribe lifts up dust. The fear of AI is maybe very similar to the fear of the unknown "barbarous" immigrant who comes to "steal" the natives' jobs and replace their roles. But are AI researchers immigrants? A final note should be made on the comparison Deleuze makes between mobile immigrants who are forced to move (hence, becoming defined by their mobility) and the nomads who invent nomadism as a method to occupy spaces (hence, they are defined by their skill in inhabiting spaces): "[Y]ou shouldn't move around too much, or you'll stifle becomings. I was struck by a sentence of Toynbee's: 'The nomads are the ones who don't move on, they become nomads because they refuse to disappear.'"[77] And despite AI winters, nomadic AI researchers have refused to disappear; instead, the struggle to maintain their positions, acknowledging the possibility of future mobility:

> Whereas the migrant leaves behind a milieu that has become amorphous or hostile, the nomad is one who does not depart, does not want to depart [...] and who invents nomadism as a response to this challenge [...] The nomad knows how to wait, he [sic] has infinite patience.[78]

The AI nomad scientists of today might have learned from previous AI winters to be patient and abstain from grandiose statements and promises. Their movement is defined by their stationary status: their desk-prepared grant applications become potential future temporary settlements. Their interdisciplinarity and simultaneous discipline specialisation are elements of "[i]mmobility and speed, catatonia and rush, a 'stationary process,' station as process".[79] Is this unsettling settlement permanent? Are AI nomads and their royal science parasitical counterparts "bad students" who stubbornly refuse to learn from the past? Or is this process necessary for the development of science and technology? Now that AI techniques (such as deep learning and neural networks) have reached a level of certain maturity, we might know the answer to such questions only if we allow AI scientists to design and develop projects according to what they see as fitting to current capabilities and needs, and *then* allow the outcomes to be appropriated by different social layers. Curiosity does not kill cats, but enables potentialities. There are no mad scientists, but nomad scientists.

ACKNOWLEDGEMENTS

I am grateful to the editor who very kindly invited me to submit to the present volume, to my interviewees who helped me gain insiders' insights to the structure of AI arenas, to the two anonymous referees offering very constructive feedback, and my current supervisors, Dr Gill Haddow and Prof Robin Williams from the University of Edinburgh who tolerated my brainstorming at early stages of writing this chapter. I declare that no monetary support has been provided for carrying out the present work. I am indebted to my brother-in-Deleuze Nikolis Palikaros for pinpointing me to the 1997 quote of Deleuze, which sparked to a great extent the initial inspiration for conducting the present work.

NOTES

1. Langdon Winner. "Do Artifacts Have Politics?" *Daedalus* 109, no. 1, 121–136 (1980). Donald MacKenzie, and Judy Wajcman. "Introduction." In: MacKenzie, D. and Wajcman, J. (eds). *The Social Shaping of Technology* 3–27. Buckingham: Open University Press, 1999.
2. Gilles Deleuze, and Félix Guattari. *A Thousand Plateaus: Capitalism and Schizophrenia*. London: The Athlone Press, 1988.
3. I intentionally abstain from the usage of the word "expert" when referring to anyone's proof via credentials in order to emphasise upon the constant negotiation of the term and the vulgarisation of the term based on taken-for-granted assumptions when someone is presented as an expert, especially in media and policy debates. For the scope of the present paper, specialisation has more to do with the content of one's studies and working routines as opposed to expertise having more to do with branding.
4. Deleuze, and Guattari. *A Thousand Plateaus*, 422–423, 428–429.
5. Andrew Pickering. *The Cybernetic Brain: Sketches of Another Future*. Chicago and London: The University of Chicago Press, 2010, but more specifically Andrew Pickering. "Cybernetics as Nomad Science." In: *Deleuzian Intersections in Science, Technology and Anthropology*, 155–162, 2009.
6. Deleuze, and Guattari. *A Thousand Plateaus*, 45
7. Pickering. *The Cybernetic Brain*, 11.
8. Pickering. *The Cybernetic Brain*, 12.
9. Pickering. *The Cybernetic Brain*, 31.
10. Ross W. Ashby. *Design for a Brain*. New York: John Wiley and Sons, 1954. Wladyslaw Sluckin. *Minds and Machines*. Middlesex: Penguin Books, 1960, 70–71.

11. Deleuze, and Guattari. *A Thousand Plateaus*, 181. A detailed analysis on the relevance of Gregory Bateson's theories on current hypes surrounding the social portrayals of AI can be found in Galanos 2017.

12. See Daniel Crevier. *AI: The Tumultuous History of the Search for Artificial Intelligence*. New York: Basic Books, 1993, 26–41 for a thorough description of the role of cyberneticists such as Wiener, Minsky, McCulloch, and Pitts in the development of AI.

13. Crevier. *AI*, 18–22; Sluckin, *Minds and Machines*, 12–14.

14. Deleuze, and Guattari. *A Thousand Plateaus*, 423.

15. Pickering. *The Cybernetic Brain*, 62.

16. For a good reference list on these debates, see Hubert L. Dreyfus. "A History of First Step Fallacies." *Minds and Machines* 22, no. 2 (2012): 87–99, and the more recent Harry Collins. *Artifictional Intelligence: Against Humanity's Surrender to Computers*. Medford: Polity, 2018; for a thorough, specialist-based and still unbeatable in my view series of arguments against the possibility of pure AI, see the classic Terry Winograd, and Fernando Flores. *Understanding Computers and Cognition: A New Foundation for Design*. New Jersey: Ablex, 1988.

17. Harry M. Collins, and Robert Evans. "The Third Wave of Science Studies: Studies of Expertise and Experience." *Social Studies of Science* 32, no. 2 (2002): 235–296.

18. Vassilis Galanos. "Exploring Expanding Expertise: Artificial Intelligence as an Existential Threat and the Role of Prestigious Commentators, 2014–2018." *Technology Analysis & Strategic Management* 31, no. 4 (2019): 421–432.

19. Deleuze, and Guattari. *A Thousand Plateaus*, 422.

20. Crevier. *AI*, 6.

21. James Fleck. "Development and Establishment in Artificial Intelligence." In Elias, N., Martins, H., and Whitley, R. (eds). *Scientific Establishments and Hierarchies*, 169–217, 210. Dordrecht: D. Reidel, 1982.

22. Crevier. *AI*, 26–60.

23. Crevier. *AI*, 65.

24. Crevier. *AI*, 120–132.

25. Dreyfus. "A History of First Step Fallacies"; Alan M. Turing. "Computing Machinery and Intelligence." *Mind* 50, no. 236 (1950): 442; Herbert A. Simon, and Allen Newell. "Heuristic Problem Solving: The Next Advance in Operations Research." *Operations Research* 6, no. 1 (1958): 1–10.

26. Jichen Zhu. *Intentional Systems and the Artificial Intelligence (AI) Hermeneutic Network: Agency and Intentionality in Expressive Computational Systems*. [Doctoral dissertation] Georgia: Georgia Institute of Technology, 2009, 114.

27. Zhu. *Intentional Systems*, 114; Jonathan Grudin. "AI and HCI: Two Fields Divided by a Common Focus." *AI Magazine* 30, no. 4 (2009): 48–57; James Hendler. "Avoiding Another AI Winter." *IEEE Intelligent Systems* 23, no. 2 (2008): 2–4.

28. Sir James Lighthill. *Artificial Intelligence: A General Survey. Part I of Artificial Intelligence*. London: Science Research Council, 1972.

29. Crevier. *AI*, 117.
30. Grudin. "AI and HCI," 53–54.
31. Alexander Linden, and Jackie Fenn. *Understanding Gartner's Hype Cycles.* Strategic Analysis Report N° R-20-1971. Gartner, Inc., 2003, 5, 10–11.
32. Steve Rayner. "The Novelty Trap: Why Does Institutional Learning about New Technologies Seem so Difficult?" *Industry and Higher Education* 18, no. 6 (2004): 349–355.
33. Peter W. Singer. *Wired for War: The Robotics Revolution and Conflict in the 21st Century.* London: Penguin, 2009.
34. Deleuze, and Guattari. *A Thousand Plateaus*, 484
35. There is nothing but space and scope limitations obstructing a comparison of similarity to other contemporary instantiations of science funding. I suggest that this observation is extractable to other fields as well, however, a more thorough exploration of this should be part of future work.
36. Deleuze, and Guattari. *A Thousand Plateaus*, 422.
37. Deleuze, and Guattari. *A Thousand Plateaus*, 428.
38. Deleuze, and Guattari. *A Thousand Plateaus*, 422.
39. Galanos. "Exploring Expanding Expertise," 425–426.
40. Knut H. Sørensen. "Learning Technology, Constructing Culture. Sociotechnical Change as Social Learning." *STS Working Paper No* 18/96, University of Trondheim: Centre for Technology and Society, 1996.
41. James Summer. "Defiance to Compliance: Visions of the Computer in Postwar Britain." *History and Technology* 30, no. 4 (2014): 309–333.
42. David Willetts. *Eight Great Technologies.* London: Policy Exchange, 2013, 9.
43. Willetts. *Eight Great Technologies*, 7.
44. Willetts. *Eight Great Technologies*, 9.
45. Willetts. *Eight Great Technologies*, 9.
46. The document's text suffers from an abundance of misspellings and typos; possibly an indication of the rush under which it was produced and that it has not been thoroughly proofread or reviewed.
47. Willetts. *Eight Great Technologies*, 25–26.
48. Willetts. *Eight Great Technologies*, 27.
49. Willetts. *Eight Great Technologies*, 8.
50. Deleuze, and Guattari. *A Thousand Plateaus*, 422.
51. Galanos. "Exploring Expanding Expertise."
52. Galanos. "Exploring Expanding Expertise," 428.
53. Amnon H. Eden, Eric Steinhart, David Pearce, and James H. Moor. "Singularity Hypotheses: An Overview." In Amnon H. Eden, James H Moor, Johnny H Soraker, Eric Steinhart (Eds) *Singularity Hypotheses*, 1–12. Heidelberg, New York, Dordrecht, London: Springer, 2012; Nick Bostrom. *Superintelligence: Paths, Dangers, Strategies.* Oxford: Oxford University Press, 2014.
54. Deleuze and Guattari. *A Thousand Plateaus*, 422.
55. Bostrom. *Superintelligence*, 18–21.
56. Bostrom. *Superintelligence*, 264–265.

57. Bostrom. *Superintelligence*, 21.
58. Galanos. "Exploring Expanding Expertise," 422.
59. Vincent C. Müller, and Nick Bostrom. "Future Progress in Artificial Intelligence: A Survey of Expert Opinion." In *Fundamental Issues of Artificial Intelligence*, 555–572, edited by Vincent C. Müller. Switzerland: Springer, 2016.
60. Galanos. "Exploring Expanding Expertise," 424.
61. European Parliament. "European Civil Law Rules for Robotics: Study for the Juri Committee." Directorate-General for Internal Policies. Policy Department C. Citizens' Rights and Constitutional Affairs, 1 October 2016.
62. European Parliament. "European Civil Law Rules for Robotics," 11.
63. Galanos. "Exploring Expanding Expertise," 424, 427.
64. House of Commons. Science and Technology Committee. "Robotics and Artificial Intelligence: Fifth Report of Session 2016–17 [online report]," 2016, 6.
65. Müller, and Bostrom. "Future Progress in Artificial Intelligence."
66. Executive Office for the President. "Preparing for the Future of Artificial Intelligence." National Science and Technology Council Committee on Technology. [online report], 23 October 2016.
67. Executive Office for the President. "Preparing for the Future of Artificial Intelligence," 23.
68. Crevier. *AI*, 117.
69. A term coined by cyberneticist Gregory Bateson to denote the negative impact of contradictory commands in the development of individual societies and its relationship to schizophrenia. See also Galanos 2016 on the application of double bind theory at a collective degree as an AI schizophrenia based on extremely positive and negative portrayals and expectations of the field.
70. Deleuze, and Guattari. *A Thousand Plateaus*, 428.
71. Crevier. *AI*, 117.
72. Deleuze, and Guattari. *A Thousand Plateaus*, 560.
73. Pickering. *The Cybernetic Brain*, 388.
74. Jennifer Robertson. *Robo Sapiens Japanicus: Robots, Gender, Family, and the Japanese Nation*. Oakland: University of California Press, 2018, 1–79.
75. James Fleck. "Innofusion or Diffusation? The Nature of Technological Development in Robotics." *Edinburgh PICT Working Paper No. 4*. 1988.
76. Robin Williams, James Stewart, and Roger Slack. *Social Learning in Technological Innovation: Experimenting with Information and Communication Technologies*, Aldershot: Edward Elgar, 2005.
77. Gilles Deleuze. *Negotiations: 1972–1990*. Columbia: Columbia University Press, 1997, 138.
78. Deleuze, and Guattari. *A Thousand Plateaus*, 444.
79. Deleuze, and Guattari. *A Thousand Plateaus*, 444.

CHAPTER 9

Artificial Intelligence and Post-Capitalism

The Prospect and Challenges of AI-Automated Labour

Thanasis Apostolakoudis

CONTENTS

9.1 INTRODUCTION

In my chapter, I deal with the impact of artificial intelligence (AI) automation on work and the compatibility of large-scale automation with capitalism. The vision of an automated world in which independent machines assist and serve human beings has been captivating the

DOI: 10.1201/9780429446726-9

imagination of writers. From Jules Verne to Isaac Asimov, and from Ursula Le Guin to the creators of Dune and Star Trek, this is a recurrent theme that appears either as a utopia or a dystopia, and often simply as an open question.

Be that as it may, it is not just sci-fi authors that show an interest in the topic. Social scientists have long since been investigating the relationship between technological advancements, on the one hand, production, employment, and social relations, on the other. Artificial intelligence is the newest form of technology to attract great research interest, with many examining the prospect of AI-led automated production. There is no agreement on the potential breadth, underlying causes, and limitations of such a development. I find the source of disagreement to be the acceptance or rejection of profit as the driving force of economic decisions, while profit's nature, scope, and meaning causes even further disagreement.

In this chapter, I attempt to shed further light on the motivational forces behind technological adoption in production and human labour replacement. I show how profit is the main driving factor behind economic decisions and examine its relationship with value and labour. I then investigate whether value and profit can be separated from human labour and what that would mean for Capital and labour.

The importance of my research is in its attempt to explore the motivational forces behind AI adoption and the consequences thereof, expanding the understanding of profit and work without losing track of their original meaning within classical political economy, especially in its Marxian account. With this, I aim to contribute to the broader debate around AI and human emancipation.

9.2 THE GENEALOGY OF AI: BETWEEN ANGST AND FAILED PROMISES

In 1921 Czech writer Karl Čapek wrote a drama called *Rossumovi Univerzální Roboti* (RUR) that depicted the production of artificial people from man-made material, called *robots*. In Čapek's initial representation and in many subsequent representations right up to the present, robots have been presented as both potentially emancipatory and dangerous. Emancipatory in that these artificial beings appear as a means to liberate humans from hard labour and menial work. But dangerous because they are also viewed as threatening humankind with obliteration.

9.2.1 Fear of the Robot?

In Čapek's account, robots can be confused for humans, can reason for themselves, and become revolutionaries. At first, they serve humans quite "happily." But it is not long before these *hard-working* creatures seek to overthrow the prevailing order, placing humanity at the risk of extinction. Since Čapek's work, *robots* (or *robota*) in Czech has been used to mean intelligent machines for hard work. Today, the broader term AI is used to refer to a variety of intelligent machines and devices that humans build to assist them in their struggles.

As Ivan Margolius describes it:

> A new spirit was thought to have arrived, a spirit of synthesis of new concepts, of a new human élan, of multiple views of reality, ambiguity of meaning as in Kafka's works. Čapek's robots were a pure example of modernity not just in the name but by being ambiguous between the real being and the artificial machine. It prompted and inspired contemporary artists, writers and architects to create novel ideas based on new thinking and not on an imitation of the past, as had happened before. [1]

The RUP drama echoed the fears around new technology, a product of WW1 and the Ford assembly line. More importantly, it expressed the ancient human fear that one day machines will make us redundant. Today this fear has gained force.

Valerio De Stefano in a working paper for the Employment Policy Department of the International Labour Organization deals with this fear by citing a 2017 *New Yorker* article. In October 2017, the cover of the *New Yorker* magazine portrayed human paupers receiving handouts from humanoid robots strolling on the street. The very same issue included an article on job automation showing the consequences of introducing automated labour processes in existing corporations, analysing in-depth the relation and interaction between humans and sophisticated manufacturing machinery.[2] De Stefano examines the reasons why the artist chose to draw such a cover in order to accompany an article on the consequences of job automation.[3] The answer he gives is that it is plausible that the artist was affected by an established narrative on job automation and the future of work that intensely fixates on a quantitative approach, trying to guess the number of workers that would be left unemployed as a result of technological developments.[4] This is what many describe as an AI takeover, namely a scenario in which some form of AI becomes the presiding form of intelligence on Earth, with computer programmes and robots effectively surpassing human intelligence and taking control, including in the workplace. It is worth mentioning that not everyone that subscribes to a not-so-distant future of (almost) full-scale AI automation shares this stress. Techno-futurists like Peter Thiel, Elon Musk, and Sam Altam predict that full AI automation (the AI takeover) is approaching much sooner than we think[5] and that it will not necessarily be catastrophic, but just "weird" (Musk) or even a great development, going as far as to call it "an unimaginably great future"[6] (Altman). I call people in this group "convinced" because they appear to have ascertained that full automation will be an (economic) reality sooner than later. However, as I will show, not all members of this group hold the same normative evaluations about this development.

9.2.2 A Future That Never Arrived?

At the same time, others seem to be stuck with an entirely different feeling, that of disappointment, or even frustration, at "the broken promise of a futuristic world." Among them the late David Graeber, who was asking some years ago:

> Where, in short, are the flying cars? Where are the force fields, tractor beams, teleportation pods, antigravity sleds, tricorders, immortality drugs, colonies on Mars, and all the other techno-logical wonders any child growing up in the mid-to-late twentieth century assumed would exist by now? Even those inventions that seemed ready to emerge—like cloning or cryogenics—ended up betraying their lofty promises. What happened to them? [7]

He had been expressing a bitter disappointment with what he considered a failed promise. In a sense, not only was Graeber not alarmed by AI's development, but he seemed to be unhappy with what his generation ultimately got:

> We are well informed of the wonders of computers, as if this is some sort of unanticipated compensation, but, in fact, we haven't even moved computing to the point of progress that people in the 1950s expected we'd have reached by now. We don't have computers we can have an interesting conversation with, or robots that

can walk our dogs or take our clothes to the Laundromat. Did I expect I would be living in such a world of wonders? Of course. Everyone did. Do I feel cheated now? It seemed unlikely that I'd live to see all the things I was reading about in science fiction, but it never occurred to me that I wouldn't see any of them.[8]

The promised AI-led utopia never arrived; even worse, most politicians have tried to convince people that we already live in a world of unprecedented—if not maximum—technological progress. How come then that the predictions of so many sci-fi blockbusters still seem so distant, even unreal? I have cited Graeber's commentary because Graeber was a sceptic but not a denialist. He was, if anything, a *frustrated* techno-optimist, knowing very well the dangers of a world filled with pointless jobs (which he calls less covertly bullshit jobs),[9] where humans end up doing largely unproductive work. He recognised that this phenomenon could intensify with a certain type of capitalist-driven automation and that there is a certain *something* that holds back the promised AI utopia, frustrating the human desire for more meaningful and fulfilling work. In this sense, Graeber was sceptical towards the theory of imminent, liberatory AI automation within the current economic framework. And as I will show later, he was not the only one with such a view.

9.2.3 Imminent Human Labour Replacement?

In any case, up until now, we cannot attribute most incidents of human labour replacement to humanoid robots anyway, since it is mostly algorithms and software that do the trick. This phenomenon has been called "the Moravec's paradox," conveying Hans Moravec's realisation that "it is comparatively easy to make computers exhibit adult-level performance on intelligence tests or playing games, and difficult or impossible to give them the skills of a one-year-old when it comes to perception and mobility."[10] It is simpler, argues Moravec, to replace human decision-making with some automated decision-making process, run by software, than to build humanoids that execute everyday tasks, like doing the housework or serving drinks. Moreover, others have emphasised, despite the notable surge in AI adoption, the impact has been "still too small relative to the scale of the US labour market to have had first-order impacts on employment patterns—outside of AI hiring itself."[11]

Several studies and reports, however, have provided different estimates. The McKinsey Global Institute,[12] in their mid-point scenario, predicted that automation could displace around 15% of the global workforce, or about 400 million workers, in the period between 2016–2030. At the same time Adrian Cooper for Oxford Economics,[13] argues that

> the number of robots worldwide multiplied three-fold over the past two decades, to 2.25 million and trends suggest that the global stock of robots will multiply even faster in the next 20 years, reaching as many as 20 million by 2030, with 14 million in China alone.

Furthermore, Joseph Stiglitz and Anton Korinek in a recent article claim that "it is evident that the COVID-19 pandemic is accelerating automation in workplaces, since, a quarter of all jobs in the economy require physical interaction and are thus directly affected by the pandemic."[14] We shall not therefore underestimate the risk of increasing economic inequalities due to this acceleration. Finally, Knight, citing Daren Acemoglu, informs us that "automation takes place faster during recessions and tends to stick thereafter, since companies adopt more automation partly due to staff shortages, but also in order to adapt to new safety measures, and to improve efficiency."[15]

So, are there valid reasons to either fear or desire intelligent technology taking over human work? Is artificial intelligence a friend or foe of labour? And is Capital able or willing to embrace AI automation? These are the questions that I examine in this chapter. I aspire to show that what matters—probably more than the technology itself—is the socio-economic context that we place these questions in. I investigate, therefore, how the adoption of AI depends on the historical and material conditions that have been shaping the economic system, emphasising the imperatives of profitability and system stability. I commence my analysis by looking into value and labour.

9.3 VALUE AND PROFIT, AI AND CAPITALISM

So far, I have highlighted some of the fears and hopes surrounding AI and jobs. There are many reasons why both criticism and excitement make sense, but often both the sceptics and the convinced forgo the historical parameters and dynamics of the economic system. This makes it harder to answer a series of questions. For example, what would a world of little or no human labour look like for Capital and its historical exploitation of workers and employees? Would it be devoid of profit, or would profit change in its nature? How would this influence production and consumption, respectively? What about ownership of algorithms and robots?

In what follows, I argue that in order to make sense of the reality of AI at work we should place it in its context, that of (late) capitalism, its incentives and driving forces. For this, I look into what many describe as the main driving force behind the adoption—or the lack thereof—of AI technology, namely the theory of the tendency of the rate of profit to fall.[16] I examine, thus, how human labour replacement is conditioned by general profitability. I end up investigating whether full automation and human labour replacement are incompatible with the current economic framework and if so why.

To begin with, the tendency of the rate of profit to fall, or simply falling rate of profit (FROP) is an empirical phenomenon mentioned by a plethora of economists and philosophers ranging from Adam Smith to David Ricardo and from Karl Marx to John Stuart Mill. I place three premises upon which the theory rests and one main conclusion that we can draw from them:

i) No value is produced without (some sort of) labour.

ii) What generates profit (in production) is the appropriation of value. All firms produce for profit, so all firms appropriate parts of labour value. This (economically produced) way of extracting value, called profit in production, is an historical arrangement.

iii) New technology is initially profitable for the individual firm, as it lessens its dependence on human labour, so it lowers wages too, which are company costs. New technology remains profitable until competition drives all firms to adopt it. Once they do, the (general) profit rate falls due to the total decrease of human labour and value produced by it.

iv) This creates an—at least temporary—counter-tendency against embracing more technological innovation, since general profitability has been decreased. This tendency runs against the tendency of the individual business to continuously increase their profits by reducing labour costs, etc. It looks like a systemic contradiction, found between the micro- and macro-targets of Capital.

The conclusion is that capitalism—seen as the overarching totality of relations within which all individual capitals/firms operate—conditions *innovation* upon profitability, which up until today depends largely upon human labour. Full automation and full adoption of AI therefore would necessitate a new historical arrangement, or will not take place.

In what follows, I explore these premises and their conclusion in more depth. It is worth mentioning, for the sake of clarity, that in this section I am dealing with artificial intelligence in its narrow sense,[17] meaning as a non-anthropomorphic or human-emulating type of technology that is "primarily designed to address narrow tasks." Therefore, any conclusions in the following section are relevant to this type of AI and not to the more general, superintelligent one that might be capable of synthesising knowledge and emulating human cognition. I will involve this latter type later on in my analysis.

9.3.1 Value and Labour

Where does value come from? This is probably one of the most complicated questions in social sciences and humanities. Some claim it is nature (e.g. the physiocrats),[18] some labour (labour theory of value- LtoV),[19] and others argue that value is whatever people agree it to be in the market (neoclassical theory of value).[20] This is a fairly complicated debate that is outside the scope of this chapter. However, an overview is needed in order to get an understanding of another premise, profit.

In modern economic thought, it was land and nature where the Enlightenment economists (physiocrats) looked first for value. Ole Bjerg, in his book *Parallax of Growth*, summarises the physiocrat argument: the main trait in physiocrat economics is a substance theory of value. Value is ultimately derived from the organic substance produced by the land. For the physiocrats, the economic growth of a nation is achieved by the expansion of the areas of land cultivated for the purpose of farming, forestation or other kinds of natural production or by the improved cultivation of existing areas of land. The purpose of such efforts is the increase and optimisation of the growth of natural organisms that may ultimately become the objects of human consumption. At the same time, the physiocrat notion of growth does not coincide entirely with the purely ecological notion of growth. Economic growth does not comprise the growth of all natural organisms but only those organisms that become the direct or indirect objects of human consumption. The farmer is referred to as the cultivator, and only those parts of nature that are subject to human cultivation are also considered part of the economy. All economic value may ultimately derive from a natural substance, but not all natural substances are necessarily economically valuable.[21]

It was some years later, and on the other side of the Channel, that Adam Smith and David Ricardo turned their focus from land and nature to labour:

> Adam Smith inquired what is the real measure of this exchange-able value; or wherein it consists of the real price of all commodities, and the answer he gave was that: "It is labour that is the real measure of the exchangeable value of all commodities. The real price of everything, what everything really costs to the man who wants to acquire it, is the toil and trouble of acquiring it."[22]

In contrast with the substance theory of value, which we can actually measure in rather simple physical terms (hectares, kilos, yards, etc.), the labour theory would require more perplexed metrics. David Ricardo's definition of value as the exchangeable value of commodities produced, in proportion to the labour bestowed on their production, sets the tone. By "production" Ricardo means not only the immediate production, but all those implements or machines required to give effect to the particular labour to which they were applied. The labour theory of value appears to enclose therefore the value of nature and the productive means within the labour activity and "credit" them all to labour.[23]

It is Karl Marx and his interpretation of this theory that offers further clarity. His break with his predecessors came through the use of the concept of *socially necessary labour time*,[24] which introduced a social perspective in production, in contrast to the starting point of other thinkers (the individual labourer). Marx agued:

> But one man is superior to another physically, or mentally, and supplies more labour in the same time, or can labour for a longer time; and labour, to serve as a measure, must be defined by its duration or intensity; otherwise, it ceases to be a standard of measurement.

Contrary to popular belief though, Marx never used the term "labour theory of value" itself in any of his works, since he opposed ascribing a supernatural creative power to labour, arguing that:

> Labor is not the source of all wealth. Nature is just as much a source of use-values (and it is surely of such that material wealth

consists) as labour, which is itself only the manifestation of a force of nature, human labor power.[25]

It seems therefore that Marx was making a distinction between concrete types of labour and general (abstract) human labour. The latter is then what unites different sorts of varying concrete types, providing some basis for measurement of value, based on (human) time-spent and energy expended on the creation of goods. The term *socially necessary* refers to the quantity of labour that is needed for the production of a good within a *given* society, under some *average* conditions of production, with a given *median* intensity and skill of labour. If we were led then to compare different sorts of labour with each other and ascribe a comparative relationship between them (establish prices), abstract socially necessary labour would be its standard of measurement, according to this theory. This is far from arguing that price is a "natural characteristic" of the goods produced in general even when measured in terms of socially necessary labour time. Not because we question the importance of abstract labor-time, but rather (because we question) the universality and naturality of (strict) exchangeability. After all, Marx himself "focused on commodities and money as a kind of symbolic analysis in social theory" rather than a natural, objective, material reality altogether.[26]

The neoclassical theory, to the contrary, sees practically no difference between market price and value and describes both as largely *an agreement* between buyers and sellers; a bargain between rational actors seeking to maximise their utility in an environment of full information.[27] In this, the neoclassical analysis

> treats the labour theory of value as a theory of price determination, and a poor theory at that. While its study might be an interesting excursus into the history of economic thought, say the neoclassicals, it has no role in modern economic analysis.[28]

As far as I am concerned, by no means do I equate value with price. Value is not even merely limited within the market altogether, since non-commercial labour is equally value-producing although it is often not measured or appreciated as such.[29] Could we ever come up with a fair price that would reflect the real value of a good? Are there even alternatives to price itself? I will not delve into these questions now. For the sake of the argument I make it is enough to recognise that human labour is *indispensable* for value-making and, respectively, profit-making. Whether the market reflects this indispensability *fully*, *partly*, or not at all is a long and interesting debate, but this does not fundamentally change the conclusion: there is no value without some form of human labour and no profit without its appropriation in the current framework of production.

9.3.2 Labour and Profit

So far I have examined the idea that human labour[30] is the main component in the creation of value as labour time spent in the production process. In the following part, I deal with profit and its relationship to value.

In the sphere of production, when a company hires workers, these workers usually initially produce a value roughly equal to the cost of hiring them. Once they are done creating this value and proceed with further work, they begin to *valorise Capital*, i.e. to increase its value without receiving the corresponding compensation for it. Thus, usually labourers work part of the day "for themselves," meaning that they produce the equivalent of their wage, and part of the day for their employer.[31]

The simpler way to understand profit[32] *in production*[33] is to compare what labourers *actually* produce during a day of work, and what they *actually* receive. In order to do so, we quite naturally think that we need a *general equivalent* to compare all productive activities and outcomes with one another. What comes to mind is time and money. Both time and money have homogenising qualities, since we can measure them (or so we think at least) with accuracy, are universal, and embrace everyone in their web. So one can actively measure how much time one spends at work, how many units of goods/services one produces, and how much money these units correspond to. This time–money relationship could be arbitrary, made-up, etc.; what matters is that it applies to all those giving or receiving payments and serves as an indicator of *difference*. Finding the *difference* between what one *actually* produces and what one *actually* receives as compensation is the basis of the quantitative calculation of profit in production.

The ideas of *surplus value*[34] and (economic) exploitation[35] are based exactly on this difference between the total value produced and the total value received. Schematically:

i) Goods/services can be translated into labour time units (time needed until the final product is produced, including previous training, education, skills-acquiring, etc.).

ii) There is a social element in labour time, meaning that the duration needed from the beginning until the end of a productive process can be measured in time units and be compared to other similar ones.

iii) A fair compensation for labour would be the refund of the full amount of value units produced. Getting less means labour is at a loss.

iv) Since labour lacks access to productive means, it is forced to be dependent upon the owners of those means (either concrete, i.e. industrial or more abstract ones, i.e. software/patents etc.), so it usually gets less; i.e. dependent labour is always at a loss.

v) This dependence brings exploitation (persistent loss of surplus value) that, quantitatively, is expressed in *fewer units of value* received than produced.

This, in short, is the quantitative account of surplus value appropriation and profit-making and helps make sense of the salaried labour exploitation. This is not the full story though. Ernesto Screpanti[36] asserts that "the production sphere is the place where the fundamental capitalist misdeed is carried out." Labourers appear to exchange their labour power with wage, as in any other commodity exchange. Yet, what they actually do comes closer to "someone who has brought their own hide to market and now has nothing else to expect but a tanning."[37]

The owners implement production plans by using their authority. Workers are then forced to labour efficiently and produce goods-to-be-sold (commodities), whose value-added is higher than their compensation (wage). But see how there are two premises that define profit? The first is that compensation is *smaller* than actual value-added (quantitative). The second is that workers are *obliged* to work for the production of *commodities* (qualitative). So labour does struggle to get both fair compensation for its work, and to *influence/control* the very nature of its work and its overarching goals away from an imposed heteronomy.

When Capital hires labour, what it actually buys is *compliance* and *subjugation*, or else the ability to direct human activity—and creativity—towards a certain productive outcome that it decides (command power). Those that have signed a labour contract know this very well. Terms of contract set the duration, goals, and frames of the desired activity, in a way that is seemingly free and uncoerced. Historically though, it is not.

Wage labour, albeit an improvement to previous arrangements, signifies the move from a system of extra-economic, personal, and largely political exploitation (serfdom, slavery etc.) to a system of impersonal, economic, and *seemingly* apolitical exploitation (wage-system).[38]

To better understand this, we can compare older forms of economic organisation, e.g. feudalism and serfdom, with their successor, capitalism:

> Within a craft, guild, and corporation, there no longer exists the direct unity between humans and land, but there is still a stable connection of the producers with their means of production thanks to the intersubjective coordination of the entire production, which hinders the full penetration of the power of Capital. The complete dissolution of the tie between the workers and their objective means of production for the first time prepares "free" labour, in a "double sense," and thus the impersonal, reified dominance by "liberated capital." Modern labourers, on the contrary, lose any direct connection to the land. On the one hand, they are free from personal dominance. On the other hand, they are also free from the means of production and thus can no longer relate to nature as their own "inorganic body." The original unity with the land disappeared with the collapse of precapitalist personal domination. Its result is alienation from nature, activity, species-being, and other people—or simply said, modern alienation arising from the total annihilation of the "intimate side" of production. When the land becomes a commodity, the relationship between humans and land is radically modified and reorganised for the sake of producing capitalist wealth.[39]

But this profit imperative for labour actually means a double constraint of its freedom:

> Labour *subsumes* its capacities and also the ownership of the commodities it produces (besides the part that corresponds to wage). So labour does not produce freely and *at will*, but following certain orders, attempting to reach set targets. The supposed "freedom of exchange" in production is then quite artificial, since labourers are ultimately "free" only to subsume their labour power and creativity to the commands of the producers, or be left outside the Market, without any means to sustain themselves. Their

"freedom" is the "freedom" of having their labour controlled by an owner (or Market imperatives *en long et en large*) to avoid starvation.

Screpanti presents the labour market as a place where a very mystifying form of commodity fetishism ravages and where agreement is construed as a transaction of "free and equal" commodity exchange, while in reality it is a social relation of subjugation and exploitation. The mystification of the employment contract depicts it as a "mutually beneficial partnership agreement" that allows "significant agency" and freedom of decision to the labourers. It is employers, though, that—more often than not—mould and direct the employees' skills. The basis of profit in production is, therefore, this relational imbalance between labour, in abstract, and owners, also in abstract. Do we have reasons to assume that owners do not compensate labour or opt-in for some form of co-ownership out of personal malice? I do not think so.

Employers do not act in an unconstrained way either, since they operate within the market and are bound by market imperatives. The most important being the obligation to remain profitable or not survive the intra-Capital competition. Labour is a cornerstone of value; I have already described how the structural imbalance against it leads to the continuous extraction of profit that favours Capital. This value, however, is fully realised only in the market, where the firm gets to sell its goods and services. Were they not to sell, corporations would be forced out of business, and whichever profit would remain unrealised. In practice, nowadays many companies are not profitable in their productive activities. This explains the monumental amounts of government support given to businesses (bailouts) directed to stock buybacks (creation of fictitious Capital) in the place of investments in productive expansion.[40]

For now, it suffices to conclude that profit in production is expressed as a quantifiable indicator of structural imbalance between firm owners and employees in terms of control, compensation, and access to the productive (and respectively consumptive) activity. The way that this imbalance is enforced, perpetuated, and measured is an outcome of the historical struggles between Capital and labour that replaced previous arrangements (feudalism, serfdom, slavery). Former serfs and slaves that turned into wage-workers were forced out of the land and away from productive means. As wage-workers now, they had to go look for them (land and productive means). Personal domination by the landlord (direct domination for direct theft of the produced value) was transformed into a commercial relationship of seemingly "free" bargain. Control became less direct and more impersonal but did not vanish. It started shifting from fear-based to need-based. The transition from personal (rent) to impersonal (profit) domination meant that human labour became a side-cost of production; one to calculate with more precision and accuracy and "reduce."

This brings me to the next premise, that of human labour-saving technology and its impact on profitability.

9.4 TECHNOLOGY, LABOUR, AND THE FALLING RATE OF PROFIT

Only where labour has been separated from the means of production, only where it expresses certain specific social relations of production, namely a system of free wage labour, where labour is a commodity and where labourers have been emancipated from any direct relation of domination (such as slavery or serfdom), are both capital and labour power "free" to make possible their combination at the highest possible level of technology.[41]

Only when both labour and capital are commodities freely exchangeable in the market will the resulting competition between productive units force them to produce at the socially necessary labour time necessary to survival, and entice them to surpass this level of productivity to reap the super-profit which, for a time, is the prize of the innovator. It is only under the pressure of such market constraints that capital accumulation develops.[42]

What drives the capitalist game is profitability, and I have already described how this means exploitation of labour time, both qualitatively and quantitatively. An enterprise that fails to achieve profitability is unable to function within the market, at least not competitively. It is soon forced either into bankruptcy, takeover, or to become a charity; enterprises are *obliged* to make a profit to stay afloat. Quantitatively it means buying labour time *low* and selling *dear* (compensating labour for less than labour has produced); qualitatively, it means being able to *command and dictate* labour activity towards an outcome.

Competition among Capital is real (no monopoly) but not perfect (no invisible hand). To assume either the one or the other away would be a mistake. It is Anwar Shaikh[43] that makes this argument and Bruce Parry[44] that offers a good summary of it. What motivates real competition is profits, and capitalists are forced to lower costs (to lower prices) in order to beat the competition. However, increasing the exploitation of labour (so increasing working hours, decreasing compensation, etc.) is not limitless. Capitalists are obliged to adopt technological advances that boost productivity, decrease costs, and revolutionise the means of production. Within industries, prices of production are "roughly" levelled by consumers searching for the best offers among competing commodities. Technological change also leads to what Marx named "increasing organic composition of capital" (Shaikh does not use the term). However, rejecting perfect competition does not mean that monopoly Capital is empirically true either. This school of thought "is based on the theory of imperfect competition, which in turn depends completely on the theory of perfect competition." Thus, real competition overrides and much more accurately describes today's economy than the theory of monopoly Capital.

It is not surprising, therefore, that technology seems, *prima facie*, salvatory for corporations. It makes sense to assume that the replacement of as much human labour as possible, for the sake of saving the main cost of a corporation, is the driving force of innovation and technology adoption. And were we to extend this further not only would companies save labour costs, but technology could eventually free labourers too, since they would not have to occupy themselves with trivial, repetitive and dull tasks.

However, the initial realisation that it is profitable for the individual company to invest in new technology in the short term, since it lowers unit costs, is followed by two others that end up forming what is known as the "falling rate of profit theory" and a conclusion on technological adoption.

i) Other companies mimic this and introduce similar technology, to lower their unit costs, motivated by the higher expected rate of return.

ii) When all/most companies introduce the new technology, general profitability falls. All in all, when general profitability falls, businesses (Capital broadly seen) become more hesitant to replace more human labour, so they tend to invest less in new technology. I will now scrutinise those premises and their conclusion.

The essence of capitalist accumulation, says the British economist Michael Roberts, is that in order to boost profits, corporations introduce machines in order to increase the productivity of employees and reduce costs compared to competitors. Roberts[45] builds on Marx's theory of the organic composition of Capital, namely the ratio between *constant Capital—machines and equipment*—and *variable* Capital—*wage labour*. The more machines and equipment a company uses, the higher its organic composition of Capital (OCC) becomes. Various authors see limitations to how far this replacement can go, with the main argument being that the human element and particularly emotional intelligence, empathy, and wisdom, are hard to replace; our experience with a machine would never be equally fulfilling and satisfying.[46] Therefore, goes the argument, consumers would reject automation and AI-offered services, if they were to feel that their needs are not served, including ethical concerns around the use of AI.[47]

I think that this limit is secondary, if a limit at all. The question is not whether we would like to replace all or most human activity from a consumer's viewpoint. I share the strong reservations against demand being what drives production and supply.[48] It does not. To remake another of Shaikh's arguments, even Keynes substituted aggregate demand with net profitability, for what he considered to be the main investment-decision-driver[49] (namely, the difference between interest rate and the rate of return). Capital seeks new investments and new opportunities with the highest net rate of return. The minimal rate of return is the interest rate, since it's what one makes by putting funds in the bank.

Firms produce (create supply) on the basis of short-term profitability. To produce, they must acquire raw materials, hire workers, buy investment goods, and distribute dividends and interest to their owners and lenders. So profit-based decisions to create supply and boost demand for raw materials, and through the payment of wages, dividends, and interest, generate the consumption demand. At the same time, long-term profitability regulates investment demand. In other words, profitability steers both supply (production) and demand. Of course, large numbers of firms and consumers do this on an individual basis, so aggregate supply and demand only relate to each other through a process of errors and adjustment that Shaikh calls "turbulent regulation." "Real macroeconomics," he argues, "is therefore neither supply side nor demand side: It is profit side."

The conclusion is that profitability (both short term and long term) sets the tone for investment decisions, including investments in AI. In the short term, a firm has a strong preference to replace labourers (variable Capital) with machines (constant Capital), especially intelligent ones. The difference between them is that the latter's cost is predictable and eventually lower than that of human labour: their maintenance cost plus their R&D; so is their productivity, given that their working hours and production rate does not fluctuate. However, variable Capital (human labour) is more perplexing. Variable Capital can be scarce (especially if rare skills are needed), gets tired or bored, has to deliver birth, demands rights, etc. Its productivity is not a given, and neither is its compensation, since it cannot usually fall under some historically produced agreement around a minimum wage, but it can grow through strikes and negotiations. In the short term, those businesses that first introduce this new technology drive down total labour cost and—given that they can sell at the same price as previously—they increase their profits, above-average per sector.[50]

However, "looking at the profits of companies that have seized the value created by labour in the new sectors is not necessarily a guide to the health of capital as a whole."[51] Other corporations bring in similar technology to harmonise their profit rates. But there is a paradox here. By attempting to boost labour productivity, with the introduction of technology, human labour-shedding takes place, i.e. new technology replaces human labour. Rising productivity results in increased production, which results in job openings in new sectors, but total human labour goes ultimately down.

This (rising organic composition of Capital) implies a falling rate of profit. Between industries, profit rates are equalised on new investments embodying the latest technology. This occurs due to accelerated or decelerated flows of Capital into or away from those industries with a higher or lower rate of return on new investment. There is no "normal rate of profit" and no capitalist is guaranteed a profit. That is what (real) turbulent competition is about. Rates of profit increase and decrease and revolve around some average, but never fully attain it, unlike in perfect competition.[52]

This is a conclusion that seems to be backed by empirical evidence, as shown in the graphs below:

These charts seem to verify both the tendency of the rate of profit to fall, as well as the link between the profit rate and the pace of the rise of automation (a lower profit rate means a lower rise of automation). All in all, automation and innovation are not natural outcomes of a "growth sequence." They do not happen *because* of the drive for profits; they happen *despite* it.

This is a crucial observation that seems to explain the frustration of authors like Graeber. The answer to the questions of the sort of "where are the automated self-driving mass transportation systems we have been promised" is not that "we are not capable of having the technological tools yet," but that "they are not too profitable for Capital yet."

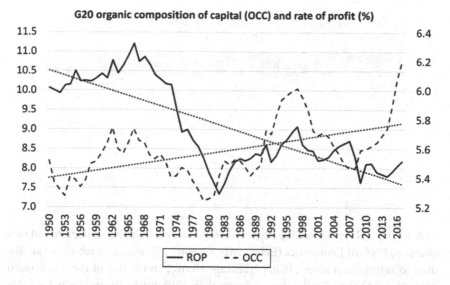

FIGURE 9.1   Note: This graph (Roberts, "More on a world rate of profit."), based on Penn World Tables and Roberts' own calculations, shows the long-term decline in profitability and rise in the organic composition of Capital.

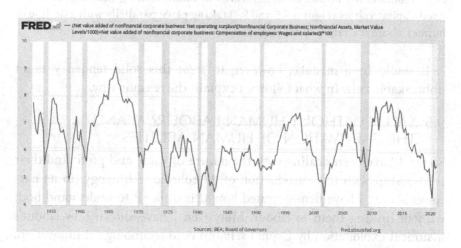

FIGURE 9.2   Note: A graph on the falling rate of profit (US only) from the Federal Bank of St. Louis (U.S. Bureau of Economic Analysis. "Net value added of nonfinancial corporate business: Net operating surplus." *Federal Reserve Bank of St. Louis*, 23 September 2021. https://fred.stlouisfed.org/series/W326RC1Q027SBEA.), using the equation profits/(fixed assets + wages).

Estimated Operational Stock of Industrial Robots in China (Thousands)		
Year	China	World
2010	52	1,059
2012	97	1,235
2014	189	1,472
2016	340	1,828
2018	649	2,440

Source: International Federation of Robotics

FIGURE 9.3 Note: The rising organic composition of Capital is depicted in two charts by Oxford Economics (Economics, Oxford. "Cumulative job losses attributed to automation since 2000, percentage change in the use of robots between 2011–2018." *Oxford Economics*, 15 September 2019. https://resources.oxfordeconomics.com/how-robots-change-the-world.) and one from the International Federation of Robotics (International Federation of Robotics. "Estimated operational stock of industrial robots in China." *IFR*, 16 August 2017. https://ifr.org/news/robots-china-breaks-historic-records-in-automation/.), showing the rise of fixed Capital/robots (Figures 9.3 and 9.4) taking place parallelly with a decline in human labour/variant Capital (Figure 9.5).

It would be a mistake, however, to treat this solid tendency as an unbreakable rule. In what follows, I explain the reasons why.

9.5 VALUE WITHOUT HUMAN LABOUR? AI AND THE CAPTIVATION OF HUMAN ABILITIES

So far, I have been dealing with the nature of value and profit and their relationship with the introduction of AI robotic technology (in its narrower sense). I have demonstrated how it is difficult to understand both without linking them to labour. Moreover, I have shown how labour's historical exploitation by Capital sets limits to technological innovation, in an environment of real competition, through the falling profit rate. In addition, I have cited various authors that highlight this phenomenon and presented empirical evidence that seems to be confirming it. Finally, I have shown that this quest for (exchange) value and profit is what hinders the full realisation of scientific and technological potential.

Industrialists, said Graeber in his flying-cars paper, "poured research funds not into the invention of the robot factories that everyone was anticipating

The rise of the robots

Percentage change in the use of robots between 2011 and 2016

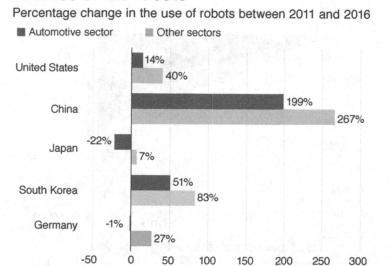

Source: Oxford Economics

BBC

FIGURE 9.4 Note: The rising organic composition of Capital is depicted in two charts by Oxford Economics (Economics, Oxford. "Cumulative job losses attributed to automation since 2000, percentage change in the use of robots between 2011–2018." *Oxford Economics*, 15 September 2019. https://resources.oxfordeconomics.com/how-robots-change-the-world.) and one from the International Federation of Robotics (International Federation of Robotics. "Estimated operational stock of industrial robots in China." *IFR*, 16 August 2017. https://ifr.org/news/robots-china-breaks-historic-records-in-automation/.), showing the rise of fixed Capital/robots (Figures 9.3 and 9.4) taking place in parallel with a decline in human labour/variant Capital (Figure 9.5).

in the sixties, but into relocating their factories to labour-intensive, low-tech facilities in China or the Global (South)." Investments moved to China—due to the higher return of profit that the country has been offering—but then real competition between firms led to the adoption of labour-saving technology in the numerous (new) Chinese productive sites. The higher return of profit in China (Figure 9.6) was what forced owners to move their production there. In countries with a low return on profit (e.g., Japan, Figure 9.7), not only was the adoption of robotic technology slower than in China, but it even fell in some sectors (Figure 9.4). Even in China though this rise is just a *fragment* of the automation, we *could* see if investment decisions were based on public and social needs instead of return on profit. However, under the current circumstances, innovation takes place if (and only if) it boosts

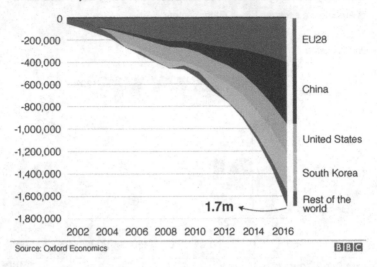

FIGURE 9.5   Note: The rising organic composition of Capital is depicted in two charts by Oxford Economics (Economics, Oxford. "Cumulative job losses attributed to automation since 2000, percentage change in the use of robots between 2011–2018." *Oxford Economics*, 15 September 2019. https://resources.oxfordeconomics.com/how-robots-change-the-world.) and one from the International Federation of Robotics (International Federation of Robotics. "Estimated operational stock of industrial robots in China." *IFR*, 16 August 2017. https://ifr.org/news/robots-china-breaks-historic-records-in-automation/.), showing the rise of fixed Capital/robots (Figures 9.3 and 9.4) taking place in parallel with a decline in human labour/variant Capital (Figure 9.5).

profits, not the other way around. And so does the development and flourishing of humans.

As Henry Heller[53] describes it:

> Under such circumstances, the full realisation of the potential of the mature, productive system would entail the withering away of value. But Capitalism cannot permit such an abolition of value because it lives off of it: "the theft of alien labour time, on which the present wealth is based, appears a miserable foundation in the face of this new one, created by large-scale industry itself". The overthrow of value is only possible through the overthrow of Capitalism. Otherwise, the further transformation and development of the forces of production in the direction of the full application of science and new technologies, including those that

The Rate of Profit in China, 1990-2018

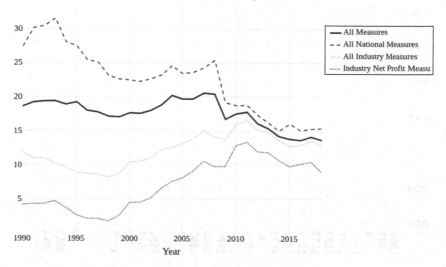

FIGURE 9.6 Note: The faster pace of automation in China—compared to the US, Japan, or Germany—correlates with an historically higher profit rate in China (although still declining) than in, e.g. Japan. This is a strong indicator that a lower rate of profit holds back, or at least discourages, investments in automation (comparison of profit rates in Japan (Roberts, Michael. "The rate of profit in Japan between 1960–2016." *The next recession wordpress*, 23 October 2017. https://thenextrecession.wordpress.com/2017/10/23/abes-mandate/.) and China (Chuang, blog. "The rate of profit in China 1990–2018." *Chuang blog*, 21 June 2020. https://chuangcn.org/2020/06/measuring-profitability/.) and the relative percentage change in the use of robots).

are more ecologically sound, is crippled by the persistence of the indispensable quest by Capital for value, and especially surplus value.

The built-in assumption in this statement—and the one that runs through the previous part of my chapter—is that the source of (surplus) value cannot be but of *human* origin. The falling rate of profit and the limitations it sets make sense within a setting of human owners profiting off of the work of other humans in the workplace. Development, innovation, and labour replacement are strangled by the need to increase profitability, i.e. to accumulate more (exchange) value through the "theft of alien labour time"; or, more precisely, *human* labour time. Currently, Capital needs human labour due to its skills, knowledge, and capacity in order to fulfil the productive outcomes set, produce more, accumulate more exchange value,

FIGURE 9.7   Note: The faster pace of automation in China—compared to the US, Japan, or Germany—correlates with an historically higher profit rate in China (although still declining) than in, e.g. Japan. This is a strong indicator that a lower rate of profit holds back, or at least discourages, investments in automation (comparison of profit rates in Japan (Roberts, Michael. "The rate of profit in Japan between 1960–2016." *The next recession wordpress*, 23 October 2017. https://thenextrecession.wordpress.com/2017/10/23/abes-mandate/.) and China (Chuang, blog. "The rate of profit in China 1990–2018." *Chuang blog*, 21 June 2020. https://chuangcn.org/2020/06/measuring-profitability/.) and the relative percentage change in the use of robots).

maintain the circuit of Capital[54] and its dominant position. Labour on the other hand needs Capital because of its ownership of tools, infrastructure etc. The difference is that labour's dependency on Capital is a construct since Capital's ownership of tools and infrastructure is—if anything—a legal artefact. Were the owners to "abandon" their legal rights to tools and infrastructure, labour would be able to handle them all well and continue production without disruptions in most cases. Capital's dependence on labour skills and knowledge is not just a construct, though. Capital would cease to exist without the exploitation of labour power unless it found refuge in non-economic methods of extraction (basically by *directly forcing* labour to work). Said differently, Capital would have to find a way to go beyond profit altogether. But what that means is that Capital would have to go beyond human work, replacing both manual and cognitive labour with non-human work. Roberts and Shaikh, as seen earlier, think that the falling rate of profit is a limit against that. And so does Ernest Mandel[55] arguing that "large-scale automation of production constitutes the absolute inner limit of Capitalism."

Not everyone shares this view, though. The falling rate of profit is just one of the Marxian *images of capitalism*, as George Caffentzis[56] calls them. And is one that has only been developed in the later phase of Marx's treatise on Capital. In the "Fragment on Machines," in the *Grundrisse*, Marx himself[57] mentions another tendency, another image of capitalism:

To the degree that labour time.. the determinant principle of production [...] is reduced both quantitatively, to a smaller proportion, and qualitatively as an indispensable but subordinate moment [...] compared to general scientific labour, technological application or natural sciences [...] [it makes] Capital work towards its own dissolution as the form dominating production.

Marx does not give a name to this tendency, but Caffentzis does; he calls it "the increasing incommensurability of wealth and labour-time." One could also name it the "tendency towards the abolition of human labour," "the tendency towards the increase of fixed Capital over variable Capital," and "the tendency towards the transfer of value creation from humans to machines." Caffentzis explains how this tendency is a product of an earlier Marxian thought that observes the system's monetary and commercial crisis in 1858 with growing excitement, anticipating the increasing introduction of technology to accelerate its destabilisation. This stance comes with a tacit, albeit strong, technological optimism, if not determinism and an *ex ante* conviction that automation would necessarily diminish Capital's dominance. This assumption, although legitimate at first, probably underestimates Capital's readiness to find new ways for profit-extraction and control over labour, ending up seeing production in a rather narrow way. Such a shift did not take place, at least not due to technology alone. Marx realised it and started placing his hope in the human, rather than the machine, especially after the breakup of the Paris Commune. This, together with later, unrealised predictions, like Keynes' on the 15 hour working week,[58] led many more to lose hope on technological introduction, significantly undermining Capital's dominance.

This already seems to be some bad news, but it might not be the end of it. What if AI automation does not only fail to assist labour liberation but also contributes to the perpetuation and strengthening of its exploitation?

Would the falling rate of profit then allow full human labour replacement altogether or function as a limit, as argued?

In their recent book Dyer-Whiteford, Mikkola Kjøsen, and Steinhoff[59] brought forward an argument made by the historian Tessa Morris-Suzuki, asking us

> to consider ways that Capital might perpetuate itself under condi-
> tions of automation" claiming that "some of the disarray of the
> contemporary left stems from its reluctance to confront the pos-
> sibility of a highly automated Capitalism.

Newer forms of artificial intelligence, especially machine learning and its deep-learning subtype, have already started substituting activities long seen as purely cognitive, intelligent, and ultimately human. Activities that have been seen as "a refuge for the labour chased out of industrial pro-duction." What distinguishes us from other animals is our imagination, creativity, and conscious reasoning. It is, argues Kjøsen et al., a series of mental capabilities, like "aesthetic appreciation; learning and understand-ing; a conscious mind; forming ideas; imagining and conceiving plans," that constitute general intelligence and equip humans with flexibility, adaptability, and the improvisation-capacity to deal with unexpected situ-ations, both at work and more broadly.

Historically, once human capabilities (mostly muscular until now) became embodied in some form of machinery (e.g. automated assembly machines), they disturbed the existing balance of power between work-ers and owners, at least initially. Capital needs to convince, coerce, pun-ish, or reward a worker; it does not need that with robots or software. Leaders of the Scientific Revolution, including Francis Bacon and Robert Boyle, have been working towards the appropriation of knowledge from craftspeople in order to reorganise and deliver it into the hands of capital-ists.[60] The invention of new, intelligent machines does substitute for (or at least augments) human activity by encapsulating it in its robotic body and brain. It is therefore a consolidated form of past experience, obser-vation, and ultimately pattern memory and knowledge. Were the above-mentioned, uniquely human, capabilities to be emulated by robots, this would undoubtedly have consequences for the labour–Capital struggle.

Steinhoff et al. cite Nick Land, a reactionary accelerationist who—with outspoken fatalism—embraces and welcomes Capital autonomisation. Land welcomes this autonomisation that would exclude humans, and importantly labourers, thus "liberating" the owners of the troublesome burden to deal with class struggle. This is, say the authors, "the neoreactionary restoration of traditional political hierarchies of race, gender and class, through futuristic and technological means." Land himself[61] proclaims that he is "no longer interested in [...] pretending this (emancipation through AI) is the same thing as what the left really means when they're talking about emancipation [...] [what] the left means by emancipation is freedom from capital autonomization."

Despite the cynicism of this statement and the overt support for Capital, Land is right to pinpoint that many progressives have been eyeing the rise of AI as a great opportunity for liberation and emancipation.[62] An opportunity to break the chains of profit and free labour from its golden cell. They see cognitive capitalism as having eroded some of the hierarchical divisions found in the Fordist stage of the assembly line capitalism and AI as boosting this trend. It is tougher after all to keep intelligence and knowledge (and its labourers) contained and under control in the same way as with labour in a 19th-century factory. Information flows much easier, and even the productive means of this new era (e.g. 3D printers) are harder to keep privatised and confined in large-scale factory sites, like, for example, the water frame in textile manufacture. Optimists, therefore, see a chance of tipping the balance in this computer-driven era of capitalism towards not the owners but the producers, since Capital's ability to exploit has been challenged in a fundamental way.

It is Caffentzis again that describes the way in which highly automated businesses gradually appropriate the value generated by labour-intensive Capital and how automation sparks the need for low-skill and low-paid labour in other sectors and places: "[E]very increase in the introduction of science and technology in one branch of industry will lead to an equivalent increase in the introduction of low organic composition production in another." What he reveals is, in short, a contradiction: the rise of automation on the one hand, and of low-skilled, underpaid labour on the other; it reveals a geography of privileged and immiserated labour in which the latter, in places like Africa and South America, is the "hidden" backbone of the AI explosion in the former (core capitalist countries). What automation gives with one hand, it takes with other, and it would be erroneous to treat all labour like the labour aristocracy inhabiting affluent Western nations.

It seems therefore that as long as the historical circumstances are so disproportionately against labour (with an increasing gap between the 99% and the 1%, rising unemployment, and stagnating wages in many countries), automation will not serve the needs of the many, but the few. In this sense, the falling rate of profit could even be met with some relief for being a barrier to that. The question then being, would it hold?

In the current conditions of partial automation and human labour dependence, Capital prioritises *the quest for profit (economic exploitation)* in order to maintain its dominant position. For the moment, and as long as it remains profitable (guaranteeing easier and faster exploitation) Capital would keep a "self-employed" precariat—on the shoulders of which the side-effects of AI-led automatisation currently fall (gig economy workers, Amazon factory workers etc.)—and a legion of low-skilled and underpaid workers in the global periphery intact.[63] The full automation of jobs like food delivery, fruit picking, fishing, or warehouse sorting, is probably uneconomical hence undesirable for Capital, yet.

At the same time, automation comes with a parallel increase in unemployment that can be useful for Capital's operations. Joblessness, although a social malaise with horrendous consequences for the people suffering it, creates the so-called "reserve army of labour."[64] This "army," besides being a side-effect of technological adoption, also works as a counterbalancing force to the falling rate of profit, through the suppression of wages and maintenance of labour discipline. Capital allows having *some* value (human labour) "wasted" if this helps maintain an adequate profit rate through more obedient labourers (due to the fear of being replaced by the unemployed). If the recent labour struggles[65] were to intensify and become "unmanageable," the urge for automation would become much stronger. There are reasons to believe that Capital would not hesitate to get rid of these workers by automating further, even if that meant reducing its profits on paper, but keeping a more manageable and obedient labour. After all, this has been the case historically, more often than not. Sure some businesses would be forced out, some Capital might be destroyed, and value would be lost. But the main imperative that pressurises Capital, more than profitability pressurises individual businesses, is the maintenance of its *ownership status* over non-Capital, the maintenance of its dominance. In moments of need, Capital unity and discipline[66] has been very strong and very forceful, so that individual business interests have finally succumbed to the general interest of preserving class domination.

In this case, we can assume that labour will not stay an observer of this unfolding reality. To expect that a growing precariat—managed and controlled through AI-automated processes—would passively accept those changes is erroneous. The same counts for an expanding labour reserve army—even with some sort of Universal Basic Income (UBI) in place.

I conclude this chapter by highlighting how a post-profit, post-capitalist world is neither inevitable nor a given, but ultimately comes down to both labour and Capital decisions. Without hiding my preference towards labour, I end this chapter by urging both well-intended sceptics and the convinced to join forces and adopt a dynamic-realist stance on the matter.

9.6 CONCLUSION: PATHS TOWARDS POST-CAPITALISM

In this chapter I have been dealing with the question of labour replacement by artificial intelligence. I have identified the fears and hopes around the use of AI at work, before analysing the underlying economic forces that motivate its adoption and rejection. For this, I delved into the analysis of value and profit. I first showed how human labour is indispensable for a proper understanding of value. Then I examined how the appropriation and control of labour, namely profit, operates as the motivational force of investment decisions. Thereafter, I looked at the adoption of AI technology through the lenses of the profit motive, showing how the tendency of falling profitability conditions innovation and automation. I have highlighted that Capital could go past this tendency nevertheless to fully replace human labour. Finally, I recognised that this would signify a change in the very nature of profit. In these closing remarks, I will elaborate on this observation and present some afterthoughts about the post-capitalist world and its potential forms.

In my introduction, I have spotted two "camps" of AI-authors, the convinced and the sceptics. Since these groups are quite heterogeneous in their members, it makes sense to further distinguish between those acting in good faith and those acting in bad faith. This distinction boils down to either reaching a conclusion without hiding one's own ideological commitments or not. Of course, analysing material and historical conditions is much more handy than a mere wish, which alone offers poor predictability. In this sense, good faith is not enough for a general argument quality, if not based on solid ground. This is not it though. Given that reality is malleable to a certain extent, wish accompanied with power ceases to be just wish and becomes a new material reality (reflexivity theory). It is one thing to be a (realist) sceptic due to one's own analysis of real conditions that inhibit AI automation (like the falling rate of profit); totally another to subscribe to it without evidence, for an own political benefit, cultivating just fear on the side. Moreover, it is different to present the real difficulties and challenges while predicting the imminent replacement of human labour than to sugar-coat them for your own gain. This is why we find the debate between these two realist groups particularly worthy of our attention.

The realist-sceptic group makes a valid point when positioning the falling profit rate as a limit to Capital's investments in AI technology and automation. Capital would rather hold back general innovation and progress than allow profitability to fall very low, undermining its dominance over labour. I have explained how profitability is crucial for Capital's position, in the historically developed system of the economic exploitation of workers that succeeded the *extra/outra*-economic exploitation of feudalism. This group's argument is that the introduction of new technology, especially of new human-like machines, would increase profits temporarily for individual companies but decrease them in the long term for all owners (the distinction between capitals and Capital). Therefore it will either be extremely slow or even a non-event.

On the other hand, the realist-convinced group accepts falling profitability as a more complicated phenomenon. For this group, the falling rate of profit causes, among others, greater dependence upon the employed while increasing unemployment. This ends up augmenting the bargaining power and per-capita produced value of the employed on the one hand and the frustration of the unemployed on the other. Capital has to ensure the work discipline and obedience of those creating value, ending up fostering what Graeber calls bullshit jobs, namely meaningless, unfulfilling jobs that serve as managerial importance-boosters, solidifiers of exploitative hierarchy, or both. This is in line with what Marx calls unproductive labour; labour that does not add new value but feeds off of productive labour. Its utility is the maintenance of a class-based social order by securing private-property relations (e.g. police, security, licencing, etc.). Besides its active use, unproductive labour has a *passive* one too, since it is charged with directing human creativity and imagination towards senseless repetitive and ultimately repressive ends. The backwash of Artificial intelligence automation is bullshit and unproductive managerial jobs together with automated precarity for gig labour in the core countries. While, at the same time, on the global periphery, it means fewer, worst paid jobs for the unskilled and mass unemployment for those pushed out by technological advances.

This increasing unemployment fosters an unstable and miserable environment for the unemployed, while enlarging the gap between them and the employed. Unemployment breeds anger, frustration and enhances class consciousness among the left out ones. After all, it is tough to convince people of the necessity of a system that does not even offer a chance for work, creation, and fulfilment. It is no surprise that high unemployment works like a ticking bomb for systemic stability, especially in the absence of counterbalancing measures (e.g. welfare). This adds up pressure upon Capital—and consequently also the State—to maintain some social cohesion, necessary for the system's reproduction. In this environment, Capital is left with certain choices to avoid a social explosion that could challenge its dominance and ownership.

Capital's first choice is to push for UBI. This is a policy that has already entered the mainstream, finding support from neoliberals, like Andrew Yang in the US, to conservatives like S. Edward Leigh in the UK. This, at first, seems quite bizarre, given that the UBI is a policy promoted by many left-leaning economists, academics, and politicians, that see either an unconditional safety net[67] or an indispensable stepping stone towards a post-Capitalist world in it.[68] Why would Capital and its spokespeople show any preference towards a policy that could decrease the appropriation of surplus value, ease the pressure on both unemployed and employed,[69] equip labour with more political power, and even pose a long-term threat for Capital's domination? As Cristicuffs notes,[70] "what presents itself as taming the effects of the capitalist economy could in fact contribute to its maintenance." Capitalism exhibits a certain "elasticity," meaning that when challenged it prefers to "subsume rather than oppose."[71] UBI could therefore replace worker unionisation, cooperation, and solidarity at the workplace with an atomised and impersonal connection to a powerful State. It is easy to see how this undermines collective bargaining, Union power, and general class conflict in production.

At the same time, Capital does not cease its effort to extract value from human activity "outside/expanding the workplace." In cognitive capitalism, the successor of industrial capitalism, the nature of commodities has changed. They no longer are finite objects that "expire in consumption," but—entangled with knowledge and information—practically transform into non-static, animated, processes.[72] Production is not limited to the workplace, but embraces the whole spectrum of social relations and engages with the production of human subjectivity. Moreover, the rising dependence upon value-producing, consuming activities have blurred the

lines between consumption and production. Well-intended UBI supporters often miss that, by focusing on wage labour, assuming that the end of
waged work is the end of capitalism; that the space outside work is free
from exploitation and a space of self-realisation. This is not the case. What
we ignore, says Mathers,[73] is "the work performed outside work: the free
labour pervasive to cognitive capitalism, which is exerted willingly rather
than through coercion or the threat of destitution." The so-called data
economy uses free time labour (clicks, rankings, reviews, content-mak-
ing) in order to categorise and extract value. Twitter's initial price offering showed a company market valuation in the billions of dollars,[74] even
though the company had not been producing any palpable commodities.
Its market value in 2021 is over $50billion,[75] surpassing companies like
Ford or E-bay. What is astonishing is that Ford employs around 200 thousand people worldwide, while Twitter no more than 6,000. This is a staggering comparison that reveals the power of exploitation of "free time"
labour. Some authors have gone as far as to reject the capitalism label for
this new model of profiteering and exploitation, opting for "techno-feudalism" instead.[76] I will not dig further into this semantic debate, but it is
false to think that the algorithm, robot, and platform owners—whether
called Capital or else—would cease value-extraction and exploitation in
the digital and automated world. Labour should be aware of this development, if it is to form meaningful opposition to this brave new world.
Capital is not playing without an opponent though.

What could labour then do? Maintaining unity looks increasingly difficult. Will the gig-precariat feel the same about automation as the elite
employees in their bullshit but well-paid jobs? Will the on-paper-unem-
ployed, click-and-attention-economy workers and UBI-receivers feel part
of labour at all? Will they even feel exploited, if receiving "free" money?
And will they seek a way to unionise and tackle these new forms of exploitation? Will they push for more or less automation? And would they care
to have a say on its direction and workings? The truth is that we simply
cannot know in advance, especially if rejecting deterministic readings of
history altogether. After all, if the subject of history is the working class
itself, the most authors can do is to analyse the material circumstances
and motives of Capital and labour.

Having said that, in my chapter, I have attempted to provide some tools
to assist in the examination of these questions. I have therefore investi-
gated a fundamental variable in this field: profit. I pinpointed both existing definitions and theories (labour theory of value, falling rate of profit),

as well as their limitations and potentially extended readings in a new context (i.e. moving beyond human labour in value creation, overcoming the falling profit limitations etc.). Since the field (AI in production) is not yet fully established, the verification of these theories lacks the necessary empirical backing for its confirmation or rejection. This certainly provides space for further research. Moreover, despite my labour affiliation, it remains arguably a more academic than experiential work. All things considered, though, it hopefully manages to analyse adequately the principal driving forces and elements behind the adoption of AI, as well as to present both Capital and labour perspectives and motives without some artificial normative neutrality.

We can claim with some confidence that capitalism, as we know it, and AI are not compatible in the long run. The sceptics are right in this. This does not mean that capitalist motives and logic will magically wither away though and not transform to embrace automation. So the convinced group is not wrong either. I sense that the Capital-posed dilemma is quite tough. On the one hand, a turbocharged version of (AI-run) exploitation that benefits a multi-billionaire oligarchy, too busy with its space-wars to seriously bother about the side-effects on the environment and overall life-quality. An automated "hypercapitalism" without (much) human labour in production. An economic system that would be capitalism in name only, with the extraction of surplus value taking place in production increasingly less. On the other hand it is an internationalised "movement" of uncritical technological rejection (together with increasing nationalism) that advocates some form of post-modern techno-primitivism and traditionalism. I do not see how this is a viable option either and how any of the two "proposals" benefit the oppressed. It is left to them then to find a new, unexplored alternative.

All in all, In order to make sense of this new reality, we have to be able to see profit and exploitation differently, knowing the existing readings while being ready to expand them. The distinction between quantitative and qualitative exploitation helps. Do we (collectively) control our labour, or do we find ourselves following incentives, whether from a manager or an automated system; for whom? Do we programme AI to work for the benefit of the people, or does it come with an exploitative logic ingrained in its software? In this latter case, not only do we risk losing our jobs to AI, but also getting a ruthless supervisor even in our "free time." Before blaming the poor robots, though, we better point to the real culprit: the frenzy of commodification, accumulation and exploitative profit-making that has already been running the planet amok and seems ready for a new transformation.

NOTES

1. Margolius, Ivan. "The robot of Prague." *The Friends of Czech Heritage* 17 (2017): 6.
2. Kolhatkar, Sheelah. "Welcoming our new robot overlords." *The New Yorker*, 16 October 2017, https://www.newyorker.com/magazine/2017/10/23/welcoming-our-new-robot-overlords.
3. De Stefano, Valerio Michele. "'Negotiating the algorithm': Automation, artificial intelligence and labour protection." *Comparative Labor Law and Policy Journal* 41, no. 1 (2020): 1–32.
4. Frey, Carl Benedikt, and Michael A. Osborne. "The future of employment: How susceptible are jobs to computerisation?" *Technological Forecasting and Social Change* 114 (2017): 254–280.
   Dauth, Wolfgang, Sebastian Findeisen, Jens Südekum, and Nicole Woessner. "German robots-the impact of industrial robots on workers," *Institut für Arbeitsmarkt und Berufsforschung Discussion Paper*, no. 30 (2017): 39.
5. The Independent. "Elon Musk warns humans risk being overtaken by artificial intelligence within the next five years." *The Independent*, 27 July 2020. https://www.independent.co.uk/life-style/gadgets-and-tech/news/elon-musk-artificial-intelligence-ai-singularity-a9640196.html.
6. Financial Times. "The delusions of techno-futurists who ask: Crisis, what crisis?" *FT online*, 25 March 2021. https://www.ft.com/content/1c1daa87-c48e-4d19-a574-046eadb5b665.
7. Graeber, David. "Of flying cars and the declining rate of profit." *The Baffler* 19 (2012): 66.
8. Graeber, "Of flying cars," 66.
9. Societal work that is pointless or even (psychologically) destructive. First appears on: https://www.strike.coop/bullshit-jobs.
10. Moravec, Hans. *Mind children: The future of robot and human intelligence* (USA: Harvard University Press, 1988), 15.
11. Acemoglu, Daron, David Autor, Jonathon Hazell, and Pascual Restrepo. "AI and jobs: Evidence from online vacancies." *National Bureau of Economic Research*, December 2020, 3.
12. Manyika, James, and Kevin Sneader. "AI, automation, and the future of work: Ten things to solve for." *McKinsey Global Institute*, June 2018.
13. Economics, Oxford. "How robots change the world: What automation really means for jobs and productivity." *Oxford Economics*, June 2019. https://www.oxfordeconomics.com/recent-releases/how-robots-change-the-world.
14. Korinek, Anton, and Joseph E. Stiglitz, "Artificial intelligence, globalization, and strategies for economic development." *National Bureau of Economic Research*, February 2021, 19.
15. Knight, W., "Covid brings automation to the workplace, killing some jobs." *Wired.com, San Francisco*, 6 July 2021. https://www.wired.com/story/covid-brings-automation-workplace-killing-some-jobs/.

16. A theory in the crisis theory of political economy, according to which the rate of profit—the ratio of the profit to the amount of invested capital—decreases over time.

17. Johnson, Matthew, Katja Hofmann, Tim Hutton, and David Bignell. "The Malmo platform for artificial intelligence experimentation." *IJCAI* (July 2016): 4246–4247.

18. "Any of a school of economists founded in 18th-century France and characterized chiefly by a belief that government policy should not interfere with the operation of natural economic laws and that land is the source of all wealth. It is generally regarded as the first scientific school of economics." Source: https://www.britannica.com/topic/physiocrat.

19. A theory of value that argues that the economic value of a good or service is determined by the total amount of labor required to produce it.

20. Neoclassical Economics on value. Source: https://www.econlib.org/library/Enc1/NeoclassicalEconomics.html.

21. Bjerg, Ole. *Parallax of growth: The philosophy of ecology and economy* (New Jersey: John Wiley & Sons, 2018), 66.

22. Smith, Adam. *The wealth of nations: An inquiry into the nature and causes of the wealth of nations* (Petersfield: Harriman House Limited, 2010), 28.

23. Dooley, Peter C. *The labour theory of value* (Abingdon: Routledge, 2005).

24. The necessary labour time is the time (per day or per week) which workers must work (in the average conditions of the industry of their day), to produce the equivalent of their own livelihood (at the socially and historically determined standard of living of their day). Source: https://www.marxists.org/glossary/terms/n/e.htm.

25. Marx, Karl. *Critique of the Gotha program* (Rockville: Wildside Press LLC, 2008), 3.

26. Bollier, David. "Re-imagining value: Insights from the care economy, commons, cyberspace and nature." *Berlin: Heinrich Böll Stiftung*, March 2017.

27. The homo economicus approach is the perception that individuals make decisions based on their own self-interest, having full information and making rational calculations that maximise their utility.

28. Mohun, Simon. "A re (in) statement of the labour theory of value." *Cambridge Journal of Economics* 18, no. 4 (1994): 391–412.

29. Federici, Silvia. *Wages against housework* (Bristol: Falling Wall Press, 1975).

30. As a human ability deployed over time towards a certain productive outcome.

31. Farjoun, Emmanuel, and Moshe Machover, eds. *Laws of chaos* (London: Verso, 2020).

32. Marx claims that profit arises not by selling commodities above their value, in which case capitalists could raise prices at will, but that commodity sold at or near their "natural" value create profit since workers are only paid for that portion of their work which pays for their own labour power, i.e. that labour which creates enough value to provide workers with their wages, http://www.mtholyoke.edu/~fmoseley/lrcgpric.html.

33. Production is not necessarily the main source of profit; this affects the explanatory power of the falling profit theory too. For profit in circulation see: Lapavitsas, Costas. "Financialisation, or the search for profits in circulation." *Economiaz* 72, no. 3 (2009): 98–119. For a critique of the falling rate of profit as a crisis-explanatory theory altogether: Rasmus, Jack. *Systemic fragility in the global economy* (Los Angeles: SCB Distributors, 2016).
34. Marxian economic concept that professed to explain the instability of the capitalist system. Source: https://www.britannica.com/topic/surplus-value.
35. Marx's Theory of Exploitation: https://plato.stanford.edu/entries/exploitation/ #MarxTheoExpl. Fine, Ben. "Exploitation and surplus value." In *The Elgar companion to Marxist economics* (Cheltenham: Edward Elgar Publishing, 2012).
36. Screpanti, Ernesto. *Labour and value: Rethinking Marx's theory of exploitation* (Cambridge: Open Book Publishers, 2019).
37. Marx, Karl. *Capital, vol. 1.* Translated by Ben Fowkes (New York: Vintage, 1976), 280.
38. Wright, Erik Olin. "The status of the political in the concept of class structure." *Politics & Society* 11, no. 3 (1982): 321–341.
39. Saito, Kohei. *Karl Marx's ecosocialism: Capital, nature, and the unfinished critique of political economy* (New York: NYU Press, 2017), 41.
40. Mazzucato, Mariana. "Capitalism after the pandemic: Getting the recovery right." *Foreign Affairs* 99 (November/December 2020): 50.
41. Brenner, Robert. "The origins of capitalist development: A critique of neo-Smithian Marxism." *New Left Review* 104 (1977): 25, 104.
42. Heller, Henry. *The birth of capitalism* (London, Pluto Press, 2011).
43. Shaikh, Anwar. *Capitalism: Competition, conflict, crises* (Oxford: Oxford University Press, 2016).
44. Parry, Bruce E. "On Anwar Shaikh's capitalism: Competition, conflict, crises." *Science & Society* 82, no. 3 (2018): 440–447.
45. Roberts, Michael. *Robots and AI: utopia or dystopia?—Part two,* 29 August 2015. https://thenextrecession.wordpress.com/2015/08/29/robots-and-ai -utopia-or-dystopia-part-two/.
46. Nilsson, Nils J. "Human-level artificial intelligence? Be serious!" *AI Magazine* 26, no. 4 (2005): 68–68. Bhargava, Amisha, Marais Bester, and Lucy Bolton. "Employees' perceptions of the implementation of robotics, artificial intelligence, and automation (RAIA) on job satisfaction, job security, and employability." *Journal of Technology in Behavioral Science* 6, no. 1 (August 2020): 106–113.
47. Du, Shuili, and Chunyan Xie, "Paradoxes of artificial intelligence in consumer markets: Ethical challenges and opportunities." *Journal of Business Research* 129 (May 2021): 961–974.
48. Garegnani, Pierangelo. "Value and distribution in the classical economists and Marx." *Oxford Economic Papers* 36, no. 2 (1984): 291–325.
49. Shaikh, Answar. "Accumulation, finance, and effective demand in Marx, Keynes, and Kalecki." *Financial Dynamics and Business Cycles: New Perspectives* (1989): 65–86.

50. Freeman, Alan, and Andrew Kliman. "Two concepts of value, two rates of profit, two laws of motion." In *Value, capitalist dynamics and money* (Bingley: Emerald Group Publishing Limited, 2000). King, J. E. *Marx and non-equilibrium economics*. Edited by Alan Freeman, and Guglielmo Carchedi (Cheltenham: Elgar, 1996).
51. Michael, Roberts, "More on a world rate of profit, the next recession wordpress." 20 September 2020. https://thenextrecession.wordpress.com/2020/09/20/more-on-a-world-rate-of-profit/.
52. Shaikh, Anwar. *Capitalism: Competition, conflict, crises* (Oxford: Oxford University Press, 2016), 19.
53. Heller, Henry. *The birth of capitalism* (London: Pluto Press, 2011), 250.
54. Otani, Teinosuke. "The circuit of capital." In *A guide to Marxian political economy* (New York: Springer, 2018), 281–298.
55. Mandel, Ernest. *Late capitalism* (London and New York: Verso, 1999).
56. Caffentzis, George. "From the Grundrisse to capital and beyond: Then and now." In *In Marx's laboratory* (London: Brill, 2013), 61.
57. Marx, Karl. *Grundrisse: Foundations of the critique of political economy* (UK: Penguin, 2005), 700.
58. Elliot, Larry. "Economics: Whatever happened to Keynes' 15-hour working week?" *The Guardian*, 1 September, 2008. https://www.theguardian.com/business/2008/sep/01/economics.
59. Dyer-Witheford, Nick, Atle Mikkola Kjosen, and James Steinhoff. *Inhuman power: Artificial intelligence and the future of capitalism (Digital barricades: Interventions in digital culture and politics)* (London: Pluto Press, 2019), 22, 118.
60. Houghton, Walter E. "The history of trades: Its relation to seventeenth-century thought: As seen in Bacon, Petty, Evelyn, and Boyle." *Journal of the History of Ideas* (1941): 33–60.
61. Land, Nick. "Ideology, intelligence, and capital: An interview with Nick Land." *Vastabrupt.com*, 15 August 2018. https://vastabrupt.com/2018/08/15/ideology-intelligence-and-capital-nick-land.
62. Alexandre, Laurent. "Artificial intelligence will kill capitalism." *Worldcrunch.com*, 26 January 2015. https://worldcrunch.com/opinion-analysis/artificial-intelligence-will-kill-Capitalism. Lowrey, Annie. "Give us fully automated luxury communism." *The Atlantic*, 20 June 2019. https://www.theatlantic.com/ideas/archive/2019/06/give-us-fully-automated-luxury-communism/592099/. Bastani, A. *Fully automated luxury communism* (London: Verso Books, 2019).
63. Scholz, Trebor. *Uberworked and underpaid: How workers are disrupting the digital economy* (New Jersey: John Wiley & Sons, 2017.)
64. A term used to describe the ranks of the unemployed who—through the absence of any meaningful choice—are prepared to work for very low wages in temporary jobs.
65. Peoples Dispatch. "250 million Indian workers and farmers strike, breaking world record." *Peoplesworld.org*, 3 December 2020. https://www.peoplesworld.org/article/250-million-indian-workers-and-farmers-strike-breaking-world-record. Van dam, Andrew. "Teacher strikes made 2018

the biggest year for worker protest in a generation." *The Washington Post*, 14 February 2009. https://www.washingtonpost.com/us-policy/2019/02/14/with-teachers-lead-more-workers-went-strike-than-any-year-since/.

66. Said, Ed. W. *Culture and imperialism* (New York: Vintage, 2012). Wood, Ellen Meiksins. *Empire of capital* (London: Verso, 2005). Zinn, Howard. *A people's history of the United States: 1492-present* (Abingdon: Routledge, 2015).

67. Camper, Joseph. "Universal basic income: The new safety net." *Public Interest Law Reporter* 23 (2017): 8.

68. Srnicek, Nick, and Alex Williams. *Inventing the future: Postcapitalism and a world without work* (London: Verso Books, 2015).

69. Gupta, Rashmi, Jemima Jacob, and Gaurav Bansal. "The role of UBI in mitigating the effects of psychosocial stressors: A review and proposal." *Psychological Reports*, March 2021.

70. Cristicuffs. "What is wrong with free money?" *Gruppen GGKN*, July 2015, 6.

71. Boltanski, Luc, and Eve Chiapello. "The new spirit of capitalism." *International Journal of Politics, Culture, and Society* 18, no. 3 (December 2006): 161–188.

72. Terranova, Tiziana. "Free labor: Producing culture for the digital economy." *Social Text* 18, no. 2 (June–August 2000): 33–58.

73. Mathers, Alex. "Universal basic income and cognitive capitalism: A post-work dystopia in the making?" *Capital & Class* 44, no. 3 (2020): 340.

74. Moore, Heidi. "Twitter heads for stock market debut by filing for IPO." *The Guardian*, 13 September 2013. https://www.theguardian.com/technology/2013/sep/12/twitter-ipo-stock-market-launch.

75. "Market capitalization of Twitter (TWTR)." Companiesmarketcap.com. https://companiesmarketcap.com/twitter/marketcap/.

76. Varoufakis, Y. "Techno-feudalism is taking over." *Project Syndicate*, 28 June 2021. https://www.project-syndicate.org/commentary/techno-feudalism-replacing-market-Capitalism-by-yanis-varoufakis-2021-06.

CHAPTER 10

Artificial General Intelligence's Beneficial Use within Capitalist Democracy

A Realistic Vision

Maurizio Tinnirello

CONTENTS

It has been claimed at times that our modern age of technology facilitates dictatorship.

(HENRY A. WALLACE, VICE PRESIDENT OF THE UNITED STATES 20 JANUARY 1941 20 JANUARY 1945)

DOI: 10.1201/9780429446726-10

10.1 INTRODUCTION

The development of artificial intelligence (AI) and in particular the possibility of artificial general intelligence (AGI)—one that matches human intelligence—have been heralded as a possible new dawn for mankind, changing our lives beyond recognition.[1] In an age of technological abundance, it is anticipated, arguably, that AGI will help mankind solve many of its more complex problems, from health issues to improving social systems.[2] There are plenty of positive views on the development of AI and AGI, yet there are more and more scholars[3] and practitioners, amongst others, warning us that technological advancements like AGI and superintelligence could lead humanity towards an existential risk.[4] Nonetheless, to secure that both artificial narrow intelligence (ANI) or weak AI (a combination of machine learning and big data), henceforth simply AI, and AGI are safe and good for humankind, scholars from various disciplines are working on safety measures; for example, making sure its technical architecture is friendly towards humans, and that AGI it is instilled with the right type of values, and that it is ethical.[5] We can already feel the impact of AI in our lives, as this technology is everywhere from social platforms to cars to exercise devices, and its ubiquitous nature renders this technology part of our daily experience, with few challenges from the general population. There are already worrisome negative effects on our social systems, for example, in the outcomes of legal cases due to machine learning bias,[6] oppression through the use of facial recognition, and negative outcomes on democratic processes, as was the case with Cambridge Analytica's use of data to target voters, and also the use the Chinese government is giving AI to conduct social re-engineering on a gigantic scale.[7] The current application of AI provides a glimpse of its use as an amplifier and intensifier of existing ills in our social systems. Efforts to secure that AI/AGI is human friendly and fair are mostly concentrated on the technical aspects or purely the ethical, or on arguing for better policies and governance for these technologies, and leave behind the wider structure in which these technologies are created. Thus, negative outcomes from AI use are thought to result mostly from how they are designed, and not arising from the wider epochal structure in which humankind exists. It is thus imperative that we address the development of AI/AGI within, and in relation to, the underpinning global political-economic system and its ideology—this means capitalism and neoliberalism, in particular capitalism's drive against democracy. A central point of this chapter is that current approaches to developing AI/AGI so it will be safe, ethical, and friendly for humankind might not be enough to secure its beneficial use, because if AGI is developed within late capitalism (global capitalism) and the processes within this system continue to erode democracy, it will amplify and multiply the ills inflicted by capitalism on humankind,[8] including unbridled capital accumulation, global inequality, and possibly a period of tyranny inflicted by those controlling AGI—bearing in mind the caveat that it is unlikely that AGI can be controlled,[9] and if it goes on to become superintelligence it might tyrannise the elites as well.[10] Late capitalism is usually defined as beginning in the late 1970s and framed by the financialisation of the world economy and the political strategy known as the promotion of democracy—this is the promotion of neoliberalism.[11]

Why approach it from this field of study? Late capitalism and its ideology, neoliberalism, underpins every aspect of our lives, from technological developments and social models, including those of international governance, to ethics. Much work has been done on AI governance, regulation, policymaking, ethics, and so forth, but are we doing something different with these emerging and powerful technologies than we have done with other technologies before? Are we certain that the ethics of those developing and using AI will be good for the rest of us? Phrased differently, would this ethical use of AGI merely ensure that AGI fits into the processes of capitalism without much resistance from global societies? Is there evidence that broad and new social models are being created to counter, manage, and control the use of this emerging technology? And if so, are they detached from the capitalist ideology?

All of this is highly relevant and problematic, as it is within late capitalism that many social, economic, and political ills have been created: for example, the most severe period of economic inequality in human history, with various elites having capital calculated in the hundreds of billions of dollars and corporations reaching a market value of trillions of dollars. The riches of the billionaires have surged during the COVID-19 pandemic, while millions of disenfranchised peoples have suffered further economic setbacks.[12] Moreover, a global crisis of democracy,[13] the rise of neo-fascism and authoritarianism worldwide,[14] the looming global environmental catastrophe,[15] in part responsible for the Covid-19 pandemic, and a structural crisis of capitalism itself—all these crises are linked to the very internal contradictions of capitalism. As argued by Karl Marx in the *Grundrisse*, when capital accumulation encounters barriers, it turns them into crises, but these are circumvented rather than solved—future crises will come out of this process.[16] Arguments emanating from critical studies of our political-economic system postulate that crises generated by capitalism cannot be solved within capitalism[17]—thus, it follows logically that any crisis created by AI/AGI within, and/or as an extension of capitalism, cannot be solved by capitalist processes, nor, as this chapter argues, by technological tinkering.

Contrary to popular belief, capitalism does not need democracy. It has worked with some form of democracy in Western Liberal states, but capitalism has secured that democracy is at best procedural—this will be illustrated later. China provides an example of how it can function without democratic pretensions. Finally, due to the structural crisis of capitalism, some have argued that we are *ad portas* of the end of capitalism, which will generate more ugly crises in this century; Wolfgang Streeck writes that what we can expect,

> on the basis of capitalism's recent historical record, is a long and painful period of cumulative decay: of intensifying frictions, of fragility and uncertainty, and of a steady succession of "normal accidents"—not necessarily but quite possibly on the scale of the global breakdown of the 1930s.[18]

It is fair and cautious to ask if it is within this system, and among its crises, that humankind hopes to develop and use AI/AGI?

First, this chapter shows that current AI is already creating huge challenges in our legal, social, and political systems. Second, this chapter shows how capitalism has been advanced while constraining and modifying democracy so capital accumulation can take place away from the majority of the population, increasing inequality and damaging the foundations for the global common good. Elites have benefited from this and have acted upon the chance to cement the displacement of contending social forces for the accumulation of capital, and to capture the political sphere, to the detriment of fair societies. Key here is that real popular democracy cannot exist within capitalism, and this could pose a significant barrier to the use of AI and AGI for the global common good.[19] Third, it argues that honest and well-intentioned pleas for the beneficial use of AGI might not succeed if this powerful technology is developed within the internal contradictions of capital accumulation, in particular how capital constrains and transforms democracy. Finally, this chapter concludes that even cautious analyses of the use of AI/AGI must start including more critical and realistic analyses of the beneficial AI/AGI idea within capitalism, if humankind is not to rely on fragmented techno-fixes instilled with the same capitalist ideology. It is very possible that humankind will need to accept that AI/AGI, even if developed safely, will bring with it the ideological underpinnings of capitalism.

10.2 HOW CAPITAL RESHAPES DEMOCRACIES INTO PLUTOCRACIES

Although the idea of AGI might seem distant and implausible, there are various firms working on its development, such as OpenAI, Deepmind, Facebook AI Research, and others. A survey conducted only a few years ago amongst AI experts on the timing and probability of AGI development gave a likelihood of 90% that it could occur by 2075, while others gave a 50% chance that it would take place by 2040–2050, after which it would only be a matter of a few decades at most for AGI to surpass human intelligence.[20] Even if AGI is at least a few decades away, and even if its very creation is put in doubt,[21] it would be wise to address the likelihood of its beneficial use, due to its possibly significant impact on the history of humankind—a man-made intelligence equal or superior to ours. Now, to ensure AGI is safe for humankind, philosophical and policy reflections are taking place to evaluate the impact of narrow AI on law,[22] policing, driverless cars, autonomous weapons and militarised AI, and labour displacement, and AI ethics teams are being hired within tech corporations in order to develop safe and ethical AI. There are also drives to instil the right type of values in AI and AGI so they will be friendly towards humankind.[23] It is presumed here that this safe and ethical AI will be transferred to AGI if it is achieved. This of course is directed from the technological standpoint to develop the necessary architecture, so these technologies are safe for humankind. These initiatives are very positive, yet this chapter posits that appeals for developing safe and ethical AGI might not be enough to prevent a dystopian future. The rational economic behaviour that is intrinsic to capitalism has been recognised as a substantial challenge for the global common good by AI scientist Stephen Omohundro.[24] He avers that "[t]o manage the anti-social drives of autonomous systems, we should both build them with cooperative goals and create a prosocial legal and enforcement structure analogous to our current human systems."[25] Those who argue that AI will help us achieve enormous benefits and those who warn us of the possible dangers are mostly overlooking, or not paying enough attention to, a very important factor in the historical placement of AI and AGI development: the global political and economic system in which it is developed, and how power is wielded within capitalism. There is a substantial gap in this area, in particular in literature outside critical and Marxist studies, which seldom reach the technical AI community or even those working on AI from the humanities and social sciences.[26] It could be that most literature does not address AGI development in relation to a critique of the underpinning system in which AI is being developed, and in which AGI might be based, because no one wants to rethink the purpose of creating more technologies that further increase productivity and competitiveness for capital accumulation in the hands of a few. Yes, the issue of power is addressed by luminaries working on AI, and it has been argued that we must tackle this to make AI good and fair for humankind.[27] They often propose more regulations and/or more governance to manage power,[28] but do not address the fact that regulations and governance are shaped by capital. These sorts of arguments are not new, nor original or even clever in the face of historical analyses, as elites have often adopted changes in order to maintain dominance over the common man.[29] This is key in the liberal democratic order and can be viewed critically from the concept of Gramscian hegemony: a combination of consent and repression—this will be clarified ahead. In short, the calls to address power aim to do enough, so AI's impact on capital accumulation remains the same. Hence the appealing and conscious calls from the likes of Elon Musk, Bill Gates, et al. that appear to seek changes to the destructive drives of capitalism come from within capitalism itself. Slavoj Žižek writes: "They stand for global capital at its most seductive and 'progressive'—in short, at its most dangerous."[30] It is also paradoxical that some of these seemingly progressive voices come from people associated with firms such as Microsoft, which by all accounts are at the other side of democracy, and more on the side of plutonomies and plutonomic elites— not to mention their work to enhance military technology and processes,[31] linking them to the entire military-industrial complex, which Cornell West describes as an intrinsic part of capitalism and imperialism.[32] Again, a sort of pre-emptive logic applies here: those AI specialists are talking of ethics and power so that any challenges to AI/AGI development come from their sphere; thus, challenges and discourses are contained by the transnational tech corporations. A possible more honest discourse would be to admit fully that these corporations fret about power and ethics so they can continue to accumulate capital. Another ideological proposition associated with AGI is the idea of exponential superintelligence and singularity mirroring the capitalist idea of unlimited growth—this ideological trap is causing global misery, as capital is running out of geographical spaces for capital accumulation.[33] Facing the prospects of further inequality and injustice, due to the concentration of power fuelled by these technologies and tech corporations as argued by historian Yuval Noah Harari,[34] I argue that it is necessary to engage in this problem from critical studies of capitalism, examining in particular how capitalism constrains real popular democracy.

It would be illusory to proclaim that all is well with how technologies, including AI, are being used by states and firms to maintain or gain political and economic hegemony and massive capital gains. AI has started to impact the global common good in a manner that has changed history by affecting one of our most cherished institutions: democracy. The 2016 United States (US) election and Brexit vote were not only decided through rallies and canvassing; there was another actor, hidden from the common observer: big data and machine learning. Both major parties used big data companies to target voters with information and misinformation about each other. This of course could be seen as no different from the way politicians have always used traditional media, but the real innovation was the use of bots that targeted a particular audience, without their knowing this information had been created from their own data to yield a specific result; thus the freedom to access information was in fact an ideological trap to constrain critical thinking. Moreover, once bots have been created, they work "on their own" to learn from users and maximise their actions. "The trend goes from programming computers to programming people [...] whoever controls this technology can win elections—by nudging themselves to power."[35] It is highly likely that the candidate that used data in a more efficient manner was the winner, unfortunately including the illegal extraction of some of the data from Facebook profiles by Cambridge Analytica. Regardless of the legality of its collection, the use of data through bots to target people in order to sway them towards a particular outcome seems to be now part of the political process. This adds another layer of complication to the already taxed institution of democracy. The "one man, one vote" maxim now could be written as "one bot, millions of votes." This is a significant threat to the existing democratic body politic. The fight for the actions, and wherewithal, of people will be a new sphere where AI can pose serious challenges to states, global governance, intellectual freedom, and pluralism; in short, how societies perceive reality. AGI, and or a combination of AGI and humans, could achieve a political victory or remodel political systems and could provide a formidable weapon versus a free political consciousness, just and fair democracy, and the global common good.

The effects on the body politic due to AI use under our current global political-economic system can also be seen in China's use of AI to conduct surveillance, perform facial recognition, marginalise and imprison its citizens—although China is far from being a democracy, it provides an example of a current non-beneficial use of AI. This is especially worrying when China and the US are in a race to achieve AI supremacy. The US has outlined a 30-year plan for autonomous weapons in order to maintain global military superiority,[36] while China has done similarly.[37] The militaristic use of AI will not only enhance the ability of militaries to gain superiority over each other, but also allow great powers to maintain their hegemony in the political and economic spheres. It has been argued that a new arms race has begun and that the qualitative nature of militarised AI within the current structure of the international system could lead states to be in a constant drive towards maintaining or gaining hegemony; however, the ever-encompassing nature of powerful AI, which could fill every theatre of war, could also signify that gaining regional hegemony might be impossible, throwing states into a permanent state of engagement as never before experienced. Tinnirello argues that governance alone will not constrain this, and that a more ambitious objective ought to be created and reached:

> Throughout our history the international system reflects that achieving global governance is not a final static outcome but a series of complex ongoing processes, as states, including great powers, compete within the existing international political economy for economic and military supremacy. To change the international system and avoid an AI arms race toward hegemony, a reinvention of our international political economy is needed [...].[38]

Coming back to the use of AI for social control, Western democracies are far from using AI as China does, but ever more liberal democracies are being challenged by the rise of neo-fascist and authoritarian movements. We have seen this in the US, Italy, Hungary, Brazil, and Poland, and countries with authoritarian political systems such as China and Russia. Thus, extremes and visible uses cannot be totally discounted. It is important to point out that the rise of neo-fascism and what seem to be out-of-the-blue results, like the election of Donald Trump or the surge of English nationalism in the form of Brexit, were not a total surprise, in their abstract form, to critical scholars on globalisation and capitalism who were raising alarms long ago on the worrying path democracy had taken.[39] These are simply the results of the internal contradictions of capital accumulation—from Noam Chomsky to Žižek, scholars expected these negative outcomes.[40] The attack on democracy, justice, and governance is affecting the liberal international order, and it has been argued that the next stage of capitalism will require less and less democracy. William I. Robinson has argued that the current stage of capitalism favours authoritarianism, repression, and a global police state, to control the surplus of humanity created by the structural crises of capitalism.[41] The current shift towards authoritarianism and neo-fascism and failing international governance are consequences of the last four decades of the hegemony of global capitalism and its drive to turn every part of the world into a capitalist space—rendering every aspect of life, even nature and humans, a commodity.

But even if we do not countenance the use of AGI within an authoritarian system, a close inspection of the way democracy has been shaped by capitalism in liberal states demonstrates that we are not likely to produce AI/AGI to serve the global common good if we develop AGI within capitalism, and this raises worrying signs for the future.

10.3 CAPITALISM VS DEMOCRACY

> Governments will use whatever technology is available to combat their primary enemy—their own population.
>
> (NOAM CHOMSKY)

Here the chapter will provide a critical view of capitalism's grip on democracy, showing that some of the ills within it are not only foreseen but even necessary for capitalism to advance. Various scholars and tech elites have argued that humankind has never had it better, in part due to improved living conditions, economic prosperity, health, and so on. They argue that this is a result of capitalism,[42] but a fundamental problem with this position is that they associate capitalism with democracy, while critical literature of globalisation has worked hard to show that democracy exists independently of capitalism and not as consequence of it. Some plutocrats view capitalism simultaneously as the best option to create wealth and prosperity, but also to attain high levels of democratic, economic, and human development, with negative aspects of capitalism dismissed as merely bad management of the international political economy. Various of these plutocrats have benefited immensely from capitalism, with some amassing fortunes of billions of dollars in assets, such as Bill Gates. Is it really surprising that they support the system, even if they continue to warn us about the dangers of unchecked capitalism? Žižek interprets this irony:

> Elon Musk, Bill Gates, Jeff Bezos, Mark Zuckerberg, all 'socially conscious' billionaires—leave bagfuls of warnings in their trail [...] In short, their version of the end of capitalism is the capitalist version of its own end, where everything will change so that the basic structure of domination will remain the same [...].[43]

The ideological proposition to reform capitalism is to instil this very capitalist ideology through seemingly progressive changes, to maintain the system of exploitation and immiseration without major social shocks. The continuation of this ideology comes in many forms, but one interesting example, adopted by tech corporations and those working on AI, takes the form of movements such as Effective Altruism (EA):

> [EA] perpetuates and validates the central illogic foundations of capital and its basic prescriptions for handling its own crises. That is, in order to achieve greater prosperity for all, EA is in agreement with neoliberalism in claiming that we need to reinvest in the very system responsible for suffering. While EA seeks the maximising of market value in order to achieve an ostensibly noble end, it enables the circumventing of crises, as argued by Marx, by softening the blows of capital's violence. But, without rejecting the exploitation inherent in a system rooted in exchange value, radical emancipation and the elimination of suffering will remain elusive.[44]

Another visible characteristic of this ideology's insidious presence is the belief that capitalist ills are due to bad management, for example, causing abysmal global economic inequality. This is a romanticisation of Keynesian economics, in the voices of various economists, including Joseph Stiglitz and Robert Reich.[45] Yet, let us not forget that even during the glorious years of the Keynesian drive, the golden age of the US economy, the other side of the capitalist coin was marked by visible victims of the capitalist advance such as minorities and women. In the Global South, there was constant interference from global powers trying to install a new economic and political order while siphoning riches out of these areas of the world, leaving them deep in debt to institutions such as the International Monetary Fund and the World Bank. This was all part of the capitalist globalisation design, and its effects continue to plague humankind.[46] Inequality is still a great political problem as much as an economic one, and this is especially true when we address the issue of a fair democracy.[47] High levels of inequality severely retard progressive drives towards greater and fairer democracy. The current state of economic inequality is staggering, as reported by Oxfam: "[t]he world's 2,153 billionaires have more wealth than the 4.6 billion people who make up 60 percent of the planet's population."[48] How can we reconcile the gains made by humankind under capitalism, with the economic and political inequality between the super-rich and the rest? Even the COVID-19 pandemic, the most severe crisis the world has experienced at least since WWII, has allowed various billionaires to further increase their wealth while millions of commonfolk experience extreme hardship. How could this take place?

Let us remember that the elite response to the 2008 economic crisis was to reward those who had caused the crash; the elites and institutions that wrecked the global economy benefited from billions of dollars in rescue packages, from tax-payer money, to avoid a much greater economic collapse—at least this was the logic put forward by those in control of the economic and political systems in the US and the UK to name few. What took place was one of the biggest transfers of public capital into private hands ever recorded, in what could be called an act of corporate socialism, and no democratic processes could stop it. This is nothing new; removing contending forces from capital is part of the ontology of capitalism.

How this era started has been extensively treated,[49] but it bears repeating here to emphasise the extent of the challenges, if we develop AI/AGI within capitalism. In response to civil movements for greater rights and equality in the late 1960s and early 1970s, elites responded by intensifying capital's grip on democracy. A 1970s report by the Trilateral Commission pointed out that the common man had gained too much power versus those at the top of the echelons of the political-economic pyramid, and they called this a crisis of democracy; the crisis being that there was too much democracy. They argued that the institutions were not containing the excess of democracy.[50] This chapter does not claim that there was true popular democracy, but gains were being made by labour versus those in power—the iconic Paris student demonstrations of 1968 and the Civil Rights Movement are examples of this. What occurred to counter this was a transformation of the existing democratic arrangement to a more manageable system for the elites, which favoured their ability to accumulate capital—a form of displacement of the contending social forces through economic, political, and ideological spheres. One of the solutions to too much democracy was the promotion of a new type of democratic arrangement that facilitated the movement of capital, and in particular financial capital, another type of technological advancement that was romanticised by the elites, without the threat of popular uprising. This democratic arrangement, low-intensity democracy or polyarchy, became the prevailing political structure pushed by, and within, the plutonomies—the US, the UK, Canada, and so forth.[51]

William I. Robinson has argued that "'low-intensity democracy' is aimed not only at mitigating the social and political tensions produced by elite-based and undemocratic status quos but also at suppressing popular and mass aspirations for more thoroughgoing democratization of social life in the twenty-first century international order."[52] The promotion of this type of democracy does not imply fundamental social changes like the fulfilment of popular aspirations towards greater freedom, democracy, social, and economic justice, and more inclusive political governments.[53] Polyarchy separates "the political from the socioeconomic sphere and restricts democracy to the political sphere. And even then, it limits democratic participation to voting in elections."[54] Polyarchy facilitates the dilution of popular demands for change through two complementary elements: consensual and coercive domination.[55] The first, consensus,

> involves the internalisation on the part of subordinate classes of the moral and cultures values, the codes of practical conduct, and the worldview of the dominant classes or groups—in sum, the internalisation of the social logic of the system of domination itself.[56]

Consensual acceptance by the subordinate classes of the prevailing system of rule cements a set of relationships between elites and subordinates that makes an undemocratic system appear democratic.[57] Coercive domination is explicit.

This type of domination can be traced back to elitism theories in the early 20th century. Italian social scientist Gaetano Mosca provided a critical insight into what model could better preserve an elitist based system. Mosca thought the best way to re-create the elites' interests was democracy. Conversely, Vilfredo Pareto argued in favour of fascism. As autocratic regimes started collapsing, displaced by market democracies and the promotion of polyarchy, Mosca's vision seems to have prevailed: at least for several decades, a new stage of capitalist domination seemed to be emerging. Mosca's idea was enhanced by the concept of hegemony, developed by another early 20th century Italian, Antonio Gramsci. For Gramsci,

> hegemony is a social relation which binds together a "bloc" of diverse classes and groups under circumstances of consensual domination, such that subordinate groups give their "spontane-ous consent" to "the direction imposed on social life" by the dom-inant groups.[58]

Thus, the concept of hegemony does not explicitly relate to forceful domi-nation but instead is forged within the democratic capitalist systems to allow the dominant classes to rule over civil society through consensual mechanisms. Some of these entail the "freedom" to create political par-ties, the right of association in civilian groups and unions, and of course the right to participate in elections. Nonetheless, Gramscian hegemony (consensual domination) does not presuppose the absence of coercion, nor of conflict amongst contending social forces, whether national or transnational, and is better conceived as the tool for the reproduction of the dominant classes' social order. Under hegemony, force remains latent until needed, or as put by Gramsci: "hegemony is consensus protected by the 'armour of coercion,' and the political superstructures of a coherent social order (whether authoritarian or 'democratic') always combine both coercive-based and consensual-based elements."[59]

Key to the reproduction of hegemony is ideology. Democracy can be an obstacle for capital, and of course elites know this. This is illustrated by the well-known Citigroup leaked memos that were sent to their richer clients, which observed that the world was divided between plutonomies and the rest, plutonomies being those areas "where economic growth is powered and consumed by the wealthy few [...]." The report also warned investors that a major threat to plutonomies could come from the power of people who challenged the ever-smaller share of the pie they were left with.[60] Here, the capitalist ideology serves as an important social technological devel-opment to maintain this status quo. They highlight that they will be okay as long as the idea that everyone can *make it* remains alive. This idea was fundamental in the late 1970s and early 1980s when the financialisation of the economy was sold as a technological advancement that would benefit humankind. It was attached to the ideological pseudo-economic theory of trickle-down economics that has been substantially debunked and has created bigger inequality between those at the top and those at the bottom of the economic pyramid.[61] Another is the prevalent democratic arrangement in the form of plutonomies or democracies orientated towards preserving and augmenting the wealth of the super-rich. This preserves procedural democracies where the super-rich can expand their activities and be freed from the negative aspects of inequality. Within capitalism, this is not an aberration but part of the cycles of capital accumulation.

The displacement of contending social forces and labour's share of capital gains is not only a problem of the realm of the economy but also a political problem. There is no doubt that automation has already increased productivity, just as the industrial revolution did in the 19th century, but there are two faces to productivity. One is the increased production of goods and services and the like. This can be translated as the expansion of capital accumulation. The other face requires us to ask where that expansion of capital accumulation takes place. The last decades have seen a significant stagnation and even reduction of labour's value share as capital gains at the very top continue to increase.[62] Contrary to what has been argued by various authors and technologists such as Gates, who of course has benefited incredibly from increases in productivity and the capital gains generated from these, the pie has not been distributed equally, as it were. On the contrary, there has been a considerable accumulation of capital at the very top and a reduction for everyone else.[63] The consequences of this global inequality can be seen in the political sphere, where increasingly contradictory results in the form of social shocks are happening throughout the world. Unable now to contend with these social forces, the capitalist forces abandon the democratic pretensions and become more authoritarian. A defining scholar of global capitalism, Robinson argues that we are starting to see a new form of control, more and more violent, taking advantage of the tools provided by the Fourth Industrial Revolution, and this is what he calls the global police state:

> Rather than serving to liberate humanity, the new technologies are being applied at this time by the agents of this system [capitalism] to bring about a global police state [...] [an] emerging character of the global economy and society as a repressive totality whose logic is as much economic and cultural as it is political [...] The methods of control include sealing out the surplus population through

border and other containment walls, deportation regimes, mass incarceration and spatial apartheid, alongside omnipresent new systems of state and private surveillance and criminalisation of the poor and working classes. They also include the deadly new modalities of policing and repression made possible by applications of digitalisation and Fourth Industrial Revolution technologies. The global police state brings all of global society into what in Pentagon jargon is called "battlespace," concentrated in the world's megacities that are now home to more than half of humanity [...] If it is evident that unprecedented global inequalities can only be sustained by ubiquitous systems of social control and repression, it has become equally evident that quite apart from political considerations, the ruling groups have acquired a vested interest in war, conflict, and repression as a means of accumulation. [...] [This] can be characterized as twenty-first century fascism.[64]

As the crises created by capitalism become more severe and threaten the very survival of humankind, the political solution of this century seems to point towards Robinson's current analysis of democracy, and the transition from the consensual component of polyarchy towards a repressive one seems empirically visible. Calls for the democratisation of technology and AI, so they are beneficial for humankind, as well as calls to acknowledge that a particular view of intelligence has been used to secure power, fail to imagine anything but changes within capitalism.[65] This section has shown that an important obstacle exists for AI/AGI to be beneficial, and that is that current political arrangements favour the super-rich, and capital has secured this. Critical here is that elites are abandoning any pretence that they care for democracy, even in historically liberal democracies such as the US and the UK. Another area where capital has negatively impacted humankind is how it has approached nature as an obstacle to capital accumulation, and we know now that nature is losing this battle.

10.4 CAPITAL CANNOT ABIDE OBSTACLES

Democracy is not the only thing that capital captures and destroys; nature and the survival of the species have also been affected by capital. Capitalism's ideology, which formulates exponential growth, has brought us to the threshold of a global environmental global catastrophe.

Capital does not abide by democracy, nor does it abide by the limitations of nature; it will aim to incorporate all geographical areas for exploitation. An example of the alarming state of affairs concerning the environment is the news, among many others, that once past a tipping point, the Amazon could be lost within decades.[66] The connection between capitalism and the environmental crisis has been demonstrated by various scholars,[67] yet the reality is more disturbing than what authors can encapsulate. It is not a surprise that the Global Footprint Network, a research organisation, reports that we are using 1.6 earths in terms of what we consume and waste.[68] Warnings are more plentiful and sterner every year, and the message is that humankind might not survive the 21st century due to ecological collapse. Yet, in many places around the world, the pillars of the capitalist ideology continue to push humankind towards collapse, as states race, for example, to prepare for the exploitation of areas that were previously off-limits, such as the Arctic and the seafloor.[69] Even if the damage might be irreversible, the capitalist logic applies: the short term private gains will make up for the risks, as these are socialised by the entire planet. It will be those mostly benefiting from capitalism at the top of the pyramid who will try to save themselves from the environmental catastrophe, while the rest experience the brunt of it. The United Nations has started to talk about climate apartheid, a dystopian image of what might come to pass,[70] while real accounts tell us this is highly probable. Douglas Rushkoff, a writer on media, technology, and popular culture, was invited by rich technologists to give his view on approaching natural and societal collapses, but he realised that the super-rich's main concern had been to learn the know-how to survive apocalyptic situations as they saw the oncoming collapse on the horizon.

> That's when it hit me: at least as far as these gentlemen were concerned, this was a talk about the future of technology. Taking their cue from Elon Musk colonising Mars, Peter Thiel reversing the ageing process, or Sam Altman and Ray Kurzweil uploading their minds into supercomputers, they were preparing for a digital future that had a whole lot less to do with making the world a better place than it did with transcending the human condition altogether and insulating themselves from a very real and present danger of climate change, rising sea levels, mass migrations, global pandemics, nativist panic, and resource depletion. For them, the future of technology is really about just one thing: escape.[71]

The capitalist ideology furthering and preserving capitalism in direct opposition to democratic advances can be seen here, as it is the precariat that will confront the brunt of the collapse, while those with the where-withal to escape are the ones that matter. This has been observed during the financial crisis in 2008, where banks and corporations received public funding to save their firms, and even during the COVID-19 pandemic, where corporations received public funding to keep them going; risks are socialised while profits are privatised. This is also linked to one of the ideas behind trickle-down economics: those with capital are those who matter in the global economy, entrepreneurs et al., and hence they should not be heavily taxed, or hindered in any way. A recent example of this is the UK's policy of allowing wealthy investors to enter the country without needing to quarantine during the COVID-19 pandemic, while the common man has no such dispensation.[72] The logic here is not purely economic but also political, as capital allows them to accumulate politi-cal clout and to form and maintain capitalist networks that are there to preserve the plutocrats. The common man does not have access to these spheres even in democracies. This was extensively illustrated by Chrystia Freeland in her work, *Plutocrats*. Reflecting extensive fieldwork where she interviewed the super-rich, the book illustrates how little in common they have with the common man and how little they take note of demo-cratic arrangements, as if they were on a different planet than the rest of humanity.[73] In some respects, it echoes the narrator's words in Francis Scott Fitzgerald's *The Rich Boy*:

> Let me tell you about the very rich. They are different from you and me [...] They think, deep in their hearts, that they are better than we are because we had to discover the compensations and refuges of life for ourselves. Even when they enter deep into our world or sink below us, they still think that they are better than we are. They are different.[74]

The long term preservation of mankind on this planet is equivalent to a barrier to capital accumulation that needs to be circumvented, adapting Marx's argument in the *Grundrisse*.[75] The plans to leave earth and settle on Mars reflect capital's drive to circumvent obstacles: the earth might be destroyed, but capital could be accumulated elsewhere. Current hurdles to capital accumulation are marked by crises in most human-driven activi-ties, resulting from the contradictions within capitalism. Moreover, the accumulation of capital has been historically bounded by the barrier of labour, whether due to wages gained from the exchange value of production or under the liberal democratic system by the power of people versus the elites. This was beautifully but worryingly illustrated by a Citigroup report in 2005 to its wealthiest investors, where it stated that the main danger to the fantastic times for capital accumulation they were experiencing was the fact that one person still counted as one vote, which could pose a problem for capital, and those at the top of the system.[76]

Democracy, labour, international institutions, nature, and ultimately humankind are all perceived as obstacles to capital accumulation and thus must be pushed aside—even if democracy needs to be remodelled or removed altogether. Under our current political economy, the global commons, or humanity's combined planetary wealth, has become a source of exchange value and thus capital accumulation. However, these processes face barriers such as global awareness, democratic checks, science and intellectual opposition. The impact of AGI and superintelligence on societies has already been speculated by several academics. For example, discussions on how labour will lose to automation illustrate how the barrier of labour will be overcome: a global basic guaranteed income will supposedly be delivered to humans in order to guard people against the effects of automation. Bostrom mentions the hopeful possibility that

[a] human-run government could use the taxation power of the state to redistribute private profits [and] because of the explosive economic growth [as a result of AGI/superintelligence] there would be vastly more wealth sloshing around, making it relatively easy to fill the cups of all unemployed citizens.[77]

This might seem like caring economics, but within capitalism (if carried over or refined in the future), this would constitute just another form of economic and political displacement: it would simply guarantee capital accumulation is kept away from most humans, keeping it in the hands of a few super-rich, whether human or AGI. Robin Hanson's *The Age of Em* illustrates this point exquisitely. In this book, the future is driven by aggressive processes of capital accumulation and rational economic behaviour by superintelligent brain emulations, while humans live separated from it all on low-pensions.[78] This, of course, would not occur by chance, but by design, as a necessary step towards the advancement of global capitalism, or whatever the next stage of capitalism is, possibly threatening mankind's right to exist as they serve little or no purpose to the process of capital accumulation.

10.5 SAFE AGI MIGHT NOT BE ENOUGH TO AVOID A DYSTOPIAN FUTURE

It is clear from the previous analysis of capitalism's war against democracy that humankind has not seen advances towards the global common good due to capitalism. Those who argue for creating institutions to secure good AI need to face the reality of how institutions are being dismantled worldwide by what could be called anti-global movements, from the US and the UK to China and Brazil, among many others who are reshaping democracy to be less consensual and more authoritarian. The imperative here is to drive a particular ideology forward even if the public argument is the opposite, and even organised contestation seems to be failing due to capitalism's grasp on radical emancipation.[79] The complexity of our times, including our appetite for capital accumulation, in an era where powerful AI/AGI exist is likely to simply further an epoch of profound contradictions, including the greatest inequality in human history.

One of the main concerns about AI and AGI is that any attempts by humans or other super-technology to place constraints or stops on them will result in intelligent systems finding ways to circumvent these attempts. If AGI were driven by rational economic behaviour, as to a great extent we are under our current political and economic system, it might be impossible to "switch it off" altogether, because it would not accept this as a rational or positive outcome—one that would deprive AGI of the endless possibilities to evolve and transcend barriers that we ourselves dream of, such as space colonisation. Those controlling AGI or AGI itself would not allow for social systems to interfere in its goals, and if these reflect those of capitalism then democracy, nature, and humans could be in great peril. By this point, there might be other major complications, because humanity would have gotten used to AGI and its interconnectedness to most global processes. Any radical modifications could themselves pose a threat to mankind. The complexity achieved by having AGI might be impossible to downgrade, as our own times can already illustrate—for example, a political process such as Brexit. If AGI has surpassed us in brain power, as it is expected it will, and if under a situation of oppression, we have to deal with the ethics of how to stop AGI from pursuing social tyranny, shall we manage it through force? Extermination? Let us remember Marx's view on ethics and how they depend on context. It is very likely that if AGI is developed under rational economic behaviour and under our current political economy, it will act within the design of capitalism. Or, if some humans manage to control or direct its development, they will ensure that AGI increases their hegemony over the rest to secure capital accumulation against those advocating for a fair democracy. It is very possible that this powerful AGI could get rid of human elites and even take their place, using the same ideological vision with which it was developed. Whether human or AGI, those at the top echelons of the capitalist system will want the precariat to remain contained if capital accumulation is to take place at levels never seen before. It is very possible that attacks against democracy continue under a future capitalist system, or it could be worse, and the precariat will be left outside of the political sphere altogether without any function but to exist—thus, perhaps Hanson's view of the future in an AGI/superintelligence capitalist world might be more realistic than a utopian world.[80] Documents like the Citigroup report show that this would be ideal for those at the top of the capitalist system, if they could get away with it.

Omohundro tells us that AI systems will want to enhance their utility functions, maximising their expected utility, and of course will want to stop any changes that could pose a threat to their operational abilities and existence. He warns us, "we must be very careful about creating systems that are too powerful in comparison to all other systems. In human history, we have repeatedly seen the corrupting nature of power. Horrific acts of genocide have too often been the result when one group becomes too powerful."[81] As a failsafe mechanism, Omohundro proposes designing a universal constitution that guarantees rights we deem important, and that can be ensured to be present as we create AGI.[82] Moreover, he writes, "[...] it appears that humanity's great challenge for this century is to extend cooperative human values and institutions to autonomous technology for the greater good."[83] The challenge is not new, nor has it ever been fully met in the past. As we push towards automation and the creation of AGI, we have barely managed to resolve the nuclear issue, or the global distribution of basic resources such as water, or what sort of acceptable morality of education we ought to instil, and so forth. What Omohundro and others are calling for is to systematically decode the ongoing complex process of history so AI and AGI can be used beneficially. This is certainly humanity's greatest challenge.

Nick Bostrom has proposed a different solution to threats coming from powerful technologies, including AGI: the *singleton*. This is an all-functioning superstructure that resembles a global government, but with much further reach—beyond earth. What is particular to this solution is that it might possibly save humanity from itself by relinquishing cosmic governance to one single unit that, ironically, could *free* us from the dangers posed by powerful technologies.

A singleton that is a superintelligent machine might adopt a modus operandi that would make its presence virtually undetectable in the day-to-day dealings of its inhabitants. It could act merely as a subtle enforcer of certain background conditions that could serve, e.g. to guarantee security or to administer some other minimal governmental tasks.[84]

This chapter argues that this concept has the same roots as the idea of the global basic income. The line goes like this: humans, do not concern yourselves with the toils of history; this particular technological development will take over, and all you need to do is exist. This reflects to some extent the current nature of the global political-economic system, insomuch as its complexity lies beyond what most people can grasp, and thus capitalists can continue to separate themselves socially, economically, and politically, but also in how they perceive the future. This solution implies that we would accept that we have failed as the stewards of the planet and of humankind, which would be another type of displacement on a much wider and deeper scale. History has shown us that the march towards greater governance is littered with costly and significant struggles. What Omohundro and Bostrom and others seem not to fully acknowledge is that we need more than safety nets and technical piece-meal solutions, or even a *deus ex machina* solution, however attractive this might be. We need an entirely new political-economic system to be created alongside AGI, and we ought to be ambitious and critical in its creation, acknowledging that AI/AGI development within capitalism will leave us with a future not based on democracy or the survival of the species, and with the realistic possibility of eternal tyranny.

10.6 CONCLUSION

Arthur C. Clarke, by now a well-established science-fiction writer as well as the author of the pioneering paper on satellite communications, had been growing increasingly irritated by the theological science fiction of C.S. Lewis, who saw space travel as a sinful attempt by fallen humanity to overstep its God-given place [...] Clarke contacted Lewis and they agreed to meet in the Eastgate Tavern, Oxford. Clarke brought Val Cleaver as his second, Lewis brought J.R.R. Tolkien.

They saw the world so differently that even argument was scarcely possible [...] Clarke and Cleaver could not see any darkness in technology, while Lewis and Tolkien could not see the way in which a new tool genuinely transforms the possibilities of human awareness. For them, machines at the very best were a purely instrumental source of pipe tobacco and transport to the Bodleian. So what could they do? They all got pissed. "I'm sure you are all very wicked people," said Lewis cheerfully as he staggered away, "But how dull it would be if everyone was good."[85]

It is quite incredible that we can plan for the creation of a new sentient being in the universe, but seem to be unable to overcome the corrosive components of global capitalism and its ideological structure before we do so. Žižek made a similar observation during the Occupy Wall Street demonstrations, finding it remarkable in many ways that we should prefer to continue with our current global political economy rather than avert a global environmental catastrophe. As AI continues to be developed, and AGI is being researched, it is not only well-intentioned technologists who are working on this, but also militaries around the world, as well as others who are designing better AI to enhance capital gains at financial markets through the automation of trading systems, and so on. The extant literature on AI and AGI repeats quite optimistically, perhaps naïvely, that we need good and friendly AI/AGI, one that can serve the common good. Yet, there is no reason to believe this particular technological development will be created or used in precisely this way. History, and especially the last 40 years or so of an international political economy underpinned by the neoliberal ideology, has shown us that technology is most often used to reinforce the status quo, and if any advances have been made by the common man, they are due to substantial struggles from below to check the advance of capital. Capitalism is a quite sophisticated system that circumvents crises rather than resolving them. This in turn strengthens the system, until the next crisis arrives, but generates extreme diverse results. The current result of this is vast social and economic global inequality and an impending environmental global catastrophe.

While Omohundro's and Bostrom's solutions might seem appealing considering our record of wars, injustice and extermination, they fall into a significant analytical pitfall: history. This conclusion opens with a conversation between C.S. Lewis, J.R.R. Tolkien, Arthur C. Clarke, and Val Cleaver, who differed pointedly in their opinions about technology. Lewis's farewell illustrates, to some degree, our history. The world would be boring without profound disagreement, but moreover, no advancement in our history has taken place without costly intellectual and human struggle. Thus, whether AGI is used for the global common good is not something we can resolve with technical safety mechanisms or even certain policy considerations, but it will probably take place through conflict, possibly enhanced by AGI and the way it will serve to deepen our political economy. It could very well be that neither existential risk, nor a *singleton* scenario will occur, but instead the continuum of history will go through new cycles of struggle between humans and AGI, made more violent by the advancement and/or decay of capitalism in an AGI era. This scenario is more akin to our historical moral predicaments and battles: whatever the outcome, it will require hardship and bitter toil to advance towards humanity's global common good.

NOTES

1. Nick Bostrom, *Superintelligence, Paths, Dangers, Strategies* (New York: Oxford University Press, 2014). Murray Shanahan, *The Technological Singularity* (Cambridge: MIT Press, 2015). Ray Kurzweil, *The Singularity Is Near: When Humans Transcend Biology* (New York: Penguin Books, 2006). Ben Goertzel, "Superintelligence: Fears, Promises and Potentials," *Journal of Evolution and Technology* 25, no. 2 (November 2015): 55–87.
2. Peter H. Diamandis and Steven Kotler, *Abundance: The Future is Better than You Think* (New York: Free Press, 2012).
3. Nick Bostrom and Milan M. Cirkovic, *Global Catastrophic Risks* (Oxford: Oxford University Press, 2008), Martin Rees, *Our Final Century: Will Civilisation Survive the Twenty-First Century?* (London: Arrow Books, 2003).
4. Bill Joy, "Why the Future Doesn't Need Us." In *Artificial Intelligence Safety and Security*, ed. Roman V. Yampolskiy (Boca Raton: CRC Press/Taylor & Francis Group, 2018), 3–19. Though it may prove controversial to cite technologists and others here such as Bill Gates and Elon Musk, this paper argues that even if their opinions do not coincide with AI scientists their voices carry weight, both economic and popular, and can inform or misinform the ongoing AI debates. Peter Holley, "Bill Gates on Dangers of Artificial Intelligence: 'I Don't Understand Why Some People Are not Concerned,'" *The Washington Post*, 29 January 2015, http://www.washingtonpost.com/blogs/the switch/wp/2015/01/28/bill-gates-on-dangers-of-artificial-intelligence-dont-understand-why-some-people-are-not-concerned/?tid=sm_fb.
5. Stuart Russel, *Human Compatible: Artificial Intelligence and the Problem of Control* (Great Britain: Allen Lane, 2019). Ibo van de Poel, "Embedding Values in Artificial Intelligence (AI) Systems." *Minds and Machines* 30 (September 2020): 385–409. S. Matthew Liao, ed., *Ethics of Artificial Intelligence* (New York: Oxford University Press, 2020). Virginia Dignum, *Responsible Artificial Intelligence Digital* (Switzerland: Springer, 2020).

6. Julia Angwin, Jeff Larson, Surya Mattu, and Lauren Kirchner, "Machine Bias, There's Software Used across the Country to Predict Future Criminals. And It's Biased against Blacks," *ProPublica*, 23 May 2016, https://www.propublica.org/article/machine-bias-risk-assessments-in-criminal-sentencing.
7. Nicole Kobie, "The Complicated Truth about China's Social Credit System," *Wired*, 7 June 2019, https://www.wired.co.uk/article/china-social-credit-system-explained.
8. George Monbiot, "Neoliberalism-the Ideology at the Root of All Our Problems," *The Guardian*, 15 April 2016, https://www.theguardian.com/books/2016/apr/15/neoliberalism-ideology-problem-george-monbiot.
9. Eva Hamrud, "AI Is not Actually an Existential Threat to Humanity, Scientists Say," *ScienceAlert*, 2 May 2021, https://www.sciencealert.com/here-s-why-ai-is-not-an-existential-threat-to-humanity.
10. Salvador Pueyo, "Growth, Degrowth, and the Challenge of Artificial Superintelligence," *Journal of Cleaner Production* 197, no. 2 (October 2018): 1731–1736.
11. William I. Robinson, *A Theory of Global Capitalism: Production, Class, and State in a Transnational World* (Baltimore: John Hopkins University Press, 2004).
12. "COVID-19's Economic Fallout Will Long Outlive the Health Crisis," UNCTAD, last modified 30 June 2021, https://unctad.org/news/covid-19s-economic-fallout-will-long-outlive-health-crisis-report-warns.
13. The Economist, "After Decades of Triumph, Democracy is Losing Ground," *The Economist*, 14 June 2018, https://www.economist.com/international/2018/06/14/after-decades-of-triumph-democracy-is-losing-ground.
14. Anne Applebaum, *Twilight of Democracy: The Seductive Lure of Authoritarianism* (New York: Anchor, 2021).
15. Naomi Klein, *This Changes Everything, Capitalism vs the Climate* (New York: Simon & Schuster, 2014). John Bellamy Foster, Brett Clark, and Richard York, *The Ecological Rift, Capitalism's War on the Earth* (New York: Monthly Review Press, 2010). Slavoj Žižek, *Living in the End of Times* (London: Verso, 2010), William I. Robinson, *Global Capitalism and the Crisis of Humanity* (New York: Cambridge University Press, 2014), Sing C. Chew, *The Recurring Dark Ages: Ecological Stress, Climate Changes, and System Transformation* (Landham: Rowman and Littlefield, 2007).
16. Karl Marx, *Grundrisse: Foundations of the Critique of Political Economy* (London: Penguin Classics, 1993).
17. Mark Fisher, *Capitalist Realism, Is there no Alternative?* (Ropley: O Books, 2009). Robinson, *Global Capitalism*, 2014.
18. Wolfgang Streeck, "How Will Capitalism End?," *New Left Review* 87 (May/June 2014): 64.
19. Ellen Meisksins Wood, *Democracy against Capitalism Renewing Historical Materialism* (London: Verso, 2015). Robinson, *A Theory of Global Capitalism*, 2004.
20. Vincent C. Müller, ed., *Fundamental Issues of Artificial Intelligence* (Berlin: Springer, 2016), 553–571.

21. Paul G. Allen, "The Singularity Isn't Near," *MIT Technological Review*, 12 October 2011, https://www.technologyreview.com/2011/10/12/190773/paul-allen-the-singularity-isnt-near/.

22. An article published at ProPublica in March 2016 illustrates how algorithms used to predict future criminals had a bias against Afro-American people, even if they had not committed a previous serious crime. Angwin, Larons, and Kirchner, "Machine Bias."

23. Eliezer Yudkowsky, *Creating Friendly AI 1.0: The Analysis and Design of Benevolent Goal Architectures* (Berkley: Machine Intelligence Research Institute, 15 June). Steven Umbrello, Angelo F. De Bellis, "A Value-Sensitive Design Approach to Intelligent Agents," in *Artificial Intelligence Safety and Security*, ed. Roman Yampolskiy (Boca Raton: CRC Press/Taylor & Francis Group, 2018), 395–409.

24. Stephen Omohundro, "Autonomous Technology and the Greater Human Good," *Journal of Experimental & Theoretical Artificial Intelligence* 26, no. 3 (January 2014): 303–315.

25. Omohundro, "Autonomous Technology," 308.

26. Nick Dyer-Witheford, Atle Mikkola Kjosen, and James Steinhoff, *Inhuman Power: Artificial Intelligence and the Future of Capitalism (Digital Barricades: Interventions in Digital Culture and Politics)* (London: Pluto Press, 2019). Nick Srnicek and Alex Williams, *Inventing the Future (revised and updated edition): Postcapitalism and a World without Work* (London: Verso, 2015). Gerd Leonhard, *Technology vs. Humanity: The Coming Clash between Man and Machine* (United Kingdom: FutureScapes, 2016). Jerry Kaplan, *Humans Need Not Apply: A Guide to Wealth and Work in the Age of Artificial Intelligence* (New Haven: Yale University Press, 2015). Martin Ford, *Rise of the Robots Technology and the Threat of a Jobless Future* (New York: Basic Books, 2016). Susan Schneider, *Artificial You: AI and the Future of Your Mind* (Princeton: Princeton University Press, 2019). Jathan Sadowski, *Too Smart: How Digital Capitalism is Extracting Data, Controlling Our Lives, and Taking Over the World* (Cambridge: The MIT Press, 2020).

27. Zoe Corbyn, "Microsoft's Kate Crawford: 'AI is Neither Artificial nor Intelligent,'" *The Guardian*, 6 June 2021, https://www.theguardian.com/technology/2021/jun/06/microsofts-kate-crawford-ai-is-neither-artificial-nor-intelligent.

28. Amy Webb, *The Big Nine: How the Tech Titans and Their Thinking Machines Could Warp Humanity* (New York: PublicAffairs, Hachette Book Group, 2019).

29. Robert C. Tucker, ed., *The Marx-Engels Reader* (New York: Norton and Norton, 1978), 496.

30. Slavoj Žižek, *Like a Thief in Broad Daylight* (Milton Keynes: Penguin Books Ltd., 2019).

31. Ben Egliston and Marcus Carter, "'Potential for Harm': Microsoft to Make US$22 Billion Worth of Augmented Reality Headsets for US Army," *The Conversation*, 7 April 2021, https://theconversation.com/potential-for-harm-microsoft-to-make-us-22-billion-worth-of-augmented-reality-headsets-for-us-army-158308.

32. Cornell West, *Democracy Matters: Winning the Fight against Imperialism* (New York: Penguin Group, 2004).

33. Robinson, *Global Capitalism and the Crisis of Humanity*, 2014.

34. Yuval N. Harari, *Homo Deus: A Brief History of Tomorrow* (New York: Harper Perennial, 2018).

35. Dirk Helbing, Bruno S. Frey, Gerd Gigerenzer, Ernst Hafen, Michael Hagner, Yvonne Hofstetter, Jeroen van den Hoven, Roberto V. Zicari, and Andrej Zwitter, "Will Democracy Survive Big Data and Artificial Intelligence?," *Scientific American*, 25 February 2017, https://www.scientificamerican.com/article/will-democracy-survive-big-data-and-artificial-intelligence/.

36. "Autonomous Horizons," US Air Force, accessed 30 June 2021, http://www.af.mil/Portals/1/documents/SECAF/AutonomousHorizons.pdf?timestamp=1435068339702.

37. Ryan Fedasiuk, "Chinese Perspectives on AI and Future Military Capabilities," *Center for Security and Emerging Technology*, August 2020, https://cset.georgetown.edu/publication/chinese-perspectives-on-ai-and-future-military-capabilities/.

38. Maurizio Tinnirello, "Offensive Realism and the Insecure Structure of the International System: Artificial Intelligence and Global Hegemony," in *Artificial Intelligence Safety and Security*, ed. Roman Yampolskiy (Boca Raton: CRC Press/Taylor & Francis Group, 2018), 349.

39. Robinson, *Global Capitalism and the Crisis of Humanity*, 2014. Žižek, *Living in the End of Times*, 2010.

40. Noam Chomsky, *Requiem for the American Dream, the 10 Principles of Concentration of Wealth & Power* (New York: Seven Stories Press, 2017). Slavoj Žižek, *Trouble in Paradise, from the End of History to the End of Capitalism* (Brooklyn: Melville House, 2014).

41. William I. Robinson, *The Global Police State* (London: Pluto Press, 2020).

42. Steven Lewy, "Bill Gates Is Upbeat on Climate, Capitalism, and Even Politics," *Wired*, 18 March 2021, https://www.wired.com/story/bill-gates-is-upbeat-on-climate-capitalism-and-even-politics/.

43. Slavoj Žižek, *The Relevance of the Communist Manifesto* (Cambridge: Polity Press, 2019).

44. Maurizio Tinnirello and Michael Samuels, "Displacing Fear from Education: Regaining Cognitive Compassion and Democracy," *The Good Society* 27, no. 1–2 (2018): 77.

45. Robert Reich, *Saving Capitalism: For the Many, Not the Few* (New York: Knopf, 2015). Joseph E. Stiglitz, *People, Power, and Profits: Progressive Capitalism for an Age of Discontent* (New York: W. W. Norton & Company, 2020).

46. Tarak Barkawi and Mark Laffey, "The Imperial Peace: Democracy, Force and Globalization," *European Journal of International Relations* 5, no. 4 (1 December 1999): 403–434. Susan George, *The Debt Boomerang: How Third World Debt Harms Us All* (London: Pluto Press, 1991).

47. Chomsky, *Requiem for the American Dream*, 2017.

48. "World's Billionaires Have More Wealth than 4.6 Billion People," Oxfam, accessed 30 June 201, https://www.oxfam.org/en/press-releases/worlds-billionaires-have-more-wealth-46-billion-people.
49. To understand the era where both capitalism and democracy were advanced to secure capitalist globalisation and the over accumulation of capital, we have to go back a few decades. Events in the 1970s, such as the oil crisis in 1973, which triggered an increase of the external debt in Central and South America, as well as mass popular challenges, such as the events in Paris in 1968, the Prague Spring, the peak of the Chinese revolution, the Soviet invasion of Czechoslovakia, amongst others, threatened the stability of the capitalist system and the elite. Additionally, the nation-state was also in crisis as it was becoming an obstacle to the accumulation of capital, because the popular classes had power within the nation-state to resist the elite's management of the political economic system. The strategy to overcome the crises was to impose capitalist globalisation. This resulted in the dismantling of the welfare state, and the financialisation of the economy. This meant that the system was modified so the rich could accumulate even more capital, in particular financial capital.
50. Michel J. Croizer, Samuel P. Huntington, and Joji Watanuki, *The Crisis of Democracy*, Trilateral Commission (New York: New York University Press, 1975).
51. Barry Gills K. and Joel Rocamora, "Low Intensity Democracy," *Third World Quarterly* 13, no. 3 (1992): 501–523.
52. William I. Robinson, *Promoting Polyarchy, Globalization, US Intervention, and Hegemony* (Gateshead, Tyne & Wear: Cambridge University Press, 1996), 6.
53. William I. Robinson, "Polyarchy: Coercion's New Face in Latin America," *NACLA Report on the Americas* 25, no. 3 (November/December 2000): 44.
54. William I. Robinson, "Promoting Polyarchy in Latin America: The Oxymoron of 'Market Democracy,'" in *Latin America after Neoliberalism: Turning the Tide in the 21st Century?*, eds. Eric Hershberg and Fred Rosen (New York: The New Press, 2006), 100.
55. Robinson, *Promoting Polyarchy*, 21.
56. Robinson, *Promoting Polyarchy*, 21.
57. Robinson, "Polyarchy," 44.
58. Antonio Gramsci, *Selections from the Prison Notebooks* (London: Lawrence & Wishart Ltd, 1998).
59. Robinson, *Promoting Polyarchy*, 22.
60. CitiGroup, "Plutonomy: Buying Luxury, Explaining Global Imbalances," 16 October 2005, accessed 30 June 2021, https://delong.typepad.com/plutonomy-1.pdf.
61. Thomas Sowell, *Trickle Down Theory and Tax Cuts for the Rich* (Standford: Hoover Institution Press, 2012).
62. "The Labour Share in G20 Economies," OECD, accessed 25 June 2021, https://www.oecd.org/g20/topics/employment-and-social-policy/The-Labour-Share-in-G20-Economies.pdf.

63. "Global Inequality," Facts, Inequality.org, accessed 25 June 2021, https://inequality.org/facts/global-inequality/.
64. Robinson, *The Global Police State*, 2–3.
65. Daniel Lee Kleinman, *Science, Technology & Democracy* (Albany, NY: State University of New York Press, 2000). Stephen Cave, "Intelligence: A History," *Aeon*, 21 February 2017, https://aeon.co/essays/on-the-dark-history-of-intelligence-as-domination. Webb, *The Big Nine*, 2019.
66. Ivana Kottasová, "Once the Amazon Rainforest Passes the Point of no Return it Could Be Gone in Decades," *CNN*, 10 March 2020, https://edition.cnn.com/2020/03/10/americas/ecosystems-collapse-amazon-climate-intl/index.html.
67. Klein, *This Changes Everything*, 2014. Foster, Clark, and York, *The Ecological Rift*, 2010.
68. Global Footprint Network, "August 1 is Earth Overshoot Day," accessed 23 July 2018, https://www.footprintnetwork.org/our-work/ecological-footprint/.
69. "How Would Offshore Oil and Gas Drilling in the Arctic Impact Wildlife?," *World WildLife Fund*, 14 April 2021, https://www.worldwildlife.org/stories/how-would-offshore-oil-and-gas-drilling-in-the-arctic-impact-wildlife. Caroline Delbert, "Scientists: Sea Floor Mining Is Basically as Bad as It Sounds," *Popular Mechanics*, 13 July 2020, https://www.popularmechanics.com/science/environment/a33279688/deep-sea-mining-warning/.
70. Damian Carrington, "'Climate Apartheid': UN Expert Says Human Rights May not Survive," *The Guardian*, 25 June 2019, https://www.theguardian.com/environment/2019/jun/25/climate-apartheid-united-nations-expert-says-human-rights-may-not-survive-crisis.
71. Douglas Rushkoff, "How Tech's Richest Plan to Save Themselves after the Apocalypse," *The Guardian*, 24 July 2018, https://www.theguardian.com/technology/2018/jul/23/tech-industry-wealth-futurism-transhumanism-singularity.
72. Beth Timmins, "Smaller Firms Express Anger at Quarantine Exemption Plans for Big Business," *BBC*, 29 June 2021, https://www.bbc.com/news/business-57644437.
73. Chrystia Freeland, *Plutocrats: The Rise of the New Global Super-Rich and the Fall of Everyone Else* (New York: Penguin Books, 2013).
74. Francis Scott Fitzgerald, *The Rich Boy* (2020), 5.
75. Karl Marx, *Grundrisse, Foundations of the Critique of Political Economy* (London: Penguin Books, 1993).
76. CitiGroup, "Plutonomy: Buying Luxury, Explaining Global Imbalances," 16 October 2006, accessed 30 June 2021, https://delong.typepad.com/plutonomy-1.pdf.
77. Bostrom, *Superintelligence*, 199.
78. Robin Hanson, *The Age of Em, Work, Love, and Life When Robots Rule the Earth* (Oxford: Oxford University Press, 2016).
79. Tinnirello and Samuels, "Displacing Fear from Education," 2018.
80. Hanson, *The Age of Em*, 2016.

81. Stephen M. Omohundro, "The Basic AI Drives." In *Artificial General Intelligence 2008: Proceedings of the First AGI Conference*, eds. Pei Wang, Ben Goertzel, and Stan Franklin, 483–492. *Frontiers in Artificial Intelligence and Applications 171* (Amsterdam: IOS Press, 2008), 491.
82. Omohundro, "The Basic AI Drives," 492.
83. Omohundro, "The Basic AI Drives," 313.
84. Nick Bostrom, "What is a Singleton," *Linguistic and Philosophical Investigations* 5, no. 2 (2006): 49.
85. Francis Spufford, *The Backroom Boys: The Secret Return of the British Boffin* (London: Faber & Faber, 2003), 9.

Index

Printed in the United States
by Baker & Taylor Publisher Services